The Political Economy of Consumer Behavior

Consumption forms a major part of people's lives. As such, geographers, historians of technology and sociologists have devoted much attention to trying to figure out what makes consumption meaningful. By contrast, economists have been content to hold onto theories of consumption that depend on a self-interested representative agent making utility maximizing decisions.

Pietrykowski develops this alternative account through the recovery of past attempts to forge a different analytic approach to the study of consumption. In particular, theories of consumption espoused by home economists, psychological economists and Regulation school theorists are critically reviewed. These research projects, marginalized by the mainstream, are the precursors of contemporary scholarship in feminist, behavioural and radical political economics. Reclaiming this work greatly enlarges the scope for contemporary research in consumer behavior. Pietrykowski then provides a richly textured set of case studies of green automobility, Slow Food and alternative/local currency, in order to explore the diversity of user cultures and to highlight resistant forms of consumer practice. By carefully interweaving historical and interdisciplinary research, Pietrykowski creates a lively and incisive critique of mainstream economics.

This monograph will be of interest to academic economists, sociologists, historians and graduate students. In addition, the economics of consumption would also be of interest to readers in management, marketing and schools of business administration.

Bruce Pietrykowski is currently Professor of Economics and Director of Urban and Regional Studies at the University of Michigan-Dearborn where he teaches courses in urban and regional studies, labour relations, and economic geography.

Routledge Advances in Social Economics

Edited by John B. Davis, Marquette University

This series presents new advances and developments in social economics thinking on a variety of subjects that concern the link between social values and economics. Need, justice and equity, gender, cooperation, work poverty, the environment, class, institutions, public policy and methodology are some of the most important themes. Among the orientations of the authors are social economist, institutionalist, humanist, solidarist, cooperatist, radical and Marxist, feminist, post-Keynesian, behaviouralist, and environmentalist. The series offers new contributions from today's most foremost thinkers on the social character of the economy.

Published in conjunction with the Association of Social Economics.

Previous books published in the series include:

The Political Economy of Consumer Behavior

Contesting consumption

Bruce Pietrykowski

Routledge
Taylor & Francis Group

LONDON AND NEW YORK

First published 2009
by Routledge
2 Park Square, Milton Park, Abingdon, Oxon OX14 4RN

Simultaneously published in the USA and Canada
by Routledge
270 Madison Avenue, New York, NY 10016

Routledge is an imprint of the Taylor & Francis Group, an informa business

© 2009 Bruce Pietrykowski

Typeset in Times New Roman by
Value Chain International Ltd
Printed and bound in Great Britain by
T.J.I. Digital Ltd, Padstow, Cornwall

British Library Cataloguing in Publication Data
A catalogue record for this book is available from the British Library

Library of Congress Cataloging in Publication Data
Pietrykowski, Bruce
   The Political economy of consumer behaviour: contesting consumption/
Bruce Pietrykowski
      p. cm.—(Routledge advance in social economics; 12)
   Includes bibliographical references.
   1. Consumer behaviour. 2. Consumption (Economics)—Social aspects.
3. Sex role—Economic aspects. 4. Social structure—Economic aspects.
5. Social values. I. Title. II. Title: Political economy of consumer behaviour:
contesting consumption.
   HF5415.32.P568 2009
   658.8′342—dc22

                                                            2008034696

ISBN13: 978-0-415-77312-6 (hbk)
ISBN13: 978-0-203-88232-0 (ebk)

Contents

Illustrations

Figures

Tables

Acknowledgements

Back in the 1980s I was extremely lucky to find myself enrolled in graduate study at a unique academic institution, the Graduate Faculty of the New School for Social Research. While I had a vague recognition at the time, I now more fully appreciate the stimulating intellectual environment created by scholars like David M. Gordon, Robert Heilbroner, Ira Katznelson, Ross Thomson, Claus Offe, Richard Bernstein and Andrew Arato. I was truly fortunate to be able to study with them. At the New School I learned that the acquisition of disciplinary knowledge need not preclude the ability to transgress epistemic borders and explore the world beyond.

In researching and writing this book I also had the very good fortune to receive assistance and support from a variety of individuals and organizations. Over the years leading to the publication of this book I benefited from the opportunity to present various parts of the chapters to scholars in a number of settings including the Bronfenbrenner Life Course Center Colloquia Series at Cornell University, the International Association of Feminist Economics Conference, Southwest Social Science Association Conference, Union for Radical Political Economics session at the Allied Social Sciences Conference, International Conference on the History of Transport, Traffic and Mobility, the Delta Marsh Conference at the University of Manitoba and the Changing Automobilism Conference at New York University.

I am also grateful to the College of Human Ecology at Cornell University for being selected as a Fellow in the History of Home Economics and Nutrition. This Fellowship allowed me the opportunity to conduct research at the Carl A. Kroch Library at Cornell. Much of the case study material in Chapter 3 was based on this archival research. I want to give special thanks to the following dedicated and professional archival research staff members: Eileen Keating, Laura Linke, Nancy Dean and Elaine Engst, Director. It was a pleasure to work amongst them.

The staff at the Bentley Library at the University of Michigan provided assistance on several occasions and I thank them for taking the time to help me locate documents used in my research on George Katona. In addition, I am grateful to the assistance I've received over the years from Kathy Irwin and her staff in Circulation Services as well as to Carla Brooks and Teague Orblych at the UM-Dearborn Mardigian Library. Additional assistance was also provided through a University of Michigan-Dearborn Faculty Research Support Grant from the Office of Sponsored Research.

x *Acknowledgements*

The range of consumption activities addressed in this book allowed me to meet and learn from a great many people involved in alternative consumer movements and from scholars and colleagues in the field. I want to single out a few of them for special thanks. Todd Wickstrom first introduced me to several of the activities associated with the Slow Food movement. I greatly appreciate his guidance and suggestions. Nick Seccia, Executive Chef at The Henry Ford, is a passionate proponent of slow food and I enjoyed learning about his experiences with heritage cooking. Many thanks to Steve Burke, President of the Board of Ithaca HOURS, for taking the time to sit down and talk about both the recent history of the community currency project in Ithaca as well as the organizational challenges facing the alternative currency movements in general. I am truly grateful to colleagues in economics and the history of technology for stimulating conversations and discussions over the years including Fletcher Baragar, Irwin Lipnowski, John Davis, Ann Jennings, Wilfred Dolfsma, Ann Davis, David George, Martha Starr, Chris Gunn, Hazel Gunn, Annina Burns, Gijs Mom, Rudi Volti and Gert Schmidt for their support and their helpful comments and criticisms. For their timely support at strategic points throughout the proposal and manuscript writing process I wish to thank Robert Langham, Terry Clague, Tom Sutton, Beth Lewis, Christopher Hook and Eilidh McGregor at Routledge.

Finally, and most important of all, for her many gifts including wit, wisdom and warmth I am extremely grateful to Suzanne Bergeron. I will never be able to thank her enough for her encouragement and love, but I will try.

1   Consumption matters

The focus of this book is on consumer behavior and economics. In particular, I argue that consumers have been neglected characters in the theories economists construct and in the stories they tell about the way the economy works. This applies to both mainstream, neoclassical economics as well as to much of the current heterodox alternative. To talk of a single representative consumer is misleading because it flattens important differences in the practices by which individuals and groups forge a meaningful life. And yet, to assemble individuals into associative groups without recognizing the intersectionality of race, gender, class and place also has the effect of glossing over the diversity of life experiences and the complex forces that shape and are shaped by consumer practices.

The mainstream or neoclassical economic approach, as it has for much of the past century, assumes that the consumer is a fairly generic creature who searches the market for those goods and services that satisfy their individual desires. McCloskey (1994) invokes the character "Max U" – the classic, narrow-minded utility maximizer – in her assessment of the limitations of modern economic analysis. The key components of consumer demand include tastes and preferences, prices and income. Given this "data," economists fashion a "representative agent" to stand in for the variety of real-world consumers. The reduction of a heterogeneous population to a single representative agent is not assumed to cause any problems for the theory of consumption. Indeed, the elegance and simplicity of the neoclassical model is taken to be an admirable characteristic (Stigler and Becker 1977). Yet, the contribution of the representative agent to our understanding of complex economic behavior has been limited at best. As Kirman argues,

> A tentative conclusion at this point, would be that the representative agent approach is fatally flawed because it attempts to impose order on the economy through the concept of an omniscient individual. In reality, individuals operate in very small subsets of the economy and interact with those with whom they have dealings.
>
> (Kirman 1992: 132)

The consumer enacts a plurality of social relations through consumption. The same individual can inhabit multiple subject positions, roles and orientations depending on their location within their economic lifeworld. In addition, to disregard the class and gender dimensions of consumption – ignoring, for instance, who does the shopping and who produces dinner (Devault 1991) – decreases our ability to understand differential patterns of consumption and different meanings attached to the practices consumers undertake.

I argue that in order to arrive at a more compelling account of consumer behavior we need to transform the discipline of economics by opening up the borders between economics and sociology, geography, feminist social theory, science studies and cultural studies. In addition, we need to encourage cross-border traffic rather than the one-way flow outward from the economics profession that has come to dominate the social sciences. Contemporary economists pride themselves on their imperial incursions into other disciplines, usurping claims to disciplinary authority in fields such as political science and sociology (Macy and Flache 1995; Lazear 2000; Zafirovski 2000). Instead, I propose an alternative perspective by which to explore economic activity as a part of the social, political, spatial and cultural environment. The groundwork for this alternative perspective lies in past economics research deemed unacceptable, flawed, ill-suited, incompatible, disruptive, threatening, marginal or foreign to the mainstream. By exploring these roads not taken, we can re-position historical texts and discourses, provide new readings and interpretations, and re-evaluate claims, data, theories and methods in a new light.

Re-framing the subject of consumption

In addition, instead of modeling economic behavior in the abstract I am much more interested in examining the way people function as economic agents "in the wild" (Callon 2007) and how economic knowledge is constructed by academic outsiders and by those in the public sphere – what Ruccio and Amargilio (2003) refer to as "ersatz economics." As a result, I illustrate how consumer behavior can be better understood as a series of social and material relationships involving needs, desires, cooperation, conflict, compassion and power. Underlying this analysis are several critical counterclaims against the reigning economic approach that will be used to frame the discussion throughout this book.

Consumers are gendered agents

First, mainstream economics analyzes the consumer in isolation from others. Clearly, however, we make purchases not just by ourselves or only for ourselves. We negotiate our purchasing decisions with our multiple selves (choosing to splurge or deciding to demonstrate self-control) and with others (e.g. family members). We also make purchases that are not for the satisfaction of our own needs but for the needs of others. When we, acting as consumers, purchase a gift, we are using the market to acquire an object that materially symbolizes the regard that we have for the recipient (Offer 1997). From this vantage point, consumption is not an isolated act predicated on meeting the autonomous demands of isolated individuals. Rather, much of the activity of shopping is bound up with creating and maintaining social and cultural relationships (Falk and Campbell 1997; Moss 2007). Shopping for the family is intertwined with the process of creating family – performing tasks that socially and culturally signify "family" – by provisioning for their needs (Nelson 1993). It is also important to note that the allocation of shopping and provisioning for the family has not been randomly apportioned among family members. Rather, shopping and household management have historically been activities undertaken by women. But not by isolated autonomous women acting on their own or their family's self-interest. The shopping and homemaking experiences have been, and continue to be, shaped by a diverse assortment of institutional and cultural actors ranging from advertisers and multinational corporations, to home economists, labor unions, grassroots activists and government regulators (Strasser 1982; Cowan 1983; Strasser *et al.* 1998; Cohen 2003; de Grazia 2005).

Choice is a social process

The process by which one comes to decide what to purchase – the process of preference formation – is left unexplored in mainstream economics. The assumption is that preferences are determined exogenously – outside of the models that economists construct. What matters is that we reveal our preferences through our actions and choices in the market. If those choices are logical – I prefer bananas to oranges and oranges to apples so I better prefer bananas to apples as well – we will end up buying more of the preferred product when its price falls. Those preferences could well be biologically hardwired or they might be the result of psychological stimuli, religious convictions or the desire to have what the "cool" kids have. Those factors do not matter to economists who care only about the choices people make as revealed through their purchase decisions. In a critique of neoclassical methodology, Nobel prize-winning economist Amartya Sen stated, "The *purely* economic man is indeed close to being a social moron. Economic theory has been much preoccupied with this rational fool decked in the glory of his *one* all-purpose preference ordering" (1977: 336). The reduction of the complex, diverse, socially and culturally meaningful behavior of consumers to the consistency of choices delivers a profoundly incomplete account of consumer behavior.

It is clear that mainstream economists care about modeling changes in consumer demand as well as static levels of demand. However, those changes had better be accounted for by a change in income or prices, or a change in tastes. If consumer purchases change in the absence of a noticeable change in prices or income, economists are left to conclude that tastes must have changed. Yet, as Hirschman (1984) points out, taste captures a wide range of shifts in consumer behavior. A new-found fascination with the flavor of apples constitutes a change in taste. Yet, so too does the realization that global warming is an impending peril and that my consumption of bananas exacts a heavy environmental toll through the cultivation and transport of bananas from Central America to my local supermarket. So we have preferences that reflect our individual tastes, but we also have meta-preferences or values that underlie important changes in our consumption choices (Hirschman 1984). Perhaps these second-order preferences and the normative context of choice are worth thinking about in a different way (George 2004; Akerlof 2007).

Furthermore, not only are choices constituted socially and culturally in ways that allow us to better understand changes in behavior, but also the very process of market exchange affects our attitudes and the structure of our preferences. Economists have begun to explore the ways through which the "mere" act of participating in market exchange affects our choices and our values. Competitive, instrumental action is usually rewarded and valued in the market. Markets, as social institutions, function to select some forms of behavior as successful (Bowles 1998). Just as some organizational forms of production and finance – for example, large scale profit-oriented production funded through competitive financial markets – limit the viability of alternative forms of work organization – small worker-run cooperatives – so, too, does market exchange foreclose the creation and sustenance of alternative forms of exchange (Gintis 1989a). Yet, contemporary microeconomics treats the market as a neutral space that has no influence on our behavior.

Consumption occurs beyond the marketplace

Economists study consumer behavior up until the time that money is exchanged for goods and services. What consumers actually do with the products they purchase is not part of the economics of consumption. To non-economists this would seem downright odd. As Robert Lane put it, "Preferences are precisely what markets cater to, but economic analysis tends to stop short of the actual consummation of preferences in both labor and consumer markets, dealing instead with observable choices" (1991: 365). Compulsive shoppers aside, the use of material goods rather than the transaction itself is what matters to most consumers.[1] And while economists have attempted to model the household's consumption of goods, one of the most widely used mainstream approaches redefines consumption as production activity. Take the example of buying vegetables at the supermarket. When the produce is brought home from the market it is treated as a factor input and enters into the household's production function. Capital goods (knives, food processor, stove) together with the labor of the cook are combined with the vegetables to produce a finished product. Once the sphere of consumption is redefined as the space for production, economists are able to model the household sector (Becker 1965; Muth 1966). Despite the reductionist rendering of the household as a factory, the recognition of the household as an economic space deserving economists' attention is noteworthy. Feminist economists have gone even further to model the household by depicting relations between family members in terms of conflict and bargaining strategies (Seiz 1991; Agarwal 1997).

In addition to the need to pay attention to the ways in which social relations in the household shape and are shaped by consumer practices, there is an equally important set of relationships involving the way in which people interact with consumer goods. Consumer goods are used to satisfy a range of biological and social needs and wants. Consumer goods are used to enhance status, demarcate class boundaries, and communicate with others (Veblen 1953; Hirsch 1976; Bourdieu 1984; Coşgel 1997; Dolfsma 2007). But the goods themselves are malleable. The meanings they carry can shift and change over time or at the same moment in time as they are put into use by different groups of users. Consumer goods are elements of a particular user culture. The user culture ascribes meanings and uses to objects that may conform to the intended use of the manufacturer and the marketing agency charged with developing an advertising campaign. But consumers can also re-define, adapt and re-appropriate consumer goods in ways that subvert, undermine and potentially destabilize dominant consumer practices. In this way can consumer goods be seen as being produced differently by groups and individuals not involved in the original production process (Eglash *et al.* 2004).

The economy is plural

Economics, especially since the fall of Communism, is typically conceived of as the study of the capitalist market economy. End of story, end of history. This perspective not only fails to recognize the numerous varieties of capitalism – from neoliberal authoritarian regimes, emerging market economies and liberal market economies to coordinated market economies (Hall and Soskice 2001) – but also neglects the non-capitalist sector residing within and alongside capitalist economies (Gibson-Graham 1996; Gunn 2004; Gibson-Graham 2006).

As a result, the capitalist market economy is represented as a single, total, dominant social and economic system. As Gibson-Graham argues, "Understood as a unified system or structure, Capitalism is not ultimately vulnerable to local and partial efforts at transformation" (1996: 256). Developing an understanding of consumer behavior and consumer practices that exist outside of the sphere of capitalist market exchange means also taking account of the alternative places in which people are distributing goods and services, and the multiplicity of non-economic discourses used to challenge the habits and routines that act to universalize the practices and norms associated with the capitalist market economy. To invoke a postmodern concept, I argue for the need to de-center the capitalist consumer. Just as feminist political economists have begun to dissect the androcentric bias associated with a masculinist reading of economic behavior (England 1993; Nelson 1996; Hewitson 1999; Barker and Kuiper 2003), so, too, have economic and cultural geographers been at work to shift our gaze away from the totalizing effects of large-scale capitalist development and toward sites of local resistance (Leyshon *et al.* 2003). Attention to the type of consumers that non-capitalist exchange creates is an important task if we are to better understand the scope and shape of consumer behavior.

The importance of consumption and the paths not taken

Another reason to focus more attention on the consumer is that consumption is a major component of economic activity. In the aggregate, consumer spending makes up the largest portion of total demand for goods and services produced in the United States. Throughout most of the twentieth and into the twenty-first century consumer spending has been the foundation of the US economy. The sizable role played by consumers in the economy is one reason economists should attend to the ways in which consumers behave. An activity common to contemporary North American middle-class consumers – shopping for a home appliances and automobiles – took on monumental importance in the aftermath of the events of September 11, 2001. Consumption was heralded as an act of patriotism. Shopping became a mark of dutiful citizenship in ways that turned the Second World War era appeal for restraint, conservation and frugality on its head. In the days after the September 11 attack, economist Janet Yellen, former Chair of President Clinton's Council of Economic Advisors, worried that consumers "will sit home glued to the TV, feeling that life has become uncertain and it's not a good time to buy a car or a refrigerator" (Stevenson and Kaufman 2001). That consumption has both political and economic effects is not lost on politicians and economists turned policy advisors.

However, the economic discourse on consumption remains largely neglectful of long-standing gender divisions. If consumption consists, at least in part, of shopping and family provisioning, these are activities that have historically been undertaken primarily by women. As such, descriptions of the gendered performance of consumption activity would enrich our understanding of consumer behavior. At the beginning of the last century a cohort of female economists devoted a considerable amount of time and effort to the recording and analysis of shopping behavior and home management practices. Although they were trained as economists they were, with a few notable exceptions, excluded from faculty positions within departments of economics. They found employment in government agencies and in college and university programs in the field of home economics. These female economists outside of the academic profession of economics created separate spheres and often collaborated with economists to develop new lines of research and modes of inquiry. However, their contributions have largely been erased from the collective memory of the mainstream of the profession.

In addition, over the course of the last century, the only period during which the dominance of consumer spending was challenged was during the Second World War. Throughout the early 1940s government spending comprised a larger portion of aggregate demand than it had ever before. By contrast, the production and sale of consumer goods was rationed. Coming not long after the great expansion of consumer goods production in the 1920s and the dramatic drop in employment and disposable income during the Great Depression, the wartime economy had yet another disruptive effect on consumer practices and spending behavior. During the war, the market was intensely regulated and consumers were required to alter the ways in which they shopped and the meanings attached to their purchasing choices. Indeed, consumers were recruited to actively participate in monitoring prices on behalf of the federal government. By examining the way in which consumers reacted to price controls and rationing, we can come to better understand consumer behavior in response to alternatives to competitive markets. Therefore, we can begin to gain insight into the behavior of consumers beyond the sphere of competitive market exchange.

At that period in time, a new understanding of the aggregate economy was being formulated and applied. John Maynard Keynes represented the economy as a national system comprised of large sectors devoted to personal consumption, business investment, government spending and foreign sales (exports) and purchases (imports) (Mitchell 2004). As stated earlier, consumption composes the largest share of total national spending. For Keynes, the typical consumer behaved in a predictable way by linking spending decisions to available income. Savings represented unspent income. While Keynesian economists were generally satisfied with the role assigned to the consumer, questions remained about the composition of consumer demand and the ways in which consumers sought to maintain their lifestyle in the face of declining standards of living. The marginal propensity to consume informs us that people will consume a relatively stable proportion of any change in their current income. People should consume more as their income rises and less as their income declines. At very low levels of income people will dig into their savings account. Later, economists loosened the reigns on current income to allow for variations in spending throughout one's lifecycle: an individual typically purchases beyond his/her means during early adulthood, while saving more as he/she matures and then consuming out of accumulated saving in retirement. Spending today can be based not only on current income but also on future expected income, and at any point in time one's spending and saving behavior adjusts to maintain a stable percentage of expected lifetime income (Duesenberry 1949; Modigliani 1986). Also, in response to declines in income, rather than immediately cutting back on spending people strove to maintain their standard of living. So, what matters is one's income relative to an accustomed standard of living (Brady and Friedman 1947). Social norms and class-based patterns of consumption – what Pierre Bourdieu called *habitus* – play an important role in the theoretical understanding of the postwar consumer (Akerlof 2007). The Keynesian consumer was depicted as a more thoroughly modern character whose behavior is incapable of being reduced to "stimulus-response patterns located in all psyches" (Heilbroner and Milberg 1995: 33). Social norms, expectations and uncertainty shape the spending behavior of the Keynesian consumer. This opened the door to explorations in the behavioral foundations of consumer activity building on the survey research and psychological concepts developed by George Katona. However, this empirically based behavioral economics failed to find its way into the mainstream.

More recently, in the midst of stagnant real wage growth coupled with asset depreciation in the housing market, Americans have been spending beyond their means. Savings as a percentage of disposable (after-tax) income has fallen precipitously from 10–11 per cent during the early 1980s to a low of 0.5 per cent or less since 2005 (Figure 1.1). Consumers are dissaving on a massive scale. Since 1999 interest payments alone have exceeded personal savings as a percentage of disposable income. Perhaps mainstream economists might be inclined to argue that people are being overly optimistic in their expectation of future income, and, hence, base their current spending on that rosy scenario. Others might postulate that in this current US regime of labor market volatility there is no accurate way to calculate future income, and so people are responding by creatively and

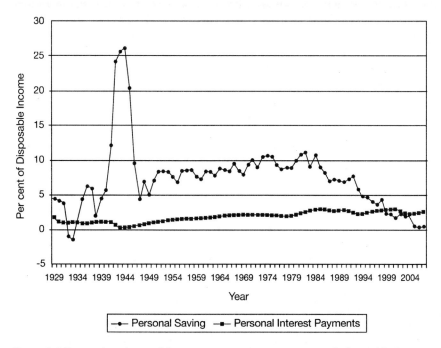

Figure 1.1 Personal saving and interest payments as a per cent of disposable income 1929–2007.

Source: Bureau of Economic Analysis, Table 2.1: Personal income and its disposition. http://www.bea.gov/national/nipaweb

desperately cobbling together alternative sources of spending beyond their income in order to preserve their standard of living. The rise in consumer debt is one indication that this is exactly what people are doing (Sullivan *et al.* 2006). In fact, since 1999 consumer debt payments (not even including mortgage debt) comprise a larger claim on disposable income than do savings. Not only are people not saving, but the amount of consumer debt they are paying off exceeds the amount that they are saving.

What is it that people are buying and how might shifts in purchasing patterns affect the overall economy? First, let's briefly talk about economic cycles of contraction and expansion, usually referred to as business cycles. It has been common practice to explain the patterns of growth and decline in the US economy by looking at changes in business investment spending. In general, it is thought that while government spending may have some effect on economic growth prospects – we need only look at the wartime boom generated by government spending during the Second World War – mainstream economists would prefer to examine the free market (absent government intervention). So, since the foreign sector has traditionally been a small portion of total GDP,[2] and since consumption spending is a relatively more stable part of GDP, any volatility in the economy must be due to changes in business investment activity (Su 2004: 29). This default position focusing on business net investment in new plant and equipment is consistent with the production-centric orientation of economics discussed above. Consumer demand is a function of income and people's income is directly related to the level of employment generated by the investment activity of businesspeople. This is a fundamental tenant of mainstream economics and one that directs our attention to changes in the rate of growth of business investment as a key determinant of business cycle turning points. In contrast to this view, UCLA economist Edward Leamer argues that downturns in residential investment and in the purchase of consumer durables (cars, household furnishings, appliances) consistently precede the onset of a recession. Instead of focusing attention on the normal constituents of long-run growth, the standard approach of mainstream macroeconomists, Leamer calculates the abnormal contributions to growth and then focuses attention on the years before a recession. He finds that since 1947 the housing sector alone accounted for 26% of the decline in eight of the ten postwar recessions.

> In the years before recessions, 20% of the weakness was from consumer durables, 10% from consumer services and 9% from consumer nondurables. Thus consumers contribute a total of 65% of the leading weakness. In contrast, business spending contributes only 10% of the weakness before recessions; 8% is from equipment and software and 2% from business structures. Most of the weakness on the business side coincides with the recessions rather than leads them.
>
> (Leamer 2007: 54)

Given this finding, Leamer prefers to call these economic changes *consumer cycles* rather than business cycles.

However, even within the sector of durable goods consumption there are recent shifts worth noting. Spending on cars and trucks has slowed down but the same cannot be said for consumer purchases of household furniture and furnishings (Figure 1.2). While it is unclear if this is a trend or not, it is suggestive of changing consumption behavior. It has become evident that the US car market has reached a saturation point and the interest in alternative fuel vehicles is altering the structure of demand within the auto industry itself (Su 2007: 19). The stimulus played by the technological system erected around the internal combustion automobile appears to be coming to an end in advanced capitalist economies (Gualerzi 2001; Urry 2008).

So, on the basis of evidence gleaned from macroeconomic data, consumers are dominant players in the US economy. Lately, the ability of consumers to maintain their accustomed levels of spending is being challenged by stagnating wages, increasing debt burdens and the subsequent diversion of income from spending to interest payments on credit cards, auto loans and mortgages. The postwar age of affluence is looking more and more like a bygone era for most Americans. But reference to macroeconomic data is only one part of the story. Just as the macroeconomists assume a standard "one-size-fits-all" theory of consumer behavior so, too, does

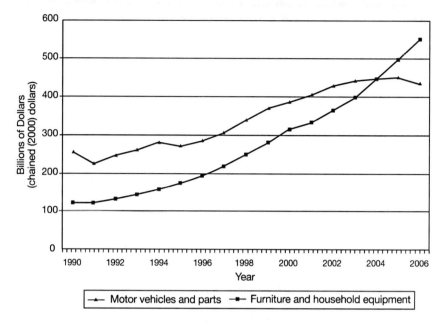

Figure 1.2 Consumer spending on key durable goods 1990–2006.

Source: Bureau of Economic Analysis, Table 2.4.6: Real personal consumption expenditures by type of product, chained dollars. http://www.bea.gov/national/nipaweb

microeconomics cleave to a stripped-down theory of consumer choice. In their model, consumers act to maximize their utility subject to the limitations imposed on them by their income and the relative prices of the goods and services they seek to buy. Another key ingredient is necessary in order to provide an analytical framework to the mainstream model: individual tastes and preferences.

Participation in green consumption is a trend that holds the potential for altering the way in which consumers think about the purchase and use of commodities. And it also offers a challenge to mainstream economics. On the grounds of cost–benefit analysis, the Prius hybrid automobile, when it was first introduced at the turn of the twenty-first century, did not provide sufficient gasoline savings to overcome the retail price differential between it and more conventional low-mileage automobiles (Holman 2005). But, the reasons for purchasing a Prius run deeper than preferences for an inexpensive form of individual transportation. So, how can economists model individual rational choices about demand when the demand for the good is itself determined by an underlying set of values that Hirschman (1984) refers to as "meta-preferences?" In this case, the preference for more environmentally sustainable forms of transportation is rooted in a deeper acknowledgement of the harmful third-party effects of individual driving behavior. Furthermore, if the motivation to buy a hybrid vehicle or fair-trade products is rooted in commitment to alter the course of future economic and social relations, the model of rational self-interested behavior tends to be unable to account for such non-instrumental goals. As Amartya Sen points out,

> ... commitment does involve, in a very real sense, counterpreferential choice, destroying the crucial assumption that a chosen alternative must be better than (or at least as good as) the others for the person choosing it, and this would certainly require that models be formulated in a different way.
>
> (Sen 1977: 328)

The formation of commitment and values is not undertaken in isolation but rather requires communication and social interaction. In addition, I argue that the process of consumption often involves not merely the acquisition and evaluation of meta-preferences (values) and commitments that shape and inform choice but that the very process of using and consuming the commodities and services that we purchase, in turn, affects our needs and desires.

So, to better understand shifts in consumer spending we need to construct a richer account of consumer practices that encompasses a broader swath of human experience that extends beyond the marketplace. In this sense I want to de-center the market as the primary focus of attention for economists interested in explaining consumer behavior. In place of isolated, atomistic individuals buying their commodities in the market, I will argue that consumption is a socially constructed set of practices. Consumption involves social relations between individuals and groups ranging from family members to retail sales workers, advertisers, transnational corporations, entrepreneurs, government regulators, and other shoppers. Markets are economic institutions that shape our attitudes, beliefs and behavior (Lane 1991; Bowles 1998). But consumption also involves a set of social practices that extend beyond the point of purchase to include the formulation of demand and the transformation of commodities by means of using those commodities. Therefore, consumption involves multiple sites of social, cultural and material interaction.

Voices of resistance to the model of self-interested consumer behavior or rational choice microeconomics do exist. On the one hand are economists who draw upon the intellectual traditions inspired by Karl Marx, Max Weber and Thorstein Veblen. From this perspective, consumption involves processes of conflict and control, group identification, status enhancement or status preservation, habitual forms of life and standards of living, and contestation over the meanings and uses of commodities. Economists sympathetic to this perspective are arrayed along a spectrum ranging from those who focus on consumption as a form of individual exploration and identity formation, to those who examine the ways in which demands and desires are artificially created and sustained by agents of the modern corporation through overt and covert (e.g. "buzz marketing") forms of product advertising. These are important contributions to our understanding of consumer behavior. But taken to their extremes they result in the depiction of consumers as either free agents able to transcend limitations of class, gender, race, geography and income in their quest for novelty, meaning and identity or as dupes acting in the best interests of corporations and against their own individual or class-based interests. Also, these approaches tend to focus on the social aspects of consumer choices without explicitly taking into account either the historical development of consumer practices or the extension of consumption beyond the point of purchase. Instead, I argue that the development of consumer practices has historically been constituted by a set of forces, not the least of which is gender.[3] Furthermore, the development of a consumer culture was predicated on the extension of consumer goods to a wider population. The establishment in the twentieth century of a mass consumer society had a profound impact on the widespread practices of consumer culture that we take for granted today. The act of shopping functions on multiple levels: material, social, cultural, political and aesthetic. For some, the shopping mall is a civic space (albeit privately owned), a place where cultural capital is acquired and social capital networks are maintained and extended. For others, the mall is an arid, monotonous commercial zone devoid of the elements of a successful, regenerative public sphere. For many, the no-frills supermarket is but a warehouse of food supplies whereas, for an increasing number of people, the local farmer's market promotes local knowledge of the source of foodstuffs and the opportunity to close the physical and social distance between producer and consumer.

This effort to widen the scope of economic analysis first entails a critical account of the process through which the boundaries between mainstream (neoclassical) and heterodox economics are created, as well as the ways in which the border between economics and non-economics is erected and defended. Claims about what counts as economics are often contested at the borders of the discipline. This is the focus of the first chapter. Next, in order to advance a political economic account of consumer behavior, I first identify some key contributions made by economists in the past. These contributions have been mostly neglected for reasons having to do with the lack of congruence between these alternative perspectives and the establishment of the neoclassical mainstream. In Chapter 3, I explore the contributions made by early twentieth-century home economists. Whatever pejorative connotations still adhere to "Home Ec," it is important to understand that early home economists were skilled professionals charged with navigating between two different worlds. On the one hand they sought to establish a legitimate academic research program in household management and consumer decision-making. Research in home economics was undertaken by economists who could not find academic employment in departments of economics. They performed economic research but were effectively shut out of participating in the development of the field. Though there were notable exceptions, the fact remains that the current state of the art in microeconomics and heterodox economics – including the dynamic and critically engaged sub-field of feminist economics – fails to fully appreciate the alternative possibilities resulting from this research.

In addition, home economists were expected to be knowledgeable consumers in their own right, alert both to the deceptive claims and blandishments of corporate advertisers and the need to educate consumers about the "proper" use of new consumer appliances and foodstuffs. Yet, they were fully aware of the importance of consumer spending to the modern economy and the strategic role of women in it. I examine the establishment of a home economics analysis of consumer practices and trace the roots of a feminist economic standpoint embodied in research and teaching through an examination of one of the nation's leading programs in Home Economics at Cornell University in the early part of the twentieth century.

The second epistemological contribution to a political economy of consumer behavior involves the representation of consumers as heterogeneous and sociable, influenced by prices, quality, income, social custom, status, fairness, and personal integrity. In the next chapter, the psychological economics of George Katona will be examined in order to trace out an alternative path of behavioral economics. By providing an account of individual decision-making that troubles the standard neoclassical assumptions of strict rationality while applying concepts drawn from outside of economics (e.g. framing and anchoring effects), research in behavioral economics has the potential to fragment economic knowledge and alter the economic landscape.

The rise of mass consumption within a regime of Fordist mass production is the focus of yet another source of economic knowledge about the consumer. Chapter 5 explores the contribution of the Regulation school toward our understanding of consumer behavior. Here, I extend the Regulation approach to include a discussion of the social relations of consumption, and more recent attempts in science studies and cultural studies to develop a theory of social practice that extends beyond the sphere of individual or group interaction to include cultural symbols and material objects and their use. In part inspired by actor-network theory and the social construction of technology, consumption will be understood as a series of practices that are capable of reproducing, weakening, resisting and subverting consumer identities, market behavior and user cultures.

In Chapters 6–8, three case studies – different sites and practices of consumption – are presented in order to highlight the ways in which these alternative strands of economic analysis can be used to provide a richer understanding of consumer behavior. Those sites and practices are: (1) green automobility, (2) slow food, and (3) alternative currency. I examine how a theory of alternative hedonism can be applied to consumer practices that resist dominant norms, while simultaneously embracing an ethos of pleasure. I conclude by exploring the behavioral dimension of ethical and political consumption.

2 Economic knowledge

Boundary-keeping and border crossing

I have come to realize that a pincer attack from a dimly remembered past and a vividly imagined future is among the best means available to academics for displacing a sense of the present that refuses to plan its own obsolescence.

(Fuller 2000a: xvi)

The discipline of economics has entered a period of exploration, self-reflection and restructuring. Behavioral and experimental economists have begun to question the bedrock assumptions of rationality and autonomous individual action. To critics of the mainstream, such as me, a serious internal review and assessment of the dominant school of thought is long overdue. The recent behavioral turn in neoclassical economics has yet to be reconciled to the foundations of rational choice microeconomic theory (Kahneman 1994; 2003). The task may well be impossible if the current regime of neoclassical economists refuse to plan for their own obsolescence. For many years economics has been immune to advances in the sociological and ethnographic study of scientific practice – science studies – and still continues to cling to a model of science rooted in nineteenth-century physics. The problem is that physics has moved beyond its nineteenth-century theorems and laws, whereas economics appears trapped in the amber of nineteenth-century metaphors and discursive practices (Mirowski 1998: 358). Yet there now appears to be a loosening of the rules governing what counts as economic analysis. Complexity theories that allow the economy to be depicted as a dynamic, evolutionary, interdependent system present both a challenge and an opportunity to re-draw the borders of economics (Davis 2006). A growing appreciation for the feedback between institutions, norms, custom and individual behavior has moved the concerns of institutional and social economists onto the agenda of neoclassical economists dissatisfied with the explanatory power of methodological individualism defined narrowly in terms of an atomistic hedonist at the microeconomic level and a representative agent at the macro level (Kirman 1992; Davis 2003; Hodgson 2007a; 2007b).

Given the current tumult, the purpose of this book, to trace out the paths toward a political economy of consumer behavior, is especially daunting. Instead of enumerating a compendium of lessons to be learned from strands of inquiry drawn from the numerous variants of heterodoxy in economics, I first intend to remark on the current state of economics with special attention to the borders and frontiers that demarcate economics from non-economics and orthodoxy from heterodoxy. The metaphor of mapping is quite appealing in this regard. I discuss the ways in which mental maps or images of economics can be construed, borrowing from the historical anthropology of Benedict Anderson and from the urban planning and design theories of Kevin Lynch.

Economists inhabit an imagined community of colleagues who collectively help to define the discipline. The term "imagined community" requires some explanation. I use it to evoke the sense of place inhabited by economists. By doing so, I adopt Anderson's (1991) characterization of the nation-state as a mental map of belonging. Anderson identifies three attributes of the nation that qualify it as an imagined community: (1) the members of the nation, even the smallest nation, can never know all its inhabitants and as such there is, at best, an imaginary bond between fellow countrymen/women; (2) in belonging to this or that nation we simultaneously exclude our membership to other nations – the nation state is limited and, dual citizenship aside, our allegiance has borders; (3) there exists a "deep, horizontal comradeship" or "fraternity" of members that binds and unites individuals into an identifiable community.

In addition to Anderson, I also employ the metaphor of spatial mapping to refer to the social cartography of academic disciplines. Much of the discussion herein will be conducted within the imagined terrain of economics. In this sense, I will adapt ideas from one of the key innovators of modern urban design and planning, Kevin Lynch. Lynch's *Image of the City*, first published in 1960, became a landmark study in the field of planning. Lynch, a sometime student of Frank Lloyd Wright, sought to understand the way cities are experienced by visitors and inhabitants alike. Lynch wanted to know the ways in which cities can be read. He ascertained that the city is a cluster of images triggered by environmental, emotional, and sensory cues. So the meaning of the city contains within it shared understandings together with idiosyncratic features replete with emotional connotations, cultural cues and symbolism. A sharp, integrated image of the city allows one to successfully navigate. Such an image helps to create a sense of emotional security ("I know the way to go."). If this all seems exceedingly simple, the idea that planners should care about the way people experience the city was largely ignored at the time of *Image of the City*. Rather, the planner was seen as the expert who understood how to control and manage the city as a complex system.[1] So, Lynch set about creating what we would today call focus groups. He would ask long-time residents of Jersey City, Boston and Los Angeles, to create their own mental maps of their hometowns. Lynch wrote about this process in a manner that presaged poststructuralist theory:

> The environment suggests distinctions and relations, and the observer – with great adaptability and in light of his own purposes – selects, organizes, and endows with meaning what he sees. The image so developed now limits and emphasizes what is seen, while the image itself is tested against the filtered perceptual input in a constant interacting process. Thus the image of a given reality may vary significantly between different observers.
>
> (Lynch 1975: 6)

We all see the city, but each of us sees a different, personal city. The issue for planners was whether they could design the natural and built environment in such a way that the personal city could also become a civic city where a collective understanding of place could help to construct a shared identity and sense of social responsibility (Duany and Plater-Zyberk 1992; Talen 1999).

By combining Anderson's concept of "imagined community" with Lynch's attempt to formulate a collective image of the city, we can begin to apply these concepts to the imagined mapping of economics. Anderson gives us the means by which to ascertain the broad parameters between the nation of economics and other disciplinary territories. We certainly don't know each and every person who identifies herself as an "economist," and yet we are alert and aware when we hear an economist on the news or listen to a colleague from another department make reference to the economic impact of this or that. How many times have we been at a professional meeting or even at a gathering of friends when someone begins to talk about economists or the economy and we, often unconsciously, get ourselves ready to represent the nation of economists? Similarly, economists know who they are by identifying who they are not: sociologists, philosophers, anthropologists, accountants. Finally, economists share in a fraternity or sorority of like-minded folk. Despite our ideological differences we all teach principles of micro- and macroeconomics and we all make reference to the "invisible hand," although not always with the same intent! There is a stock of knowledge about what constitutes the "mainstream" – even if the term "mainstream" is odd to some because, well, what else is there? This shared discourse and practice contributes to a common sense of who "we" are. This is the imagined community of economics and economists. But there is more to it than that.

Anderson's discourse on imperialism and nationalism begins to identify fissures and fault lines. Notably, among the colonized peoples there emerged individuals who were native to the colony but educated and trained by the imperial power. As such, they identified culturally – and perhaps economically – with the imperial elite. Likewise, in an analysis of national surveys of economists undertaken in the late 1970s and early 1980s, it was discovered that there were large areas of agreement among economists about the efficacy of the price system (Frey *et al.* 1984). Overall consensus centered more on microeconomic issues than on macropolicy. However, divisions were found between economists located in different countries. Economists from the US, Germany and Switzerland had the highest between-group internal cohesion, whereas the Austrian and French economists were less likely to be enamored of the price system. More recent intellectual foment among European economists, the French in particular, signals an uprising among students and faculty who have adopted the slogan "postautistic" economics. These economists argue that contemporary mainstream (neoclassical) economics has become excessively technique-driven, unnecessarily parochial and detached from empirical evidence (Fullbrook 2003).

Meanwhile, Kevin Lynch gathered data on the way people interpret the city by asking them to create their own personal map. One could do the same thing with economists. Lynch (1960: 155) asked the following questions ("urban boundary mapping") that could be adapted to mapping the economic terrain (Figure 2.1).

Urban boundary mapping	Economics boundary mapping
Draw a quick sketch map of the area in question, showing the most interesting and important features, and giving a stranger enough knowledge to move about without too much difficulty.	Draw a quick mental map of the field of economics listing what you think are the most important and distinctive features of the discipline.
Make a similar sketch of the route and events along one or two imaginary trips, trips chosen to expose the length and breadth of the area.	Make a similar sketch of an important problem area or current topic that occupies researchers in your sub-field and identify the most promising perspectives, theories and/or methods.
Make a written list of the parts of the city felt to be most distinctive.	List the key features that set economics off from other social sciences.

Figure 2.1 Urban and economics boundary mapping.

If we undertook such a task, asking colleagues to draw maps of economics, we would begin to investigate how the mapping of economics is particular and partial in ways that reflect our own standpoint. If we were to move beyond the heuristic use of this example and actually assembled maps of the economics discipline, what might they tell us? Would we, like Lynch, be able to distill uniformities among the diverse array of mental maps that would allow us to identify the key nodes and edges that characterize and frame the field of economics? Or is it more likely that the imagined community of economics would be portrayed as fragmented, uneven, discontinuous and contentious? As a heterodox economist I would prefer to believe that the latter outcome would hold. Indeed, there is evidence to suggest that the field of economics is fragmenting and that the image of a unified neoclassical doctrine is rife with inconsistencies and incongruities (Fullbrook 2003; Sent 2004; Davis 2006; Mirowski 2007). However, as David Colander (2007) reports, among freshly minted graduate students at highly ranked departments the scope of disagreement and debate over what constitutes the economic core seems to be narrowing. Perhaps this reflects the implementation of selection criteria that result in admitting students who are extremely receptive to the idea that economics education primarily entails the acquisition of techniques grounded in a few fundamental theoretical postulates. Arjo Klamer, in response to a 2005 update of a 1985 survey of graduate education by Colander, laments:

> If anything, the discipline has become more homogeneous, more single-minded, more hard-nosed about the science of economics and hence less heterogeneous and arguably less intellectually exciting. Problem solving continues to be the key to success, and so is mathematical dexterity. Intellectuals with a wide range of interest will not survive in the conversations that economists are trained to conduct.
>
> (Klamer 2007a: 230)

Klamer goes on to say that, "It remains interesting to note that even though economists are willing to study any phenomenon that strikes their fancy … their own behavior and impact of their science are not among them..." (2007a: 233). This lack of reflexivity, I argue, is part of the epistemologic legacy of modern economics that represents economics as a scientific enterprise adhering to procedures of objective, value-free inquiry.

I use the term "standpoint" in the paragraph above in the way that the feminist philosopher Sandra Harding uses the term. Harding proposes a forceful and provocative re-interpretation of what it means to be "objective." Rather than accepting the subject/object binary category made use of in the traditional scientific method, Harding argues that there are two types of objectivity: weak and strong. The weaker version of objectivity is characterized by the quest to rid one's analysis of value judgment and to apply universal standards by which to ascertain the truth (or non-falsifiability) of one's findings. By contrast, strong objectivity takes account of the subjective nature not just of the analysis undertaken but also the context in which it was developed and the particular perspective or standpoint of the investigator. Harding maintains that:

> culturewide ... beliefs function as evidence at every stage of scientific inquiry: in the selection of problems, the formation of hypotheses, the design of research (including the organization of research communities), the collection of data, the interpretation and sorting of data, decisions about when to stop research, the way research results are reported, and so on.
>
> (Harding 2004: 136)

The reason this is important is that it compels us to question the taken-for-granted claims of science to objectivity. It opens up scientific method to an analysis of the rhetoric and everyday practice of scientists themselves. This is an approach that has been provocatively implemented in science studies and in social construction of scientific knowledge explorations of the interpretive realm of scientific practice (Hess 1997). In economics, it is affiliated with some strands of an emergent feminist economics paradigm (Hewitson 1999) and it is also to be found in the rhetorical turn in economics launched by Dierdre McCloskey and Arjo Klamer (McCloskey 1987; Klamer and McCloskey 1988; Klamer 2007b). These more heterodox positions construct bridges to other disciplinary modes of investigation.

One way of translating this research into the language of economics is to suggest that strong objectivity and the social construction of science seek to examine the ways in which culture, power and norms are constitutive of the institutional framework of scientific practice, which, in turn, affects the "nature" of science itself in such a way that the preferences and the practices of scientists are taken to be endogenously determined. The rational scientific actor seeking to scrupulously apply the governing laws of her discipline to the objective search for truth is replaced with the image of workers situated in laboratories embedded in relations of power and politics, entrusted with making interpretive judgments about the problem set, hypothesis, criteria of acceptability, and about which results to report out and which to omit. Indeed, sociological studies of scientific workers reveal that scientists themselves are enmeshed in practices that include mobilizing resources, shaping attention, and speaking on behalf of scientific instruments in order to give voice to the results (Knorr-Cetina 1985; Latour 1988; Didier 2007). The corresponding role of economists conducting controlled experiments under laboratory conditions can best be approximated through the practice of selecting out dependent variables, the choice of independent variables, and the estimation of bias and error in econometric modeling or through the invocation of the claim *ceteris paribus* as commonly portrayed in introductory economics textbooks.[2] In either case most economists have yet to come to grips with the socially constructed world of their own laboratory lives.

The claim that economic knowledge is socially constructed allows for an understanding of the field as the outcome of interpretation, negotiation and contestation over the constituents of economic knowledge and the legitimacy of particular practices, methods and techniques of analysis. The practices underpinning the social construction of economic knowledge refer not to some ideal process of participatory democracy in which informed and equally well-resourced academic citizens debate the merits of competing theories and methodological approaches within a free market of ideas. In contrast to this pluralist democratic model, science can instead be depicted as an inherently political venture within which not only is the work of scientists used for political ends but the constitution of scientific knowledge and the accountability of scientists for their own research practices is itself constituted through relations of power and control over resources (Fuller 2000a). Concomitantly, economists engage in boundary disputes, erect checkpoints and employ gate-keepers in order to enforce the boundary between economics and non-economics. This "boundary-work" (Gieryn 1983) results in the demarcation of economic from non-economic research. In economics, the dominant school of thought – neoclassical economics – is referred to as the "mainstream" by those laboring on the borders of the discipline. Boundary-work is a 24/7 job because the claim to epistemic legitimacy is always already open to contestation. According to Gieryn:

> Sociological attention is centered on how the boundaries of science are episodically established, sustained, enlarged, policed, breached, and sometimes erased in the defense, pursuit, or denial of epistemic authority. As knowledge makers seek to present their claims or practices as legitimate (credible, trustworthy, reliable) by locating them within 'science,' they discursively construct for it an ever changing arrangement of boundaries and territories and landmarks, always contingent upon immediate circumstances.
>
> (Gieryn 1999: xi)

This is not to say that borders are impermeable (Lamont and Molnar 2002). In economics the status of *homo economicus*, and metaphors such as the marketplace of ideas are being questioned and challenged (England 1993; Nelson 1993; Strassmann 1993; Nelson 1996; Thaler 2000). Recently, mainstream economists have, in greater numbers, begun to join heterodox economists in abandoning strict rational choice models of human behavior to instead look at economic systems as complex networks of human interaction (Gallegati and Kirman 1999). This trend supports the claim raised earlier that economics has become fragmented and economic discourse has become increasingly contested. But economics has always been contested. Past lines of inquiry have been buried, alternative paths forgotten. What I propose is to shift attention toward these borderlands.

Warning: markets and economics courses may be hazardous to social health

The approach taken in this book reflects the heterodox perspective in economics, particularly the traditions of social economics and radical political economy. Practitioners in both of these schools of economic thought maintain that individuals and their behavior are socially, culturally and materially constituted. For example, markets are understood as social institutions that do more than merely channel pre-existing preferences and desires. Rather, market exchange inserts individuals within a set of cultural norms (e.g. market efficiency has been represented through the application of a streamlined, functional design aesthetic), social norms (e.g. competitive behavior is appropriate and expected within market settings) and power relations (e.g. the ability of one agent to get another agent to act against their own interests), which themselves assert an influence on the behavior of economic actors (Lutz and Lux 1979; Gintis 1989b; Bowles and Gintis 1993; George 2004). Recent endeavors by behavioral and experimental economists to better understand decision-making under uncertainty have begun to challenge mainstream accounts of rationality (Charness and Rabin 2002; Rabin 2002) and, in so doing, move toward theories of endogenous preference formation and social preferences that are more amenable to social economics and radical political economy approaches. One outcome of this excavation into the history of economics will be to expose alternative trajectories for behavioral economics through an examination of the research of one of the founders of psychological economics, George Katona. For now, I want to summarize one example of the type of research that raises the potential for re-socializing economic agents in general and the consumer in particular.

Middlebury College economist Jeffrey Carpenter (2005) studied the effect of market institutions on the other-regarding characteristics of individuals. His research utilizes experimental economics within a game theoretic framework. He wants to isolate the effects that changing institutional structures have on social preferences. Two precursors to his study are addressed. I will focus on one. Hoffman and colleagues (1994) explore responses to a bargaining experiment in which individuals are first identified merely as individual A and individual B, and then they are alternatively referred to as sellers and buyers. By invoking the names "seller" and "buyer," the interaction is transformed into a market exchange. The results of the bargaining game reveal that sellers' offers are appreciably lower compared with offers made in a non-market setting. This result is suggestive but does not directly explain whether social preferences themselves have changed.

The individual players could simply have formulated differently their estimates of offers being rejected under the non-market and market scenarios. But the results are suggestive in that they imply that actors may perform differently when the discursive structure of the exchange changes. For instance when buyers and sellers are identified as such, the interaction is framed by the existing stocks of knowledge regarding what constitutes a market and the behavior typically displayed or performed in markets (Schutz 1967; Pietrykowski 1996).

Carpenter instead measures social preferences *before* and after participation in various bargaining experiments. This is akin to assessing student learning not only by analyzing final grades but also by comparing students' knowledge and capacities before and then again after having completed a course (often measured with a pretest and post-test evaluation method). His pretest is a value-orientation experimental design used by social psychologists. In this experiment, individuals, randomly selected into groups of three to minimize strategic (bilateral) behavior, engage in 24 decisions to divide a monetary sum between themselves and another player. The decision ordering of the payoff options, e.g. Option A: 13.00 francs for You and 7.50 francs for Other vs. Option B: 10.60 francs for You and 10.60 francs for Other, is randomized. In addition, the payoff to Other could have just as likely preceded the payoff to You "so that players could not just focus on their own payoffs; at a minimum they needed to look at the consequences of their choices for the recipient" of their actions (Carpenter 2005: 67). The pattern of responses is then mapped onto a "motivational vector" that measures both the consistency of the choices (the longer the length of the vector the more consistent the choice pattern) and the orientation of the individual choices categorized along four dimensions: Altruistic, Cooperative, Egoistic, and Competitive. Here it is interesting to note that this procedure and the categories used by Carpenter were first developed and utilized in the field of psychology, not economics. The post-test exercise to determine a participant's social preference valuation requires individuals to play the role of dictator in distributing tokens of differing value to recipients. The objective was to use a similar, but not identical, game in order to assess the orientation of individuals toward others. Altruists "are those whose preferences for their own payoff and the payoff of the other player are substitutes because, for a given price ratio, they assign all the tokens to whoever benefits most" (69). Cooperative individuals are those who equalize payoffs, for example, if they deem a certain allocation to be fair – say 60/40 – then they consistently apply this allocation across successive plays of the game. Egoists act in such a way as to keep all of the tokens for themselves while Competitive individuals are defined as the least social (other-regarding) of all.[3] The similarity between the two games allows for comparisons of the same individuals' social preferences both before and after the experiment.

The contours of the experimental design are as follows: 36 individuals participated in the pretest and then the post-test. The results formed the basis of the control against which the games would be evaluated. In other words, the change in social preferences elicited in each of four games (to be described below) was measured against the change in social preferences resulting from the control.

The four games can be summarized briefly:

Game 1: Repeated Ultimatum Game
- Two players, one of whom is dictator. Dictator decides on payoff ratio between self and other player. If payoff is deemed too low the other player can reject the offer and both parties receive zero payoff. This game is played ten times between the same players.

Game 2: Random Ultimatum Game
- Same as above except, while the total number of games played is still ten, the players are randomly re-selected after each round of play.

Game 3: Best Shot Game
- Here the scenario involves the payment needed to provide a public good shared by all payers.
- The goal is to provide the good in an amount consistent with the highest bid.
- Each bid is costly as the highest bid succeeds in providing the highest level of provision but also requires the bidder to pay the costs of the project.
- The equilibrium solution is for first-mover to bid zero and the second-mover to bid at a level that maximizes their individual payoff (similar to estimating net benefit).

The reason for introducing Game 1 and Game 2 is to examine the role played by socialization in Game 1 versus anonymity in Game 2. The rationale for Game 3 is that with the ultimatum games (1 and 2) there is a tendency, over time, to make a higher offer in the hopes of lessening the chances of rejection (e.g. spiteful behavior in response to a perceived unfair offer), whereas in Game 3 if first-movers become more generous second-movers have an incentive to offer lower bids and free ride (receiving the benefits of the public good without paying for it).

Game 4: Market Game
- In this game there is one seller and four buyers of a good (indivisible and costless for the seller to produce or obtain).
- The good is offered for sale and the highest bid is either accepted or rejected by the seller.
- The result is similar to the ultimatum game as one player (seller, in this case) receives most of the payoff.

Carpenter's primary results can be summarized as follows: first, market competition (Game 4) and anonymous game-playing (Game 2) tend to make individuals less other-regarding. This result persists even after controlling for the effects of payoff disparities, non-equilibrium results (Carpenter refers to these as non-*homo economicus* behavior) and other endogenous determinants of preferences such as bad treatment by other players. Exogenous controls include sex, race, roles (first- or second-mover), and original value orientation. Furthermore, he finds that in games between the same players (Game 1) the higher level of social exposure to the other player results in: (a) first-mover offers that tend to become more altruistic with successive plays of the game largely in response to (b) second-movers' willingness to reject unfair offers by first-movers (80). In sum, it appears that the results suggest the more that markets resemble Wal-Mart or Costco – giant, impersonal warehouses – the greater the tendency for exchange to elicit lower levels of social preferences (other-regarding behavior). In addition, competition, because it tends to punish those whose bids are not accepted, encourages egoistic behavior and resentment "toward the market structure" itself. This effect extends beyond individual experiences. In other words, even those people who are not frequently ill-treated by the market become less other-regarding. In this way, the anonymous and competitive exchanges (markets) frame expectations and attitudes regardless of one's personal experience with market exchange (81).

The reason for such a detailed review of this experimental study is that it presents several relevant issues for the political economy of consumer behavior:

1   The analytical structure of economics seems to be moving decisively away from large-scale model-building toward what I would refer to as nanotechnology of social behavior – attempts to explain micromotives and the interaction between individuals and between individuals and institutions. I characterize this as a change in the *scale* of economic analysis together with a heightened attention to the *context* within which economic behavior takes place.
2   A profound skepticism of the explanatory power of rational choice as the basis for economic behavior is beginning to take hold of economic analysis – what Richard Thaler refers to as the move from the study of *homo economicus* to the analysis of *homo sapiens* (2000). This seems to me to represent a move aimed at unpacking the black box of human *behavior*.
3   Finally, the behavioral turn is characterized by a liberal borrowing of both statistical techniques and explanatory frameworks from other social sciences (notably psychology and sociology). This reflects a broadening of the *scope* of what counts as economic research.

Now I am fairly certain that many economists have either read about or are themselves actively engaged in research in behavioral or experimental economics. So perhaps the study by Carpenter fits within their mapping of mainstream economics, possibly as a new frontier. However, it might be surprising to discover that one of the stated objectives of Carpenter's paper was to test the hypothesis put forth by Marx that exchange tends to erode solidarity and social (class) cohesion. The paper was published in the *Review of Radical Political Economics*, a leading heterodox economics journal.[4] The behavioral turn within economics can be seen as an opportunity not only to re-draw the disciplinary map of economics but also to engage in useful border crossing and inter-disciplinary exploration.

Let me now turn to another example that deals not with the frontier of research in economics but rather the traditional and seemingly mundane topic of economic education. Economic knowledge is transmitted via several well-known routes: graduate training, undergraduate education, and popular communication through the internet, newspapers, television and radio.[5] The triumphs and travails of graduate education in the United States have been documented most notably in the 1991

Commission on Graduate Education in Economics (COGEE) Report (Krueger 1991; Colander 2001). The most sensationalistic headline one could probably create from the COGEE findings is that contemporary graduate education in economics has produced a generation of "idiot savants"[6] skilled at mathematics and abstract problem-solving but displaying little or no concrete understanding of the nature of economic institutions nor a sound understanding of the function and historical evolution of economic policy (Krueger 1991: 1044–5). As Colander (2001) notes, the Report met with stony silence from the top graduate schools in the United States. The rise of postautistic economics (Fullbrook 2003) can be characterized as a resistance movement that the authors of COGEE should have anticipated lest their call to diversify the curriculum went unheeded. Compounding this situation is that the research agenda in economics seems to be shifting away from abstract models of equilibrium, axiomatic proofs, and representative agents and toward differently rational action, endogenous preferences, experimental and, arguably, more ethnographic methods, thereby creating an ever greater rift between the core theory and the frontier of economic research. Nowhere is this chasm more clearly on display than in the undergraduate classroom. One can argue, as Davis (2003) has recently done in a thoughtful and provocative assessment of the state of orthodox economics, that there is a predictable lag between the generation of new techniques and approaches in economics research and the concomitant evolution of the standard economics curriculum. I would tend to agree. But the aspect of economics education that most interests me is the effect of economics education on the behavior of students themselves. If preferences can be shaped by institutions, then the institutional structure and content of economics education may well affect the behavior of students as measured before and after their introduction to the world of mainstream economics.

Research on the value-shaping impact of principles of economics classes suggests that the acquisition of economic knowledge helps to shape moral decision-making. Robert Frank, together with Thomas Gilovich and Dennis Regan (1993), conducted an experiment with undergraduate students at Cornell University. First, Frank and colleagues wanted to examine the behavior of economics students relative to other participants in a Prisoner's Dilemma game. They found that economics majors tended to defect more frequently than non-majors. Recall that defection means that you will confess to the police and therefore get a lighter sentence than your partner as long as your partner keeps quiet. The optimal result for both parties is not to defect. Even after controlling for sex, class year and type of game played (Game 1: unenforceable promises allowed; Game 2: 30 minutes of preplay socialization; Game 3: 10 minutes of preplay socialization), the economics majors consistently behaved more selfishly than non-majors.

A particularly interesting feature of this study is that the students were asked to provide a rationale for their behavior. A statistically significantly higher percentage of economics majors referred to the rules of the game (strategy) as an explanation for their behavior. This response led Frank and his colleagues to follow up with a subset of economics students in an upper level (public finance) course. They asked the students whether, in a one-shot game, they would cooperate or defect if they knew for certain that their partner would cooperate. Interestingly, 58% of the advanced economics undergrads *would defect* compared with 34% of the non-majors. A key question remains: does economics contribute to selfish behavior or do selfish individuals select economics as their major? They found that overall the defection rate falls with years in college. However, economics majors persistently defied this trend and seniors were nearly as likely to defect as first-year students (Frank *et al.* 1993: 168).

To extend their analysis even further they surveyed students in three classes: two introductory microeconomics classes (one section employing a more traditional neoclassical approach) and one introductory astronomy course. The survey elicited student responses to certain ethical dilemmas: (1) leaving unreported a business error in your favor; and (2) returning a lost $100. The survey was distributed once in September and then again in December. The results indicated that economics students were more inclined to be less honest in December (at the end of their term) than in September, with the more traditional instructor's students leading the way. The authors conclude that "emphasis on the self-interest model tends to inhibit cooperation" and that this is indeed a problem for both economics and the world in which economics majors inhabit (1993: 170).

Beyond self-interest: heterodox alternatives

As indicated by the examples above, the model of self-interested utility maximizing behavior is under attack on a wide range of fronts. Heterodox economics offers an alternative optic through which to explore new directions for economic analysis. While the heterodox label includes a very diverse range of perspectives, there are some common threads that bind them together (more or less). First, there is a profound skepticism if not outright hostility toward the reductionism practiced by neoclassical economists. For instance, the claim that economics has effectively transformed the disciplines of the social sciences into subfields of economic inquiry through the imperial power of economic logic and technique combined with the pragmatic acquiescence on the part of our vanquished colleagues in the social sciences (Lazear 2000) ignores the postpositivist turn that has taken place within the social sciences (Fine 2002; Steinmetz 2005).[7] A second unifying thread that connects many of the heterodox approaches (social economics, post-Keynesian, Marxian, feminist, institutionalist, Austrian to name some of the major alternative schools) is an appreciation for the historical dimension of economic thought and the historical specificity of economic analysis (Hodgson 2001). Another area of rough consensus lies in the belief that heterodoxy can make a contribution to economic education and practice that serves to re-animate the normative/ethical dimension embodied in not just the moral philosophy out of which economics sprang but also the more recent engagements with political theories of justice, fairness and community of Rawls, Walzer, Sen, Habermas, Nussbaum, Putnam and Sunstein to name a few. It would not be surprising if today's students never encountered theories of fairness and justice in their economics education. The dominance of pareto optimality and the near absence of serious discussions of maximin or human capabilities as concrete alternatives places the results found by Frank and colleagues into a broader context. Am I advocating an "Ethics for Economists" course as part of the required core in undergraduate and graduate training? It certainly warrants serious consideration. But a single course is a small counterweight to the dominant paradigm. Which is why I think that advances of the type signaled in some of the work done in behavioral economics begin to call into question the basic assumptions found in exogenously given preference functions and representative agent models that allow for movement beyond the borders of mainstream economics.

What else can heterodox economics offer? In my own map of the economics landscape as I traverse my own particular research path, I see difference, power, and conflict in addition to resource allocations, profit and markets. In other words, what is of interest to heterodox political economists is the ways in which power is manifested through economic institutions and practices embodied in daily routines and discourses about the economy. This was also a concern of economists aligned with visions of the economy at odds with the dominant paradigm throughout the twentieth century. But it should be noted that a project to recover past knowledge and practices with the intent of gleaning new meanings and identifying new directions for research runs afoul of the Kuhnian vision of paradigm construction. The Kuhnian framework depicts knowledge as a progressive enterprise whereby new paradigms supplant older disciplinary lines of inquiry by dint of their superior ability to explain the panoply of anomalies that have frustrated practitioners working within the older paradigm. For all the references in *The Structure of Scientific Revolutions* to revolutionary upheavals whereby new, usually younger, scientists upend and transcend the entrenched disciplinary practices – a process likened to a Gestalt switch – the goal of scientific revolution is the re-establishment of normal science once again insulated from external critique and content to focus on puzzle solving. Therefore, past knowledge and practices incompatible with the current paradigm are deemed irrelevant to current scientific endeavors. Fuller (2000b: 235) compares this disciplinary amnesia to Baudrillard's simulacrum – a simulated presentation of reality that comes to occupy the role of the real better than the real itself (hyper-reality). The elegance, simplicity and technical sophistication of the dominant paradigm is the simulacrum that participants understand as their discipline's reality. In contrast to Kuhn's revolutionary model of paradigm change, Fuller proposes a more classical understanding of knowledge construction wherein the "openness of the future is defined by the variety of ways available to deploy the past" (2000b: 308). Adopting this perspective would require us to revisit moments in the history of economic thought in order to locate theoretical approaches and methodological insights abandoned, neglected or undeveloped. In the next three chapters of this book, the aim is to excavate alternative understandings and explanations of consumer behavior. I then proceed to introduce three case studies that will hopefully shed light on the ways in which consumer behavior is both embedded in the social and economic structures that constitute our relationships with others and with the material culture embodied in consumer goods and services, while also offering possibilities for consuming differently by contesting dominant consumption norms and practices.

3 Economic knowledge and consumer behavior

Home economics and feminist analysis

In this chapter I begin to discuss the paths that were not taken in the creation of economic knowledge about the consumer. Early twentieth-century economics displayed a wide array of approaches and techniques that equally claimed to constitute a valid scientific approach. In particular, I argue that the historical development of modern economics in the 1920s and 1930s created a space for the development of an alternative body of economic knowledge of household and consumer behavior. During this period women were trained in the discipline of economics but many were denied employment in departments of economics (Forget 1995; Albelda 1997; Folbre 1998; Madden 2002). Some female economists found jobs in other academic programs. The question this raises is: did these discriminatory hiring practices together with the maintenance of segregated academic departments mean that female economists' research was no longer economic research?

In particular, I look at the experiences of women who trained in economics but found employment in university programs in home economics. Hazel Kyrk and Margaret Reid are two of the best-known examples of female economists whose contributions, while significant, were often more readily acknowledged outside of the economics discipline (Nelson 1980; Throne 1995; Hirschfield 1997; Yi 1996; Forget 2001; Lobdell 2000; Kiss and Beller 2000; van Velzen 2003). For example, both Kyrk and Reid had a lasting influence on the development of economics within the field of home economics (Forget 1996; Kiss and Beller 2000). Evelyn Forget, in her account of the life and work of Margaret Reid, asks the following questions relevant to this investigation:

> What exactly was the relationship between departments of home economics and departments of political economy? How did pedagogy differ between the two departments and, in particular, how did the training in economics received by students differ when it was accessed through home economics departments rather than departments of political economy? And finally, would the economic research eventually undertaken by an academic who approached the study of economics through the route of home economics be different in any substantive way from that created by someone trained in a more conventional fashion?
>
> (Forget 1996: 2–3)

I want to extend the analysis of individual female economists, such as Kyrk and Reid, to include those women who received formal training in economics but whose entire professional careers were defined outside of the disciplinary orbit of economics, sometimes in conscious opposition to it. I claim that these home economists worked collaboratively in academic departments, trained graduate students, and engaged in government-sponsored economic research. Their approach combined knowledge of the discipline and methods of economics together with a fierce opposition to traditional masculinist understandings of the economy – particularly consumption activity and household production. To explore these issues in more depth, I reconstruct a chapter in the history of home economics with special reference to the program at Cornell University in the 1920s and 1930s. I maintain that a rigorous, interdisciplinary, and advocacy-oriented consumer and household economics was established and maintained at the very same time that neoclassical consumer theory was in the process of being codified. That its practitioners were excluded from affiliation with academic departments of economics does not, in and of itself, signal that these women did not identify as economists nor that their work was positioned outside of the boundaries of economics. Rather, the curricula and research in home economics at Cornell can be read as an oppositional discourse to mainstream consumer and household economics.

Uncovering the hidden and neglected narratives in consumer economics requires that we attend to the historical process of gender segregation. Segregation that, while it erected barriers to entry to the primary domain of economic discourse, may have also fostered, of necessity, the construction of alternative spheres of economic research and practice.

Setting the stage: economics and pluralism in the 1920s and 1930s

The rise of neoclassical economics to its position as the premier school of economic thought is often attributed to its superior ability to conform to the model of scientific method. Indeed, the establishment of the American Economic Association (AEA) and the *American Economic Review* was connected with the desire to define economics in terms of scientific rigor and practical relevance. As Michael Bernstein (2001), notes:

> The trick, of course, would be to balance the desire for relevance (even notoriety) of the work of the Association and its members with the determination to retain the scientific and professional status of the enterprise as a whole. If expertise was to have influence, it should not at the same time forfeit its claim to objectivity and impartiality.
>
> (Bernstein 2001: 21)

This task, undertaken through the first decades of the twentieth century, of defining economics as a distinct professional discipline involved both recruitment and exclusion. In the early years of the century the new profession urgently needed members. But they needed to be the right members. The decision was made that women involved in the emerging field of home economics were to be excluded from the AEA. According to Bernstein:

> On the one hand, it furthered the conscious effort of AEA founders to secure a distinctive place for economics as a scientifically grounded enterprise that avoided the lesser prestige of feminized occupations like 'home economics.' On the other, it actually dovetailed with efforts dating from 1900 to constitute home economics as a separate discipline in its own right ... Their very success made the 'defeminization' of economics, at the hands of profession communities like the AEA, rather easy.
>
> (Bernstein 2001: 26)

Furthermore, Helene Silverberg argues that in the early 1900s the establishment of the social sciences as a distinct realm of academic inquiry was carried out within a gendered context. Gender came to be "encoded" in the techniques and methods of the disciplines forming the social sciences. "Economists regularly represented the market as an arena of production and exchange among male workers and male employers – even as the number of working women increased and women's consciousness as consumers became politicized" (Silverberg 1998: 9).

It should be noted that the first generation of home economists were themselves recruited from traditional fields of science, including chemistry (East 1980; Nerad 1999). So, the existence of a separate sphere of home economics could serve different, and often competing interests, as a segregated space for the practice of a lesser sort of scientific studies and as a discipline of their own within which women could engage in the type of traditional scientific research for which they were trained.[1] But at this point in the development of the field of economics, home economics served mainly as a foil against which to define economics. Economics was to be concerned neither with women's activities in the home nor with women's activities in the marketplace. Indeed, though Wesley Mitchell (1912: 271, 280) suggested that more attention be paid to the ways in which women marshaled resources in the home and made decisions in the marketplace, he referred to such activities as the "backward art" of spending and deemed such investigations worthy of "domestic science" in colleges and universities. Among members of the nascent economics profession, economics was decidedly not to be confused with home economics.

The prohibition on home economists in the economics profession can be seen as one of a number of exclusionary practices that attempted to create a coherent identity for economists. Over time, neoclassical economics, in contrast to other approaches such as institutionalism, appeared to hew more closely to the standard of objectivity and value-neutrality and thus acquired its status as science. Hence, other approaches fell by the wayside. However, this story of exclusion and in-group consensus ignores: (1) historical shifts in the meaning of the concept of objectivity; (2) the only partial exclusion of women from economics; and (3) the enlarged scope of economic research undertaken in home economics programs as a result of the exclusionary practices of academic economists.

One needs first to consider the social construction of the concept of objectivity. Assuming an ineluctable march of scientific practice in economics leads to some important oversimplifications. Between the 1920s and the 1950s the meaning of objectivity changed from one of fairness and toleration to strict value-free inquiry guided by incorruptible mathematics (Morgan and Rutherford 1998: 8–9). The narrative, built around the notion that the more objective and scientific neoclassical economics triumphed over the institutionalist school, neglects important features within the schools of thought themselves. In particular, this narrative account rests on a fragile dualism. "Institutionalism versus Neoclassicism" assumes internal stability and the definition of a coherent core around which consensus is constructed.[2] Yet, institutionalism could hardly be said to be internally coherent and consistent. Morgan and Rutherford (1998) commenting on the period between the two World Wars note:

> Institutionalism, then, was a broad movement and quite nonexclusive. Institutionalists as a group had no one method to defend and no one economic theory to peddle. What they did have was a commitment to serious scientific investigation, detailed empirical work (though with no one method), serious theory building (which eschewed simple assumptions), and a commitment to understand the importance of economic institutions in determining economic outcomes. This last point relates to the institutionalists' view that new institutions or methods of 'social control' were required to overcome the economic and social problems created by the existing market system.
>
> (Morgan and Rutherford 1998: 3)

Pluralism more accurately characterizes economics in the early decades of the twentieth century. The boundaries between neoclassical and institutionalist approaches were porous and the same economist could quite confidently borrow liberally from each one. "Heterogeneity, amorphousness, and perhaps, especially, individuation of practice ruled the day" (Samuels, 2000: 141).

Philip Mirowski and D. Wade Hands (1998) argue that even within the neoclassical school, the interwar period was marked by a diversity of approaches used to explain the economic function of market mechanisms. They identify as many as five distinct perspectives on demand theory alone. One primary distinguishing marker was the extent to which empirical data collection and statistical testing – creeping econometrics – was tolerated. They maintain that diversity more than sameness marked the neoclassical approach in the period between the wars.

Research in the sociology of scientific knowledge suggests that practitioners in the sciences construct discourses that both convey research findings and define the proper content of disciplinary work. Such boundary-work often takes place via exclusion (Gieryn 1983). The exclusion of home economists from the economics profession in the 1900s and 1910s is an example of boundary-work that makes use of gender categories to define the borders of research. Yet, the apparent pluralism of interwar economics in the United States suggests that exclusionary boundary-work was minimal. Therefore, in the 1920s and 1930s the academic field of economics seemed relatively wide open. Nevertheless, the boundary around economics was not completely unguarded. Admission to the sphere of economic knowledge production was open to those who acquired the requisite educational degree.

Who gained access to economics education? Graduate training in economics was, and still is, frequently inhospitable to women. Nevertheless, as Randy Albelda (1997) notes, "Despite their minority status, women were better represented as graduate students in economics in the 1920s than they were for the next half century" (24). Barbara Libby notes that the rise of sub-specializations (sociology, social work and home economics) funneled women out of economics, and hence diminished their role in the profession.

> Before the growth of these areas of specialization many women, working and writing in the areas of social problems and reform, considered themselves – and were considered by the rest of the profession – to be economists, but they were later considered founders and/or members of other professions.
>
> (Libby 1984: 275)

However, as the social sciences began to distinguish themselves by method and technique, women's entry into the economics profession declined. Women, even when legitimately conducting academic research in economics, were pejoratively referred to as "social economists" (Albelda 1997: 28–9). Folbre (1998: 43) argues that the creation of separate academic spheres within which female economists could pursue "social economics" was a defense against the threat of growing feminization of the profession.

So, even the seemingly straightforward task of enumerating women's affiliation with economics as an academic field is muddied by this tendency (varying by academic institution and perhaps even the particular views held by the reigning department chair) to segregate women into social economics, home economics and social service administration. So, here we see home economics serving the interests of male economists, yet again, this time not as an object of research against which to define economics but as a separate homeland for female economists. A cadre of academically trained, often highly skilled, economists was separated from the discipline. Yet, these economists were deposited upon an academic terrain – home economics – in which they could chart their own course. Re-constructing a history of research on consumer behavior that reflects the work of economists toiling in their field needs to attend to the historical process of gender segregation. Segregation that, while it erected barriers to entry to the primary domain of economic discourse, may have also fostered, of necessity, the construction of alternative spheres of economic research and practice.

In the 1920s and 1930s, a cohort of female economics Ph.D. recipients entered the job market. Some, a few, were educated by female academics and had female doctoral supervisors – Hazel Kyrk at the University of Chicago being foremost among them. Many would land jobs in government agencies or with social service providers, but many others would try to find a place in the academy. The situation facing women in economics departments was daunting. As noted earlier, women economists were often segregated into the sub-field of social economics, a special terrain referred to as the "feminine gender of political economy" by Franklin Sanborn, head of the Department of Social Economy for the American Social Science Association at the turn of the twentieth century (Cookingham 1987: 65). In this location, they focused attention on the social problems of the family and specifically the economics of consumption. Foremost among these are Kyrk at Chicago, Jessica Peixotto at Berkeley, and Margaret Reid and Elizabeth Hoyt at Iowa State. Each of them set out to construct a broad understanding of consumption often in conscious opposition to the marginalist revolution (Kyrk 1923; Hoyt 1928: vi).

Social economics of consumption

Kyrk's critiques of marginal utility reveal the contours of an alternative formulation for consumer economics. She first argues that the atomistic individual is too restrictive, and, as such, does not admit influences on individual choice that emanate from social codes, customs or "organized habit." The social basis of individual choice is neglected, to the detriment of economists' ability to explain human behavior. Kyrk next criticizes the "intellectualism" attributed to individual consumers. By intellectualism, she is referring to rational choice with unlimited cognitive capacity. This automatically excludes behavior that results from "impulse, custom and instinct." She goes on to assail the hedonistic binary choice set (pleasure or pain) that motivates economic behavior. Relying on Dewey's pragmatic philosophy, she argues that sensation is neither the only nor the primary stimulus to action.[3] Furthermore, the rational calculation of sensory experience is thwarted by the unique constellation of environmental factors that frame our sensory experience (Kyrk 1923: 138–41). Finally, she charged that the model of rational self-interest may match the behavior of the capitalist business owner but need not be generalized to other spheres of economic life. "They [economists] ascribed to human nature what the institutional organization was really responsible for. Self-interest and calculation may be satisfactory clues to the business man's conduct, but they cannot be carried over to the interpretation of consumers' choices" (1923: 143).

In light of this critique of marginal utility and the rational choice framework, Kyrk eschews any prospect of rescuing this approach in favor of constructing a value theory built with insights gleaned from social psychology and pragmatist philosophy. For Kyrk, something has value if it aids in the accomplishment of a task or fulfillment of an objective. Commodities are seen as "raw materials which must be organized, or from which must be constructed the situation sought" (1923: 165). The objects that help to construct the desired situation also build up a sense of self on the part of the consumer. Furthermore, as objects can often fulfill more than one use, value is attached to the use rather than the inherent qualities of the object. Finally, the process through which values are attributed to these objects is socially determined. This social matrix envelopes the individual consumer and orients him/her toward a standard of consumption characteristic of his/her class or nationality. Here Kyrk identifies one's standard of living with one's lifestyle. One's lifestyle is imparted largely by habit and emulation of those around us: "group or mass phenomena" (1923: 177). Standards of consumption particular to a social group are enforced through the desire to avoid ostracism so as to stay in good standing with the group. In addition, group cohesion is maintained, the group's position within the social structure is reproduced, and group prestige is secured through the adoption of the group lifestyle. In this way, conspicuous consumption acts to signal group affiliation and emulation promotes group cohesion. Only in the case of economic stratification are the markers of difference and distinction divorced from their functional or useful qualities (226).[4]

The interplay between lifestyle and consumption practices shares some of the same features as Pierre Bourdieu's concept of *habitus*. *Habitus* stands for a system of classificatory schemes and codes that correspond to social and cultural tastes. The goods that people acquire reflect their particular assessment of their position in this classificatory system. "*Habitus* thus implies a 'sense of one's place' but also a 'sense of the place of others'" (Bourdieu 1989: 19). Clusters of consumption practices can serve as markers of difference and distinction. But, for Bourdieu, the symbols inhere in the social group and are coded so that in-group members are best able to crack the code. Bourdieu, however, is critical of Veblen's depiction of consumption driven by conscious attempts to engage in conspicuous consumption. Rather than refer to conspicuous consumption as a force driving changes in standards of consumption, Bourdieu argues that patterns of consumption are structured by one's economic position. The cluster of commodities (symbols of distinction) characteristic of each group, although socially constructed, appear to individuals as an objective reality (1989: 20).

In another anticipation of more contemporary depictions of the consumer from outside the bounds of mainstream economics, Kyrk argues that the analytical rigor with which economists can chart consumer behavior is stymied by the lack of a measure of what constitutes successful consumer activity. Profitability and competitive pressures toward innovation signal the success or failure of producers but consumers have no similar benchmark. In addition, this places the consumer in a vulnerable position *vis-à-vis* merchants.

> It is this situation in regard to the standards and purposes which govern consumption, which more than anything else places the consumer as purchaser, in a distinctly disadvantageous bargaining position in his encounter with the producer. He does not know at all what he wants, or he does not know exactly, or he does not know it when he sees it.
>
> (Kyrk 1923: 188)

In this way, Kyrk characterizes the consumer as an unmanageable subject.

In a strikingly similar account, Iowa State economist Elizabeth Hoyt described the ways in which consumers' purchases hew to social norms and cultural practices through processes of emulation, experimentation and learning (1928: 9–10). Like Kyrk, Hoyt describes consumers as active participants in crafting a lifestyle through their consumption practices. This tension between the active consumer (agency) and social norms and institutions (structure) is a recurring theme in both accounts.

Hoyt, influenced by Veblen, argues that habit and custom guide consumer decisions, but only up to a point. Of equal importance are frames of reference that
she labels conventions. To the consumer, conventions are contemporary and more
flexible forms of consumption than ingrained habit or tradition. Conventions are
influenced by one's current cohort of social peers and, as such, they impose a
constraint on the range of choices consumers make. Another influential force is
producers' efforts to steer buyer purchasing decisions.

> Man is not a bundle of unsatisfied interests; on the contrary, he has to learn
> his interests, and usually he learns hard; but if he has a teacher he learns more
> readily than he learns by himself. The business man who wants to sell his
> product becomes perforce a teacher. He is engaged in the process of teaching
> interests. The teaching of interests is a necessity for businesses needing to
> create demand for new products.
>
> (Hoyt 1928: 101)

The acknowledgment that consumers come to the marketplace without preformed
interests denies the claim that preference formation lies beyond the realm of
market exchange by recognizing the effect of learning and persuasion.

Once again, consumers' interests are portrayed as inchoate, diffuse, fungible
and multivalent:

> The consumer, however, is a difficult person to deal with, for he sometimes
> acts in an unexpected and unaccountable way. He – or more likely she –
> sometimes shows a perverse disposition to buy more when the price is high
> and buy less when the price is low. The psychology behind this is, of course,
> the consumer's belief that high price is an indication of quality, or sometimes
> her more illogical conviction that the payment of a high price gives her a
> certain prestige. This failure of the consumer to act as the economist expects
> her to act cannot be shown to affect the demand for large classes of goods,
> such as food, clothing, luxuries, in the long run; but it can be shown to affect
> the short-time demand for many special classes of goods, particularly the
> demand of a limited class of consumers.
>
> (Hoyt 1928: 131)

The extent to which these portrayals of consumers deviate from the rational choice
model suggests a much broader scope of investigation for social economics. Kyrk
and Hoyt variously describe consumption as a process involving identity formation, group solidarity, and status display, as well as the attainment of useful products. Additionally, the process of choice is depicted as one moment within a series
of activities that involve learning one's interests, exploring the range of available
products, assessing family needs and desires, monitoring the family budget and
engaging with the products through use in the household. These activities include
the values and interests of others in assigning value to commodities in the market.
Habits and traditions are joined by conventions to underscore the volatile, contingent

and flexible conditions affecting consumer choices. Interestingly, neither Kyrk nor Hoyt explicitly attend to the ways in which consumption – notably shopping and household activities – was subject to a gender division of labor within the home.[5] Efforts to construct the consumer as female were left to the home economists.

The unpredictable character of consumer behavior noted in both Kyrk's and Hoyt's writing is the outcome of the multiplicity of often conflicting forces working to determine – indeed, to overdetermine – choice.[6] In this way, both Kyrk and Hoyt implicitly call into question the modernist impulse to discover a general covering law that explains consumer choices and the evolution of living standards. The possession of a surplus of income over and above that which meets physical survival requirements makes a precise rendering of consumer behavior impossible. There emerge a multiplicity of consumption standards, which can be analyzed in such a way so as to identify patterns and practices representing the lifestyles associated with different social, economic and cultural groups.

Kyrk identified three distinct approaches to the study of the consumer in economics: (1) price theory, (2) business management and (3) household budgets in relation to income. Over the course of the twentieth century, the first approach evolved into mainstream neoclassical microeconomics. The second came to be attached to theories of marketing. The final approach was taken up variously by home economists and survey researchers increasingly located outside the field of economics.

Boundary-crossing: home economics as economic research

Departments of home economics were quite diverse in the early twentieth century. Commonly associated with maintaining and preserving the cult of domesticity, home economics programs emerged from multiple sources including progressive political reform of public health, labor conditions, and household management (Stage and Vincenti 1997; Berlage 1998; Goldstein 2006). In the 1920s and 1930s, the traditional associations of home economics with the domestic arts were broadened and redefined to include economists; chemists and nutritionists began to enter the field. Home economics programs were a diverse lot. Some schools, following the lead of Ellen Swallow Richards at Vassar, devoted their research to hygiene and nutrition. But most schools also provided education and training in household management. While the University of California at Berkeley split its program into separate divisions of art (clothing design, color theory, interior design) and science (food, nutrition, dietetics) there were female faculty members also teaching social economics, notably Jessica Peixotto who offered courses on "Contemporary Socialism," "The Control of Poverty," "The Care of Dependents" and "Studies in the Standard of Living" (Nerad 1999; Cookingham 1987). As the field began to grow, academic research programs started to take root and a community of social scientists formed around the study of issues relating to the provisioning of the family.

But did the research produced by these female economists mark a new direction for the theory of the consumption? Could this proto-feminist economics construct knowledge differently? Harding (1986) discusses the possibilities for a feminist science. Does feminist science emerge only after a non-patriarchal society has been established'? Harding notes that some individuals have suggested that a feminist science can be glimpsed through the alternative practices of contemporary female scientists. Harding disagrees:

> But I think it is a mistake to search through existing or past practices of individual women scientists for the broad outlines of a feminist science ... Women scientists do violate the division of labor by gender which restricts women to domestic work or low-status wage labor. But how alternative can the practices be of isolated individuals who have somehow managed to bridge this division of labor and social identity?
>
> (Harding 1986: 139–49)

She dismisses the notion that a feminist science can be read from the isolated and unrelated practices of female scientists. But what of the counterfactual case implied by Harding? What if there existed a closely connected cadre of women scientists in communication with one another, sharing results and methodological approaches? What if these women faced ostracism from their home discipline and yet were able to establish a separate – albeit unequal – academic space? What if they were able to recruit female graduate students in order to assist in the development and sustenance of a research and teaching program? Furthermore, what if there was institutional support in the form of governmental recognition of the results of their research and a rather porous boundary between academic and government employment and research opportunities for these female scientists? If such a group existed could it not lay some claim to being a prototype for a feminist science? At the very least it would call for a detailed study of the way in which knowledge was created and diffused by these practitioners.

Such a group of women did exist in academic departments and government agencies throughout the early part of the twentieth century. They were social scientists – economists to be exact. They were mostly shunned or excluded outright from departments of economics (Madden 2002). They pursued their research agenda in a field that has largely been ignored by the discipline of economics. I am referring to the "old" home economics and particularly to the fields of consumer and household economics. The home economics program at Cornell University offers an example of the integration of female economists into home economics.

Constructing alternative economic knowledge: home economics at Cornell University

Cornell University has one of the oldest home economics programs in the nation. Originally founded in 1900 as an extension program for farm wives, it became a College of Home Economics in 1925 (Rose and Stocks 1969). By 1930 there was a clear recognition of the role of economic analysis in home economics. The 1930 *Annual Report of the College of Home Economics* describes the function of the Department of Economics of the Household:

Study of the use of money by the household has resulted in the development within the department of a specific field concerned with economics of the household. Interest in problems of consumption, and in the relationships that exist between the consumer-buyer and the producer, is an outcome of an industrial society in which production has been moved from home to factory. The homemaker has become a consumer-buyer. The goods that she buys, the understanding with which she apportions the family income in satisfying the needs of the family, and the demands she makes on the producer, are being recognized as having economic significance, not only in the home but in business as well.

(Rose 1930: 185)

Reflected in this description is the clear identification of the study of the household with the sphere of consumption. In 1930 Helen Canon, having recently earned her Ph.D. at Cornell in Economics with a specialization in the economics of the household, joined the faculty on a full-time basis. Canon was an economist intent on establishing an economic research program within home economics. She was placed in charge of creating an academic department in the "economics of the household and household management." Jean Warren, a doctoral student who wrote her thesis under Canon's direction and who later went on to join the Home Economics faculty at Cornell, had this to say about her:

She started the department and she had the idea that we were concerned with the work and business of the home, that the more we really understood what was going on in a number of homes, the smarter we would be. Much of our work would have to be based on observations of homes. This goes back to her fundamental premise that homemakers were smart – that what they were doing had a reason. If we in the academic world couldn't see the reason, this was no excuse for saying that a woman was stupid. She might be very wise about what she was doing.

(Warren 1964: 48)

At about the same time, Martha Van Rensselaer, the Dean of the College, was actively trying to recruit Day Monroe, a University of Chicago Ph.D. who studied with Hazel Kyrk. As part of her recruitment effort Dean Van Rensselaer wrote, in a letter to Monroe, "… I cannot but feel that we shall give more and more attention to the problems of consumption as a help to production and of course will involve distribution. We may be the first state to introduce this work" (Van Rensselaer 1929). It was clear that the Cornell faculty and administration saw the development of an economic analysis of consumption as a major research project for the College. In fact, in September of 1929, Canon, the new assistant professor, wrote a memo to her Dean concerning the possibility of recruiting Monroe:

When you talk with her I think you should let her know that we are reorganizing courses so that she will be doing some free thinking about the kind of thing Home Economics students need – the kind of courses that should be developed. … In other words, I think we must develop our own field – by drawing upon other fields, of course, but not by taking over blocks from other fields and setting them down in ours, which is what all the economics of the household courses which I know about have done to date, although it is not generally recognized and I do not think I should have become conscious of it had I not seen how Professor Warren has developed his own agricultural economics rather than taking over economics and setting it down in agricultural economics courses.[7]

(Canon 1929a)

Canon appears to be conscious of the limitations of contemporary economic analysis as it relates to household and consumer behavior. Trained in economics she does not want to merely apply traditional economic principles but desires instead to actively engage in the creation of new economic knowledge.[8] Therefore, rather than perceiving home economics as antithetical to economic research, Canon and Monroe jointly envision creating a new interdisciplinary program with the intent of transforming consumer and household economics. This new vision of consumer and household economics was brought into focus via teaching, academic research, and government/policy research.

The curriculum at Cornell: family life and the household economics

Although the historic association of home economics with the cult of domesticity should not be entirely discounted, the first academic programs in home economics "developed a notion of women's professionalism that departed from the older conception of separate spheres" (Strasser 1982: 207). At Cornell, the curriculum aimed to hold the activities of women and families up to scholarly inquiry and critical investigation. Indeed, a radical re-interpretation of the role of the family was suggested by the curriculum established at Cornell in the 1920s and 1930s. For example, an examination of the required readings for Course 111: Family Life (circa 1928) reveals a list that included a mixture of fiction, government statistical reports, social science texts (including Benjamin Andrews' *Economics of the Household*), as well as magazine articles from *Harpers*, *Atlantic Monthly* and *Survey Graphic*.

The core texts in the course included three novels: *A Woman of Fifty* (1924) by Rheta Childe Dorr, *So Big* (1924) by Edna Ferber and *The Home-Maker* (1924) by Dorothy Canfield. The use of novels as texts in courses outside of literature is extremely rare today in the social sciences – especially economics. As Kirsten Madden notes, in the nineteenth century, literary sources counted as a popular and "effective way to educate the masses in economic thought" and the neglect of literary sources in twentieth century history of thought discounts the role of women in creating economic literature (2002: 19). Novels allow the author to create distinct and complex characters, to explicitly represent the values of the author through the character's or the narrator's voice, and to acknowledge and elicit the participation of the reader. This contrasts with the economics text, in which the characters represent universal human agency (economic man), the assertion of values is prohibited, and the author assumes a detached reader (Bergeron and Pietrykowski 1999: 140).

While it may be anticipated that a course on family life in a home economics program would tend toward the study of "normalized" families and "appropriate" gender roles, the three novels actually subvert this agenda. In each case the traditional family is subject to critical interrogation and found wanting. *A Woman of Fifty* is a largely autobiographical account of Dorr's life as a journalist and suffragist. She chronicles her marriage, separation and eventual divorce. Her separation and divorce are depicted as an awakening. "As far as I could see I lived in a world entirely hostile to women; a world in which every right and every privilege were claimed by men" (Dorr 1924: 83). In a fascinating approach that mirrors (and precedes by over 70 years) Barbara Ehrenriech's journalistic account – *Nickel and Dimed* – from the front lines of the minimum wage labor force, Dorr recounts her decision to:

> ... take up, one after another, the historic trades of women, cooking, sewing, washing and ironing, spinning and weaving, canning, preserving, and other household arts, following from the home where they began to the factory which had absorbed them. ... My great object, of course, was to demonstrate that women were permanent factors in industry, permanent producers of the world's wealth, and that they must be considered as independent human beings and citizens, rather than adjuncts to men and to society.
>
> (Dorr 1924: 164)

Like Dorr, Selina Peake, Edna Ferber's protagonist in *So Big*, feels constrained by the traditional role assigned to her as a truck farmer's wife living near Chicago. Ferber depicts Selina as a warm, wise and loving wife and mother, a woman content with her simple life yet unwilling to submit willingly to patriarchal norms. The relationship between Selina and her son Dirk is the focus of the story. Dirk's progress in life is fueled by ambition and dreams of prosperity in 1920s Chicago. Ferber sets these ideals against the values of connectedness and the human-scale aspirations of Selina. Yet when Salina's husband Pervus dies, Salina knowingly violates community standards and begins to work the fields and cart the produce to market herself one week after her husband's death. Maria Mootry (1995) remarks of Ferber, "Her men and women characters have both 'masculine' and 'feminine' traits. Emotion, intelligence, scientific planning, appreciation for beauty, achievement, rigidity, parochialism, and sexist ideas are not gender-specific" (xv). Finally, Dorothy Canfield's *The Home-Maker* offers a portrait of family life that also troubles gender norms. Lester and Evangeline Knapp are poorly suited to their gender-assigned roles – she a woman of great vision, acumen and business-sense who rules the home with strict efficiency; he a contemplative sort imbued with a child-like fascination with the world around him. An accident provides the opportunity for their roles to reverse. Evangeline takes a job in the very mercantile store in which her husband was employed before an injury that left him paralyzed. She proves to be an expert at selling women's clothing and communicating with female clientele.

She is soon promoted and given more responsibilities. Lester, meanwhile, savors his role as househusband. Indeed, with Lester at home the children no longer exhibit the horrible emotional outbursts and physical maladies that beset them prior to the accident. The story turns on the need for Lester to remain an invalid in order that both husband and wife can enjoy their new roles – roles that society would prohibit if Lester were able-bodied. When Lester miraculously recovers, both husband and wife – with the aid of a sympathetic doctor – determine to keep this a secret in order to continue this otherwise unacceptable social arrangement. Not only does Canfield illuminate the damage done by gender stereotypes and the cost of maintaining a gendered division of labor, she also poignantly depicts the relationship between husbands and wives, children and parents as relationships based on power and control.

In all three novels the gender division of labor is directly confronted and over-thrown. Gender roles and gendered attributes become blurred and the appropriate place for a woman in society is enlarged and expanded. These books formed a core of readings in the Family Life course at Cornell University's Home Economics program. The Department of Family Life was a gateway into the study of home economics for students at Cornell. During this period the Department of Family Life and the Department of Household Management were engaged in collaborative teaching and research, and the idea of integrating the two programs was considered (Rose and Stocks 1969: 73). The values imparted to students in Family Life 111 reflected the teaching and research program taking shape in the household management program.

Helen Canon and Day Monroe restructured the curriculum in household man-agement to explicitly attend to the dual identity of homemakers as consumers and producers. Their courses stand in marked contrast to standard neoclassical consumer price theory. Examples of courses include:

Problems of the Household Buyer (Monroe)

This is a survey of the problems of the household buyer endeavoring to make intelligent selections of goods in the modern market. The following topics will be considered: the difficulties of the buyer in a market where fraud and adultera-tion may mean pecuniary advantage to the seller; attempts to influence consumer demand, such as advertising and salesmanship; the inadequacy of the informa-tion available as to quality and comparative prices; the guides upon which the consumer may depend for aid, as grades, labels, and other standards; the protec-tion given by law and other forms of social control; the structure of markets and the channels of distribution; marketing expenses and price policies with special reference to buying habits, which tend to increase costs.

The Marketing System and the Consumer – graduate-level (Monroe)

This course includes an analysis of the structure of markets and a study of market functions and functionaries from the standpoint of their relation to the household. An attempt is made to give the student a basis for evaluating the present-day market as a means of meeting the needs and desires of consumers. The effects of the market upon consumption and of consumer demand and the attitudes upon the market are considered, as is the problem of social control, or the regulation of markets in the interests of consumers.

(Rose 1930)

These course descriptions highlight the way in which Monroe conceived consumer economics. The consumer is portrayed as an active agent in the construction of the market. These courses highlighted the costs associated with using the market mechanism, prefiguring the transaction cost theory of Coase. In addition, an institutionalist perspective is apparent in the curricular focus on the necessity for market regulation and social control. This curriculum appears to have been replicated at other colleges as well. For example, Margaret Reid's undergraduate education in home economics from 1916 to 1921 differed significantly from the course of study pursued by Iowa students majoring in economics:

She knew not only the theory of markets and their operation and the theories of consumer behavior, but also had some knowledge of how those theories took shape in the world of the consumer. The clinical distance of the economist was tempered by the experience of the well-trained consumer/observer ... The home economics graduate applied economic analysis to a narrower range of problems, but drew on a broader range of disciplines to augment economic analysis in the solution of these problems.

(Forget 1996: 7)

The focus on consumption as a complex process of negotiation involving questions of power and control, gender and class, persuasion and manipulation was also reflected in the research projects undertaken by the faculty and graduate students at Cornell.

Academic research and thesis supervision

From its inception, the field of household management at Cornell was consciously developed in relation to the discipline of economics. In an assessment of the contributions of household management to the field of home economics, the authors of an internal Cornell report state:

While economics is only one of the fields of subject matter involved in household management, it is one of the most important, and strength in this field reinforces the sub-structure for building a fund of subject matter for management. A vigorous new interest became evident in what was called 'economics of the household' or 'family economics.' Possibly this new interest was due in part to the adjustments that home economics has experienced during and immediately following the world war, and in part to the concurrent and rapid

development of statistics which was putting economic facts before people in
more concrete terms than formerly.

(Canon 1942: IV)

Home economics programs got a boost from the need to persuade families to
decrease consumption during wartime. In 1917, the US Food Administration was
established under the leadership of Herbert Hoover (Rossiter 1982: 120). Located
within this temporary agency was the Home Conservation Division headed by
Sarah Field Splint, editor of *Today's Housewife* and Martha Van Rensselaer, then
head of the Department of Home Economics at Cornell. Beginning in 1925 with
the passage of the Purnell Act, federal money to promote research in the field
became available. This prompted research in the field of household budgeting and
family provisioning.

Helen Canon's dissertation research on the size of market centers and their
effect on family purchases was emblematic of this new research focus. Her work
was used in subsequent studies of consumer spending. In addition, Margaret Reid
made use of Canon's research in her textbook *Consumers and the Market*. Other
faculty members followed suit in developing a pragmatic research agenda that
addressed the needs of public agencies by charting the budgeting and consumer
purchasing decisions of families. Day Monroe wrote articles on consumer expenditure and national economic growth, including a scholarly review of consumer
income analyses prior to the work of Engel (Monroe 1974). By and large, academic research in consumer economics by home economists was likely to be
advocacy-oriented. Although not completely eschewing the language of economic
science and mathematical formalism, economists working in Cornell's home economics program viewed themselves as activist scholars. In a 1944 *Journal of
Home Economics* article entitled "Preparing for Social Action," Monroe makes an
argument for an expanded and engaged role for home economists in preparing for
postwar reconversion. She argues that home economists need to be familiar with
current statistics on income distribution and should be able to convey information about adequate family income to their students. "'Statistics on income and
its distribution belong in economics,' some say. True, such facts are included in
some economics courses, but few emphasize their significance in terms of family well-being" (Monroe 1944: 66). The focus on well-being as a distinguishing
marker between economics and home economics is consistent with a narrowing
of the scope of mainstream economics toward an emphasis on growth rather than
human development (Sen 1993). It also points out Monroe's conception of home
economics as an interdisciplinary field in which economic knowledge was created
not just conveyed.

In this 1944 article she argued that the provisions of the Social Security Act be
taught to students who, in turn, needed to educate women and families about the
details of the legislation.

The widespread publicity given the Beveridge plan has stimulated interest in
action for postwar security here. Do our students know the provisions of the

Beveridge plan, the careful effort to safeguard the nation's treasury against unwarranted "raids" while protecting its citizens against economic hazards over which they have no control? Or do they, without reading its provisions, brand it as "communistic"?

(Monroe 1944: 66)

She was clearly aware of the need to carefully analyze the economic impact of legislation and to defend social policy against free-market ideology. This is not to imply that Monroe was uniformly hostile to market forces. With respect to postwar housing she advocated for the removal of restrictions on competition in order to lessen the control of vested interests (contractors, subcontractors, and labor unions) over the price of housing (Monroe 1944: 67).

Again with reference to the 1944 *JHE* article, Monroe returns to her interest in consumer practices and the study of the market as a social arena in which gender and class interact:

Over-the-counter buying also is given considerable time in food courses ... But the war has demonstrated that education still has far to go in giving homemakers an understanding of their social responsibilities as buyers. For example, everyone knows there is a labor shortage. A woman accustomed to think in terms of her role in socioeconomic situations would see the need for lessening her demands upon the time of the retail staff, depleted by the war.

(Monroe 1944: 67)

Here we see Monroe suggesting that the product market is loaded with decisions that extend far beyond the decision to buy ground sirloin or chuck. The very act of purchasing products entails microdecisions about how to spend time, who to interact with, the quality of that interaction and how much of their time to take up. Indeed, Monroe explicitly acknowledges the marketplace as a sphere in which homemakers have some capacity to exert control and power over the retail store staff. She sees the act of purchasing products as an interpersonal relationship that has direct macroeconomic impacts.

The work that Monroe undertook with one of her graduate students further illustrates the kind of alternative microeconomic analysis being constructed outside economics departments. Consider the 1935 doctoral thesis of Leila Muriel Doman entitled "A Study of Price Variations in Retail Grocery Stores." As part of her thesis, Doman collected and analyzed price data in grocery stores by looking at identical products sold in competing establishments. Her analysis involved comparing the sale price to the everyday price, looking at the content of advertising, the timing of advertisements, the effect of distance and dispersion of store location on price variations and variation in the level of retail services provided. Her research examined:

- whether in fact announced sale prices were lower than everyday prices (in 73% of cases they were).

- whether price variations increased with distance between stores (they do).
- the content of advertisements (91% mention brand name; only 45% identify the quantity offered on sale).

Doman maintained that the objective of the study was to examine "the immediate benefits which the buyer may gain by taking advantage of low price quotations." However, she also noted that competition may "in the long run increase the costs of marketing and the general level of prices of consumer goods" (3). In other words, Doman suggests that the very act of competitively induced price-cutting may lead to forms of non-price competition (such as advertising, provision of extra services or inducements to shop) that result in higher prices overall. On the one hand, this displays an appreciation for the type of strategic retail behavior that traditional microeconomic price theorists formally discuss in theories of price discrimination and monopolistic competition.

On the other hand, the detailed store-level data and the investigation of the complex role of advertising, and the depiction of consumers as active participants in the selling process conveys a richer and potentially more persuasive account of consumer behavior than traditional economics had been able to provide. Furthermore, shifts in the composition of household production away from home-produced goods and toward the increased patronage of retail establishments also contributed to the importance for women to cultivate the traits of a skilled shopper. Doman's thesis was cited in Reid's *Consumers and the Market* ([1938]1942: 494) as evidence of deceptive pricing strategies employed by retailers.

As neoclassical rational choice approaches – and men (Rossiter 1997) – made inroads into the home economics program in the 1950s and 1960s, there remained a core of faculty committed to institutionalist and feminist approaches. For example, in the late 1960s Kathryn Walker released results of a time use survey indicating that married women who work over 30 hours outside of the home report the longest total working day when both household labor and market work are added together (Walker 1969: 624). In this sense, home economists can be said to have produced early statistical evidence of the double day for working wives (Ferree 1991; Floro 1999; Hochschild and Machung 2003).

Government research

Female economists who encountered barriers to employment in the academic workplace sometimes found employment in the government. In particular, many of those in the generation of female Ph.D. economists who graduated in the 1920s settled into jobs requiring data collection and statistical analysis. The Bureau of Labor Statistics and U.S. Department of Agriculture, in particular, hired female statisticians under the job title "social economist." Women constituted approximately 10 per cent of all statisticians and mathematicians hired by the federal government (Rossiter 1982: 232). The tasks they worked on involved the creation and elaboration of a body of knowledge relating to social survey methodology, especially those involving standards of living, prices and consumer expenditure. It could well be said that in the 1920s and 1930s women conducted the majority of statistical research on consumption (Stapleford 2007: 422).

Day Monroe left Cornell to lead the Economic Research Division of the Bureau of Home Economics. While working at the Bureau, Monroe directed the first Study of Consumer Purchases in 1935–6. This was a major multi-million project funded by the National Resources Planning Board and the Works Progress Administration and requiring the joint effort of the Bureau of Home Economics and the Bureau of Labor Statistics.[9] Monroe worked closely on the Study with Faith Williams, a Ph.D. recipient from Columbia University's Economics program and former assistant professor in home economics at Cornell in the 1920s, at the Bureau of Labor Statistics. She also worked with Hildegarde Kneeland of the National Resources Committee's Consumption Research staff. Other NRC staff members included Erika Schoenberg and Milton Friedman. Kneeland was a graduate student at Chicago and studied with Hazel Kyrk. During the 1910s and early 1920s, while still pursuing graduate studies, Kneeland taught home economics at the University of Missouri, sociology and statistics at Barnard, and was head of the department of household economics at Kansas State before becoming director of the Economics Division at the Bureau of Home Economics prior to Monroe.[10]

The 1935–6 Study of Consumer Purchases provided a wealth of detailed information. It represented the ambitious, coordinated efforts of the Bureau of Labor Statistics, Bureau of Home Economics, National Resources Committee and the Central Statistical Board in providing, what *Monthly Labor Review* reported as a "complete picture of American living levels" (Anonymous 1938: 610). Families were categorized by race, income level, occupation of wage earners and geographic region. Survey data was collected from 300,000 urban and 80,000 rural families. A subsample of 60,000 families provided detailed information on the quantity of goods and services purchased and the prices paid for each product. These families also revealed their savings and their borrowing activity for the year.

The expenditure study actually provided a less than complete picture of the American consumer. Foreign-born families were excluded from the study. So, too, were families who received relief within the year of the survey. Finally, only married couples constituted a family in the eyes of the Study designers. By contrast, an earlier study of families in Chicago, conducted by Monroe (1932), made a concerted effort to include "broken" families in the data set. These families comprised nearly 14 per cent of the total Chicago families surveyed in Monroe's study. In addition, by using the traditional, two-parent, heterosexual normative family as the unit of study, the authors of the Study of Consumer Purchases obscured the role of gender in mapping consumer spending practices even as the purchasing consumer remained a gendered subject in the eyes of the home economists who helped to prepare the study.

Upon its publication, the Study of Consumer Purchases became an important social text that was itself consumed by various groups to advance their interests. This research effort provided the social scientific data used to provide the narrative context for the Farm Security Administration and Resettlement Administration photos and documentary film depicting the lives and experiences of ordinary Americans during the Depression. Notably, in terms of the New Deal political agenda, the study revealed that one-third of the nation was ill-fed and ill-housed. This fact was subsequently used by President Roosevelt to rally public opinion around the need for increased government assistance during the Great Depression (Ewen 1996: 264).

The study data was also used to estimate the reaction of consumers to changes in income. For example, Elizabeth Gilboy, an economist who earned her doctorate at Radcliffe in 1929 and was a long-standing member of Harvard's Social Science Research Committee, used data from the Study of Consumer Purchases to estimate income elasticity by product, occupation, and geographic location (city, village). Her disaggregated statistics revealed variations in consumption and saving. She made use of her results to question the stability of the Keynesian relationship between consumption and income. Of particular interest is her claim that the empirical results are themselves a product of the particular distribution of income in the United States. Specifically, the savings generated by the wealthy, who tend to consume less and save more as their income increases, more than offset the spending in excess of income (dissaving) undertaken by the poor and the middle-class. If the distribution of income were tilted in favor of greater income equality, she argues, savings would diminish.

> It is highly questionable whether there is any fundamental psychology which will lead the individual to save, when governments tend more and more to guarantee his security against old age, unemployment and other economic risks, and when the power of modern business is concentrated upon urging him to spend.
>
> (Gilboy 1938: 140)

Keynes wrote a personal letter to Gilboy, which was then reprinted in the *Quarterly Journal of Economics* along with her reply. In addition to clarifying that the psychological law underlying the propensity to consume refers only to the absolute increase in savings with income, Keynes relates his belief that savings will grow faster than consumption with rises in real income (Gilboy 1939: 633). If this psychological law is not fulfilled, Keynes states, "we have a condition of complete instability" (634). Gilboy's reply identifies a slippage in Keynes' characterization of the propensity to consume as a psychological law. She sees the law-like behavior of Keynes' propensity to consume to be an outgrowth of institutional and historical factors rather than a behavioral constant.

> In summary, I would like to say that Mr. Keynes seems to me to have stated in the propensity to consume a *statistical* and not a psychological tendency – or law – which may be true for our society as a whole but is probably not true for certain individuals or groups within that society. I should hesitate to extend the concept into other societies different from our own.
>
> (Gilboy 1939: 637)

Gilboy's reply resonated with the interest of home economists to investigate the diversity of purchasing decisions undertaken by families with similar levels of income.

The consumer purchases data provided the opportunity for researchers to segment and dissect the US consumer in a radically different way. One important feature allowed for detailed analysis of the particular type of products purchased. Using this data, Dorothy Dickins, a home economist at Mississippi State College, conducted several studies that brought to light cleavages in the American buying public. She used data from the Study of Consumer Purchases to initiate a detailed study of farm families in Mississippi and compared the composition of food purchases in 1936 to that in 1948. She examined two types of families, those who operated their own farm and sharecroppers. She also looked at differences between white and black families. Dickins categorized food usage into primary foods if over 75 per cent of the group used that item during the week. Only four staples (lard, sugar, flour, cornmeal) were common to all groups over both time periods. In fact, whereas in 1936 white farm operators and white sharecroppers consumed similar types of primary foods (correlation coefficient, $r = 0.82$) by 1948 they were eating differently ($r = 0.43$). The same can be said for black operators and black sharecroppers ($r_{1936} = 0.84$, $r_{1948} = 0.58$). Furthermore, whereas in 1936 both white and black farm operators had several primary foods in common ($r = 0.49$) by 1948 they had divergent patterns of food consumption ($r = -0.17$). Increasing differences among food purchases by race were also showing up among the group of sharecroppers ($r_{1936} = 0.50$, $r_{1948} = 0.35$). Indeed, by 1948 the group differences between black operatives, black sharecroppers and white operatives were so large that one could begin to talk about distinct food practices.[11]

Although the Study of Consumer Purchases was constructed in such a way that spending behavior was differentiated by geography, race, family size and income, it was flawed to the extent that consumer purchases were assumed to take place without regard to differences in the social relations governing market exchange. For instance, while the availability of foodstuffs widened for farm operators during the postwar period, sharecroppers could not participate in the same markets.[12] The structure of sharecropping involved seasonal payment for work performed that was insufficient to meet the year-round needs of the sharecropper family. In order to make up the shortfall, credits were given to tenants for use at the landlord's commissary. However, credits were not cash and, as such, could be used to purchase only what the landlord had on offer. Control over the type of foodstuffs available established the power of the landlord over the nutrition levels and foodways of the sharecropper (Thompson 1975; Kayatekin 2001). But whereas sharecroppers were included in the survey, spending by families receiving governmental or charity assistance was excluded on the grounds that their purchases were less indicative of free choice (Stapleford 2007: 433). This highlights one of the problems faced by government economists, home economists and statisticians. Namely, that the process of counting and classifying consumers and their spending practices required a myriad of interpretations and judgments at each stage of the process.

Nevertheless, the Study of Consumer Purchases created new knowledge about consumer behavior. To the extent that the data was intended to be used by New Deal economic planners to create meaningful estimates of aggregate demand, the complexities of the collection and interpretation process created time lags that militated against its use. On the other hand, the data was very useful for those interested in consumers as variegated, heterogeneous and diverse. Corporations and marketing agencies made use of the Study of Consumer Purchases data in order to look into the market baskets of American consumers (Stapleford 2007). By contrast, the neoclassical theory of demand was moving in the opposite direction, away from the type of empirical estimation of consumption (Mirowski and Hands 1998) and culturally conditioned theories of demand (Kyrk 1923; Hoyt 1928) adopted by economists influenced by the institutionalist approach. One example of this emerging division within economics can be seen in the research on interdependent preferences.

In his 1949 publication, *Income, Saving, and the Theory of Consumer Behavior*, Harvard University economist James Duesenberry made use of the 1935–6 consumer purchases data set to probe variations in consumer spending and saving behavior across families. In this work he made explicit his criticism of current neoclassical consumer theory. The received theory was faulty to the extent that it failed to unearth the psychological motives underlying consumer choice (Duesenberry 1949: 17). In particular, it failed to acknowledge the interdependence of consumer preferences. Preferences, argued Duesenberry, are directly influenced by others in our reference group, especially those who are immediately above us in economic and social rank. If someone in our group purchases a new car our preferences are shaped by observing the car and noting its features, and hence, in this way, our aspirations are fueled independent of changes in income or prices (Mason 1998: 97). This "demonstration effect" spurs emulation and the diffusion of new products throughout a social group. Duesenberry based the psychological impulse to match the consumption levels of our social neighbors on the desire to preserve one's self-esteem. So, if achieving a high standard of living is a social goal that improves self-esteem and the acquisition of higher quality goods and services increases the standard of living, then buying more and better goods and services brings about higher levels of self-esteem. Duesenberry grounds the urge to preserve and promote one's self-esteem in the psychoanalytical concept of the ego-ideal (1949: 28). When interdependent preferences combine with the demonstration effect and the need to preserve one's self-esteem, Duesenberry arrives at an explanation of consumption determined by the spending of other individuals in one's reference group. This is the basis for the relative income hypothesis.

On the one hand, Duesenberry articulates a social psychological theory of preference formation by taking into account the frame of reference through which consumers make sense of their standard of living. By consciously crossing disciplinary borders, Duesenberry was acknowledging the strict limitations of neoclassical and Keynesian consumer theory. This may be the one reason why most economists abandoned the relative income hypothesis in favor of Milton Friedman's permanent income alternative (Mason 1998; Frank 2005). But for all his references to interdependent preference formation, when Duesenberry goes about constructing an analytical model that requires him to translate social psychology into neoclassical microeconomics, he conjures up a utility maximizing agent whose utility is now a function of her own consumption in relation to the impact of other individuals' consumption choices. While the relative income hypothesis offers an explanation for any one individual's consumer preferences it begs the question of how members of the reference group form their preferences. The problems resulting from the lack of a thick institutional description of consumer choice make it difficult to explain group differences in spending and saving behavior.

Take the case of differentials in black-white saving behavior. In the period from roughly 1917 until 1943, savings rates for African Americans were higher than for whites of comparable income levels.[13] Duesenberry, based on an analysis of the 1935–6 Study of Consumer Purchases data (Mendershausen 1940), notes the tendency for black families to save more than whites with similar incomes. As blacks and whites exist in separate social groups yet "these two communities are subjected to the same ways of doing things," one would assume that incomes reflect the ability to purchase goods that satisfy needs and wants. So, one would hypothesize that absolute income levels should generate roughly the same levels of saving. And yet they do not. Duesenberry explains the fact that blacks save more than whites on the basis of the lower average income of blacks. As such, $2,000 in income received by a black family in Columbus, Ohio will place it well above the average income of all black families. This will not be so for white families in Columbus, where the average income was $2,080. So, the relative standing of a white family will encourage them to save less and spend more in order to achieve their consumer aspirations, whereas the black family are relatively wealthy among members of their reference group and will save more (Duesenberry 1949: 50–2). This is an intriguing explanation.

In response to Duesenberry, Klein and Mooney (1953) first note that while the black-white saving differential is a "striking result" of the 1935–6 study, it is surprising that economists have taken interest in a phenomenon more likely to rouse the interest of sociologists. They mention the particular use to which studies of racial differences are put, namely as inputs into a more general theory of consumption. But by doing so, economists flatten the differences that exist between consumers. The white-black saving differential appears to have been one of the more unsettling findings of the Consumer Purchases Study (CPS). Sterner (1943) hypothesizes that the differences may reflect differential access to credit or to racial barriers prohibiting qualified blacks from moving into better-paying jobs. This latter explanation is intended to counter the racial stereotype linking black families with excessive and uncontrolled consumption spending.

Klein and Mooney used the CPS data along with data from the 1947–50 Surveys of Consumer Finances coordinated by economist George Katona at the University of Michigan to identify those combinations of variables that were useful in explaining racial variation in savings rates. They examined the effects of the interaction of asset, region, job security, and credit on savings rates in order to test for statistically significant group differences on savings of blacks and whites. The conclusions were both promising and inconclusive. No single attribute, demographic differences, regional differences or differences in access to credit, job security nor relative income offered a clear, conclusive or sufficient explanation for the differential in black and white savings behavior (Klein and Mooney 1953: 455–6).

Adequate explanations for differences in consumer behavior continued to elude economists seeking to apply statistical techniques to survey data. In the case of black-white savings differentials, the social structure of the credit market may well have had a role to play. Toward the end of their research paper, Klein and Mooney note that blacks were more likely to purchase items on installment. In fact, Southern blacks' purchases of durable goods far exceeded that of other groups. They surmised that this was the result of upper-income blacks' need to display their status within the community (1953: 455). So, it is telling that in spite of the economic arguments employed throughout the paper, they place their bets on the more "sociological" explanation.[14]

Empirical data, even as detailed and comprehensive as the Study of Consumer Purchases, was also unsuccessful in providing a solid foundation for neoclassical microeconomic theories of consumer behavior. Curiously, revealed preference theory (Samuelson 1938) would appear to find its empirical justification in the consumer expenditure data. Rather than relying on utility theory with its links to psychology and attempts to discern intensity of preferences, why not explain preferences by reference directly to the purchasing choices made by consumers? Samuelson presumed that, under ideal conditions, data on commodities, prices and income could be used to derive the theory (62).[15] Yet, Wallis and Friedman (1942), examining both experimental and statistical approaches, were unable to conclusively derive indifference functions from the data. The data was not cooperating with the theory. The frustrations encountered by economists wishing to make use of this data – reflecting unpredictable and unruly consumers – encouraged many to abandon the search for empirical regularities and the motives behind consumer choices. As Little maintains:

> The fact that an individual chooses A rather than B is far from being conclusive evidence that he likes A better. But whether he likes A better or not should be completely irrelevant to the theory of price, which can concern itself solely with market behavior, and not with motives.
>
> (Little 1949: 92)

Not only was market behavior alone an adequate basis for establishing a theory of consumption but the subject position occupied by the consumer was far too unstable a foundation upon which to construct a theory of demand.

> The behavior of human beings seems in fact to be less predictable than the behavior of aggregates of human beings, and, to the extent to which this is true, the theory of consumer's behavior must, at least as far as positive economics is concerned, continue to be nothing more than a logical exercise, because, in price theory, it is the aggregates, and not the individuals, which are of interest.
>
> (Little 1949: 99)

Furthermore, as the study data reported what people did rather than what people thought, the raw data was not contaminated by qualitative reports on attitudes or consumer expectations. So, yet another response was to tame the unruly data by using it as an input into econometric models wherein it could be transformed, smoothed and aggregated.

The Study of Consumer Purchases data set was capable of being utilized in a number of different ways. Government policymakers sought to use it to gauge consumer demand and, as consumption spending constituted the largest share of national expenditure, aggregate demand. Business managers were keen to use the data to better understand demographic variations in household purchasing decisions (Stapleford 2007). Economists were interested in the way in which demand responded to changes in income in order to empirically estimate the consumption function (Gilboy 1938; Duesenberry 1949; Friedman 1957; Thomas 1989). Yet, as illustrated above, while the Study of Consumer Purchases was utilized by economists it often confounded economic theories of consumer behavior.

Finally, a significant, and little mentioned, feature of the Study of Consumer Purchases is the fact that consumer spending was being surveyed and social scientists were avidly engaged in constructing a discourse about the US consumer during the depths of the Great Depression. While it is understandable that the federal government would be interested in investing resources to create a stock of scientific knowledge and empirical data pertaining to consumption, there is little recognition that the consumer being constituted through survey data was simultaneously the product of a massive economic slowdown characterized by great uncertainty and economic insecurity. By sharing details of their personal spending habits with government officials, consumers were also forced to assess their own standard of living against a checklist of consumer goods available to "typical" families. For example, the checklist covering women's and girls' clothing required consumers to state whether or not they purchased fur coats or wool coats, cotton flannel, silk pajamas, kimonos or negligees. The process of measuring consumer purchases undoubtedly prompted consumers to measure themselves and their own lifestyle relative to the world of goods available in the market. Such knowledge about their place in the wider world of consumers may well have had an effect on their satisfaction with their own standard of living. Surveys and studies of the postwar consumer would continue the methods developed in the Study of Consumer Purchases. But now the object of study constituted both by the researcher's interpretive lens and the social framework within which consumers interacted with one another and with the objects of their needs and desires was an increasingly affluent consumer society.

Summing up

Who defines the boundaries of economic research? In whose interests do those borders exist and what kinds of knowledge get silenced, ignored or left out? Separate and distinct from the emergence of neoclassical economic theory, home economists at Cornell University explored the ways in which consumer identities are sustained and transformed through the practice of buying. Researchers in home economics departments undertook time allocation studies long before new household economists claimed the household as a legitimate area of theoretical inquiry. Methodological insights developed by early twentieth-century home economists into the gendered nature of consumption and household production could be fruitfully carried forward into contemporary analyses of household and consumer behavior. If economics as a field of inquiry can be conceived of as being constructed and maintained by discursive practices, then the discourse of home economists working in departments of Household Economics and Management can be said to have created a competing, albeit partial and fluid, discourse that can help to re-frame our understanding of consumption as a gendered, complex and symbolically mediated area of economic life.

As Ulla Grapard (2001) notes, "One of the promises of the newly emerging field of feminist economics is that it enables us to go beyond an ahistorical view of gender relations while it offers us insights into the place of gender in economic discourse" (206). By investigating the diversity of economic knowledges produced, and by acknowledging the existence of "other" economists excluded from the mainstream on the basis of gender and ideology, we can recognize the power of disciplinarity in economics and, in the process, transgress the boundary drawn around "real" economics.

Home economists conducted research on consumption behavior that extended the scope of inquiry beyond the marketplace and into the home. Furthermore, the household was depicted as a site of social conflict, contested norms and a space of control. In this way, home economists directed their analytical lens toward a separate sphere of economic activity that could not be usefully reduced to the combination of factor inputs. Through an examination of the curriculum, academic research and government-sponsored research it becomes clear that the family unit was more than the sum of its individual, utility-maximizing parts. For one, children, their needs and the caring labor put forth to raise a family was an integral part of home economics training and research. This "other" economy of caring labor and personal services exists as an alternative space about which contemporary feminist economic analysis has been particularly concerned (Folbre 1995; Donath 2000). In addition, the activity of shopping was depicted as a skilled task performed within a setting marked by deception and the rhetoric of persuasion.

Finally, connections between economics and home economics were not completely severed. They were kept alive through the research agenda of women working as social economists creating an alternative foundation for consumer economic theory and new approaches for understanding consumers as plural and diverse. The key contributions of Hazel Kyrk and Elizabeth Hoyt include the construction of an interdisciplinary understanding of the consumer that drew heavily on insights from the fields of psychology, sociology and anthropology in addition to the institutionalist economics of Veblen. As a result, they described consumer behavior in terms of the social norms, group symbols and cultural conventions that combined to guide and constrain individual preference formation. They were also cognizant of the role that consumption plays in identity formation. Their explanation of consumption patterns in a post-subsistence family corresponds closely to the concept of *habitus* described by Bourdieu's sociological theory of taste. Furthermore, they appreciated that choices are not characterized in terms of some predetermined preference structure. The institutions, norms and practices within which people live affect the choices they make. Finally, both Kyrk and Hoyt voice skepticism about the ability or necessity for economic theory to advance a universal, essentialist explanation of consumer behavior. Consumer choices are often contingent, unpredictable and the consumer as a subject is incapable of being fixed to one type. This was certainly one of the major implications of the empirical research generated by the Study of Consumer Purchases. While the study data was used to forecast aggregate consumption, the data was also amenable to disaggregation and segmentation. The data represented the American consumer but not necessarily as the "mirror of nature" – a factual, objective and "true" portrait of the consumer. Rather than claiming that home economists and social economists were adopting a logical positivist method with which they observed empirical regularities,[16] I want to suggest that they were engaged in attempts to understand consumer behavior as contingent, unpredictable and overdetermined by race, class, and culture. The attempts by Gilboy and Dickins to describe differences in spending behavior by income, race, gender, occupation and location signal their interest in deconstructing the consumer. As such the empirical representation of the consumer is one of a fragmented economic subject. More importantly, it suggests that consumers are composites of their income, racial, gender, occupational and geographic "locations." This anticipates the contemporary notion of "intersectionality" by which theorists attempt to understand the multiple subject positions of economic agents. So, while the gender of consumers is an important factor in mapping the behavior of shoppers, so, too, is the race, reference group, occupation and geographic spaces through which the female consumer navigates (McCall 2005).

4 Psychology and economics
Max Wertheimer, Gestalt theory and George Katona

In the interwar period, while home economists were conducting economic analysis within a program of their own, a multiplicity of competing conceptualizations of consumer theory were on offer within economics departments – often within the same department – throughout the country. There was no clear demarcation between identifiable neoclassical economists and their rivals from the institutional school (Morgan and Rutherford 1998; Yonay 1998; Samuels 2000). However, in the decades following the Second World Ward, neoclassical demand theory converged around a unified set of principles, though still exhibiting a modicum of variation and contestation (Mirowski 2000; 2002; Kirman 2006). Resisting this trend was the economist and psychologist George Katona. Rather than seeking first principles, Katona applied insights from psychology to the study of consumer purchasing and consumer expectations. Katona remains a neglected figure in economic thought and his insights are "conspicuous by their absence in standard macroeconomics texts" (Earl 1990). Sent (2004) locates him within the first wave of behavioral economists, along with Herbert Simon, as an economist who sought to develop an alternative to the neoclassical mainstream. The psychological tradition upon which Katona drew is equally neglected in historical accounts of the disciplinary border-crossing undertaken by economists over the course of the second half of the twentieth century. Katona's research, not unlike that of the home economists and social economists, offers up a different script for use in writing an alternative history of consumer theory.

Historical accounts of the relationship between *fin de siecle* consumer theory and psychological hedonism point to their intersecting interests. The idea was that utility should be able to be quantified and that there was a scientific procedure available to measure the psychophysical response of individuals to various stimuli. Experimental psychology would provide the scientific data upon which utility theory would be based. However, with the ascendancy of ordinal utility theory, psychological motivations – requiring measurements of the psychic intensity of pleasure – could be sidestepped in favor of letting consumers rank order their own preferences (Lewin 1996; Davis 2003; Bruni and Sugden 2007). The widespread acceptance of ordinal utility marked the separation of economics from psychology. The separation continued for most of the twentieth century. More recently, the behavioral turn in economics points to a rapprochement of economics and psychology. Indeed, Bruni and Sugden ask what if the psychological underpinnings of hedonistic, sensory-based utility theory represented a road not taken in the development of modern neoclassical economics? They and others (Camerer 1999) maintain that the current contested terrain of neoclassical economics, represented most vividly by the rise of behavioral economics, re-animates the debate over the relationship between economics and psychology. But these narratives generally fail to recognize the contested nature of psychological discourse at the turn of the century, especially the divisions within the scientific community in Europe around the dual characterization of psychology as a branch of physics and as a field of philosophy. At the center of this debate was Katona's mentor, Max Wertheimer. Wertheimer was one of the founders of the Gestalt school of psychology. Katona, in turn, sought to modify the Gestalt approach for use in economic analysis.

So, it is important to note that in the field of psychology a somewhat similar process of disciplinary boundary-making was taking place during the early part of the twentieth century. A brief sketch of the intellectual contours and method-ological debates within the field of early twentieth-century psychology – with special emphasis placed on the development of Gestalt psychology – will serve to shed light on: (1) the tension between physics and philosophy in demarcating twentieth-century psychological methods; (2) the emergence of a privileged posi-tion for scientific discourse in psychological studies of human behavior; (3) the way in which Gestalt psychologists negotiated the boundary between natural sci-ence (*Wissenschaften*) and humanistic studies (*Geisteswissenschaften*); and (4) the implications for psychological and behavioral economics.

Difference and division in the emergence of Gestalt psychology

The Gestalt school developed against the grain of those seeking to connect mental perception to a direct physical stimulus. Ernest Fechner, in particular, proposed a functional relationship – Fechner's Law – to describe and then to measure the intensity of a sensation in response to the application of a stimulus (Bruni and Sugden 2007: 152; Colander 2007: 216). Edgeworth applied this key principle of psychophysics to the economics of consumption in his statement that "The rate of increase of pleasure decreases as its means increase" (Edgeworth 1881: 61). Indeed, Fechner's work was used to establish a physiological basis for hedonistic behavior on the part of individual economic agents. It promised to felicitously combine subjective states of mind to their physical determinants. It is, therefore, not surprising that Fechner had some influence on the research project of neoclas-sical economists at the time, although the majority of economists preferred to keep psychology at arm's length (Colander 2007). Although Edgeworth may have eventually rejected the strict utilitarianism issuing from Fechner's Law (Stigler, 1950: 276), the basic psychophysical response investigated by Fechner, and later Wilhelm Wundt, still finds its way into many microeconomic principles textbooks under the heading diminishing marginal utility.

In fact, as late as 1942 Wallis and Friedman cite Fechner's law as a psychologi-cal postulate upon which to design experimental studies of consumer preference between commodities. Wallis and Friedman report on a series of experiments Wallis performed while an undergraduate psychology student at the University of Minnesota and subsequently published in the *Journal of General Psychology* (Olkin 1991: 122; Wallis 1935). When different sized colored objects of the same shape are located at varying distances from the observer, the objects appear to be the same size. Similarly when differently colored shaded squares are located at varying distances, their colors merge into a single shade. "It should be noted in favor of this method that the combinations presented to the subject are blended into a homogeneous stimulus, so that he compares the two combinations as entities" (Wallis and Friedman 1942: 182). These entities are then referred to as indifference surfaces. Although Wallis and Friedman acknowledge that the actual "data" used in these experiments have "no relation to economic indifference functions," it is the process of visually "seeing" uniformities in shape and color that are held to be indicative of the consumer preference formation. "It is known that various colors produce differing size illusions, just as different commodities produce varying satisfactions" (1942: 181). Wallis and Friedman try, in a most curious way, to connect research in psychology, namely experimental psychology, with consumer choice. What is most puzzling is the use of techniques that were by then associated with Gestalt psychology. In his 1935 *Journal of General Psychology* article, Wallis makes no reference to Gestalt theory. So, the linkage between visual illusions and consumer preference is left unexplored.

Bruni and Sugden (2007) offer a retrospective analysis of Fechner's research as a way to re-introduce psychology into economics. Specifically, they identify links between psychophysics and contemporary behavioral economics. The psychological approach of Edgeworth is contrasted with the rational choice theory posited by Pareto. They argue that while rational choice won the day and came to define the key principles of neoclassical analysis, by abandoning the psychological underpinnings of economic choice an alternative path was closed off. Bruni and Sugden single out the theory of discovered preferences as an exemplar of the rational choice model. The choice process under discovered preferences is undertaken by individuals who know what actions will best fulfill their given preferences (Bruni and Sugden 2007: 163). If a particular choice misses the mark it is due to insufficient time given over to learning. With enough repetition, choices will match up with preferences. But what determines that repeated trials will do the trick? Bruni and Sugden, rightly I think, identify as a key assumption of the theory that individuals discover their preferences. Preferences, as such, are always already under the surface of human cognition and need to be brought into the open through repeated experiences. They are not constructed through the process of consumption (Bruni and Sugden 2007: 164). By contrast, deviations from predicted rational choice outcomes could be explained instead by invoking many of the explanations put forth by behavioral economists (for example, loss aversion or endowment effects). In fact, the process of repeated trials may not be independent of preferences but may act to shape preferences (Kahneman and Snell 1997). Although I certainly agree with the need to re-assess the roads not taken in the history of economics, the past contributions of psychology to economics are more pluralistic than Bruni and Sugden allow. Rather than rehabilitating nineteenth-century psychophysics, I argue that we should look, instead, at the Gestalt movement in psychology.

The origins of Gestalt psychology are to be found at the intersection of natural science and philosophy. The Gestalt theorists established common ground in their opposition to the mechanistic model of consciousness prevalent within the natural science understanding of human behavior. The natural science attempt to locate a physiological basis for the mental states that precipitated individual action supported the claim that thought could be reduced to physical stimuli. The Gestalt psychologists were generally unconvinced by such a deterministic model. On the other hand, their desire to explain human consciousness through means of experimental methods was incompatible with the philosophical camp. Gestalt theorists straddled the two approaches and each to a different degree felt more closely allied with physics or philosophy, but neither truly as a home. Wertheimer opposed the view that "exactitude and precision of chemistry and physics are characteristics of natural sciences, but 'scientific' accuracy has no place in a study of the mind and its ways. This must be renounced in favor of *other* categories" (1955 [1924]: 2). The search for alternative models is nowhere more apparent than in Wertheimer's own experimental research. Wertheimer, together with Wolfgang Kohler and Kurt Koffka, developed the conceptual framework of Gestalt theory. While Gestalt psychology is commonly understood as the study of shifting holistic frames of interpretation, Wertheimer was especially interested in the gaps or spaces that stand between the parts and the relational patterns that form our recognition of the whole picture. His experiments with visual perception revealed that subjects observe an object in motion when it was stationary. Sensory perception was constructed for the subject by the design of the experiment. The transitional process from immobility to the perception of movement captivated his attention. This middle ground fascinated him because, in his experiments, subjects exhibited a tendency to "center" an object, and these structured wholes were taken to constitute the natural, immutable building blocks of conscious thought (Wertheimer 1955: 121; Ash 1995: 128). Also, the notion that sensory responses can be disconnected from physical phenomena called into question the linkage between physical data, values and choices that underlie the utilitarian framework.

Wertheimer contrasted an ideal typical (logico-deductive) scientific method whereby general explanations are produced by discovering the laws governing their constituent elements with the Gestalt method through which the whole is perceived prior to the parts and indeed the "part-processes are themselves determined by the intrinsic nature of the whole" (1995 [1924]: 2). The whole appears to the observer as "impressions of structure" together with its "relational contexts." So, Gestalt refers to the mental structuring and ordering of disparate elements in the world as a way of coming to understand the world. Furthermore, while the structuring process is an inherent feature of human thought, the meaningful structures will themselves reflect cultural and social conditions (Ash 1995: 122–23). These fundamental tenants of Gestalt psychology were conveyed to Wertheimer's students, among them was George Katona.

Katona and the development of psychological economics

Katona held a unique position within the postwar US economics profession. He held simultaneous academic appointments in the Departments of Economics and Psychology at the University of Michigan. This "dual citizenship" allowed Katona to range much more freely outside of the traditional boundaries established by postwar neoclassical economics. Yet, compared with the pluralism of the interwar period, postwar economics comprised a much narrower vision of what counted as legitimate economic research. As such Katona, much like the home economists of the 1920s, crafted an analytical understanding of economics from the margins of the discipline.

Katona received a Ph.D. in psychology from the University of Gottingen in 1921. Two years later, economic conditions made it necessary for him to discontinue postdoctoral studies whereupon he found work in the research department of a Frankfurt bank. During this period Katona encountered first-hand the effect of rampant inflation on consumer behavior. He found a mentor in Gustav Stolper who, in 1926, invited him to become assistant editor of Stolper's new publication *Der Deutsche Volksvirt* (The German Economist). He was also the Berlin correspondent to the *Wall Street Journal* during the Weimer Republic. He fled Germany for the US in 1933, whereupon he found employment with Max Wertheimer at the New School. Wertheimer was one of the original faculty members comprising the New School's "University in Exile," which was established to provide an academic haven for refugees fleeing Nazi Germany. While at the New School, he encountered a lively group of German émigré scholars including Emil Lederer, a social economist from the University of Berlin, and Adolph Lowe formerly of the Kiel Institute of World Economics and the University of Frankfurt (Rutkoff and Scott 1986: 87–88). The Kiel Institute disbanded in Germany owing to its identification by the Nazis as an institution harboring "socialistic and Jewish sympathies" (Rutkoff and Scott 1986: 98). In 1939 Jacob Marschak, himself a former member of the Kiel Institute, was appointed to the economics faculty at the New School. After Marschak left the New School and moved to the University of Chicago's Cowles Commission for Research in Economics, he invited Katona to direct a Rockefeller Foundation funded study of price control.

Katona's first extended foray into economic theory and policy began in 1942 with the publication of *War Without Inflation*. That Katona enters the disciplinary field of economics during the Second World War is highly significant. The war economy re-structured the relationship between markets, the state and citizens in their roles as producer and as consumer. As the production of output shifted away from consumer goods, the threat of inflation loomed large if consumers were unable or unwilling to alter their spending behavior. Furthermore, with the imposition of price controls, income was no longer an important determinant in the allocation of goods to major segments of the consumer goods market. Rather, the national interest was bound up with the need to reduce the standard of living. In the language of the late twenty-first century, this was tantamount to the enactment of a national campaign to encourage "downshifting" – voluntary reductions in consumer spending and a commitment to live with less. In a speech to Congress in April of 1942, President Roosevelt declared that the American people will accept "less in the way of creature comforts than we have in time of peace." As a result, concluded Roosevelt, "our standard of living will have to come down" (Katona 1942: 92). Katona, in turn, responded to FDR's directive by questioning its popular appeal. At the time the speech was made consumer goods were in plentiful supply, so the point of reference of the average American consumer did not accord with the dire conditions one usually associates with the need for the entire population to ratchet down their living standard. This was especially the case for individuals whose income was beginning to rise appreciably above levels experienced during the Depression (Bentley 1998). The second reservation Katona raised about the effectiveness of FDR's call to decrease spending concerned the psychological reaction individuals have to a negative appeal. Katona argued that a negative command is less likely to be enthusiastically obeyed, if it is obeyed at all. Furthermore, negative actions, because they focus attention on the creation of deprivation, are more likely to be subjects of invidious comparison. Is the sacrifice borne equally? "Renouncing the enjoyment of something is relatively easy if everybody does it, but how can one know whether others, too, reduce their standard of living?" (Katona 1942: 94). The relevance of this issue to the topic of consumer behavior revolves around the attempt on the part of the government to establish an economically viable strategy to reduce consumer spending – to, in essence, refrain from consumerism in the cause of national unification around provisioning for the war effort.

While Katona wrote favorably about the campaign to enforce saving through the purchase of war bonds, he noted that these were not the only channels available to consumers: spend or save. A third option was available:

> It follows that it depends on us, the consumers, whether there will be shortages in the most important lines of foodstuffs and clothing. Before the war we used to buy a suit, a pair of shoes, underwear, whenever the need arose. If we continue this practice now, and if in addition we buy only when it becomes impossible to go without a new article, we shall have enough of many of these goods. But if we buy in advance of our needs, if we hoard and waste, if we use more than what we must have, then there will be shortages, and we ourselves will suffer.
>
> (Katona 1942: 95–96)

In addition, he notes that while the stock of consumer durable goods may diminish, opportunities remained for consumer spending on non-durable goods and services. And this was indeed the case. As spending on consumer durables declined the consumption of non-durables (food and clothing) rose, whereas spending on services remained roughly (Figure 4.1) unchanged throughout the period from 1940 to 1950 (Cohen 2003: 70). By recognizing that consumers could spend as usual, save or spend differently, Katona was also acknowledging the inherent difficulty in controlling the modern consumer. Katona was beginning to explore problems with attempts to thwart the desire to consume.

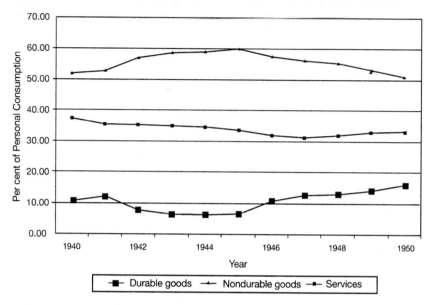

Figure 4.1 Composition of consumer spending 1940–1950.

Source: Bureau of Economic Analysis, Table 1.1.5, Gross National Product. http://www.bea.gov/national/nipaweb

In *War Without Inflation* Katona analyzes the effects of price controls from the perspectives of contemporary economic theory, associative psychology and educational psychology. Contemporary neoclassical economics held that price controls resulted in hoarding and queuing in the controlled sector and inflation in the non-controlled commodity sector. Katona criticizes this mechanistic approach. The division of labor in the social sciences caused psychological factors to be omitted from the analysis of economic phenomena, to the detriment of economics. Or, more accurately, economics was aligned with a behaviorist version of psychology, which Katona sought to critique.

> The inference that given the stimulus A the response B will follow necessarily and invariably is questionable even in the case of the so-called reflexes; it is still more questionable in behavior of a higher order, to which economic behavior belongs. More money in the hands of the people, less merchandise in the stores, these are stimuli to which sellers as well as buyers respond. How they respond depends on many factors, among which are the past experience of the responding persons, the setting of the stimuli, and the way in which the stimuli are understood.
> (Katona 1942: 6–7)

The underlying assumption held by Katona is that economic agents often lack complete and accurate information about the macroeconomic consequences of their actions. Consumers understand the world through frames of reference. The role of government is to re-frame expectations and understanding. More precisely, Katona was interested not in guiding, shaping or altering the incentive structure motivating behavior per se, he was an opponent of the behaviorist position in psychology, but rather in creating the conditions whereby individual perceptions of the scope of action could be broadened. Price controls alone were insufficient without inculcating new ways of understanding the interaction of supply, demand, income, prices and controls and their interdependence (1942: 32). To develop his analysis, Katona applied concepts in Gestalt psychology to economics.

From Gestalt psychology to economics

The Gestalt experience is characterized by a change in the field of perception. For example, a picture may be seen to represent one object, but, by volitionally altering the field of vision, an entirely different object is perceived. Often, the subject will not be able to perceive the dueling images without being told what to look for in the image when the alternative image is not immediately apparent. In addition, the field of perception privileges the whole over its parts (Wertheimer, 1955; Sokal 1989: 89). It is in this sense that Katona sought to understand the way in which individual economic agents frame the economy (Katona 1951: 8). He used the analogy of the postwar economy to illustrate the framing experience. The government's role is to provide the information necessary for individual consumers to re-frame their perception of the effects of their consumption and savings behavior. This is different from government's active control over market prices, and it is also distinctly different from attempts to modify the behavior of agents by recalibrating the incentive structure through the adjustment of tax rates. By contrast, according to Katona, the role of postwar governmental anti-inflation policy would be to engage in communication with its citizens. Katona "argued that of prime importance in fighting the war without inflation was the role of the state in the creation of a Gestalt, a comprehensive set of cultural expectations that would influence group psychology and work against price increases" (Horowitz 1998: 151). This idea that the expectations and understandings of "the public" were vital components of economic behavior shifted the analysis from the atomistic individual to the social whole. Whether the public was merely the aggregate citizen (representative agent); whether it was an amalgamation of different elements of the citizenry (composite agent); or whether it was a distinctly new and modern agent in political and economic discourse was unclear. What is clear is that Katona was re-working the building blocks of consumer economics to take into account group behavior, limited information, expectations and frames of experience.

In 1944, Katona, working at the Cowles Commission, wrote a short piece in the *American Journal of Sociology* on the importance of the "frame of reference" for understanding the responses of economic agents to wartime pricing strategies (Katona 1944). Katona utilized concepts from Max Wertheimer's and Kurt Koffka's Gestalt psychology to explain economic behavior. Using interview responses collected by the Committee on Price Control and Rationing, Katona examined the behavior of two manufacturers of men's shirts in reaction to government wartime price controls. Manufacturer A responded to price controls by lowering the quality and quantity of inputs used in making shirts. Manufacturer B, on the other hand, did not alter any aspect of production as a result of price controls. Manufacturer A explained his actions by referring to the principle of profit maximization as that which "[E]very student of economics will readily understand [as the] function of a businessman." As a result of price controls imposed in a "seller's market" – demand outpaces supply – he is forced to save on expenses. Manufacturer B adopts quite a different frame of reference. Manufacturer B cites the same prevailing conditions – a seller's market coupled with price controls. Yet the fact that B can sell as much as he produces, provides him with a sufficient level of profit in spite of the price controls. Furthermore, he acknowledges that price controls apply to his suppliers as well so his production costs have not been driven up. Finally, Manufacturer B recognizes the need to retain the patronage of his customers after the war and reductions in quality would hinder his ability to retain his customer base once the war has ended. Katona interprets Manufacturer A as clinging to an "old, traditional, pre-war context; what the economists call 'maximizing profits' rules his mind" (Katona 1944: 341). Manufacturer B has selected a new frame of reference within which the very meaning of costs, prices and profits are re-defined and re-connected in a different way.

This example is important for our understanding of economic behavior for three reasons. First, the concept of framing is directly appropriated from psychology and represents a counterpoise to the disciplinary imperialism of economics. Katona explicitly refers to Maier's 1930 *Journal of Comparative Psychology* study of human reasoning, in which Maier explores Gestalt psychologist Kurt Koffka's notion of latent attitude. The latent attitude is reflected in habitual behavior. For instance, a successful problem-solving strategy is carried over into a new context. What worked in one problem situation is relied upon in a similar, but new situation. In particular, Maier wanted to examine the responses of individuals when the latent attitude is incapable of solving the new problem. Maier argued that the solution depends upon shifting direction and modifying or completely abandoning the familiar route (Maier 1930). The example used by Maier and reproduced by Katona involves fitting a line through a set of points. Given the following arrangements of points the subject is asked to connect the points with four straight lines making sure not to lift the pencil or re-trace segments of the line. For most subjects the latent attitude perceives the 3 × 3 arrangement as a square and this then shapes the direction of the search for possible solutions (Figure 4.2). However, the actual solution requires one to see the points separately from their collective shape and to extend the line beyond the borders formed by the 3 × 3 square.[1] This "Gestalt switch" – a term later used by Thomas Kuhn (1970: 85) in describing the process of a paradigm shift (Cat 2007) – highlights the ways in which goal-oriented behavior might be thwarted by perceptual barriers.

Problem   ## Solution

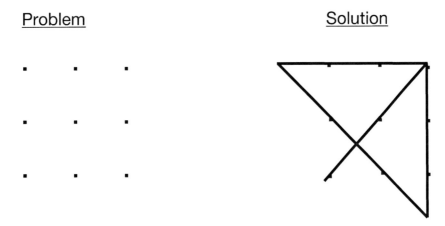

Figure 4.2 Problem solving example.

This type of habit-governed perception and cognition is also similar to the intuitive thought processes used by subjects in experiments described by the behavioral economist and Nobel Laureate Daniel Kahneman (Kahneman 2003).[2] The impression in the puzzle example (Figure 4.2) is that the points comprise a square. The image of a square is more accessible to us than is the pattern of the arrow displayed in the solution. Kahneman argues the immediate perceptions that spark intuitive responses can be combined with reason in order to organize information through the acquisition of skills over time. The co-existence of intuitive action together with reasoned action in our repertoire of possible responses to various decision-making situations renders the rational agent model of traditional economics incomplete at best (Kahneman 2003: 1453–4).

A second feature of Katona's project of reading psychological theory into economics involved his use of data drawn from survey interviews. Katona recognized from the outset that not all agents operated from the same frame of reference. However, what was important for every subject was the context within which the elements of the situation related to one another. Once again, there are similarities between Katona and Kahneman around the process of framing. Kahneman (2003: 1454) uses the example of a pair of lines that are understood to form the shape of the letter "B" when placed in a series of letters and the numbers "1 3" when embedded in a row of numbers. Here, expectations ("B" follows "A" and precedes "C"; "13" follows "12" and precedes "14") and context reinforce one another. Katona also attaches significance to the context or frame within which to make sense of phenomena. For example, Katona used responses to a 1942 nationwide survey question asking respondents: "If income taxes are increased next year, will this affect prices in general, or won't it make any difference to prices?"[3] Katona (1944: 342) reports that there were three general categories of response: (1) higher income taxes have no impact on prices; (2) raising income taxes will mean higher prices because taxes result in higher business expenses, and, therefore, higher prices; and (3) higher income taxes would stabilize or decrease prices as less income would be available to spend. This example reveals that the variables taxes and prices are incorporated into three very different frames of reference. In addition, Katona makes use of survey responses in order to shed light on the interpretive skills and subsequent behavior of economic agents. The use of information gleaned from survey questionnaires was a methodological device absent from neoclassical theory.[4] It introduces a phenomenological dimension to economic analysis to explicate the lifeworld of economic actors.

What Katona does not fully address and what is a lacuna within much of Gestalt psychology is the process whereby frames of reference are established and maintained or jettisoned. To what extent is a frame of reference a reflection of personal knowledge and tacit understanding? Is there a set of underlying social norms or class structures that pattern and coordinate the formation of frames of reference? At precisely the same time as Katona was analyzing the formation of public sentiment about postwar economic conditions, Alfred Schutz, a banker and sociologist, was seeking to understand the way in which people made sense of their lived experience.

Frames of reference and structures of relevance

Schutz's research in phenomenological sociology reflected a transitional time in his life and a tumultuous time in the US as a whole (Wagner 1983). Schutz arrived in the US in 1939. His status as an outsider no doubt influenced his work. Not only was he a relative newcomer to the US, but, as his primary occupation was as an employee for a banking concern, he was also a relative outsider to the academic profession. His appointment to the Graduate Faculty of the New School for Social Research in 1943 eventually afforded him the opportunity to focus his efforts on the construction of a phenomenological approach to sociology that linked the continental philosophy of Edmund Husserl to the pragmatism of John Dewey and George Herbert Mead. In so doing, he focused on the ways in which individuals experience their social reality in time and space. He also attended to the practical concerns of people making their way in the world populated by Others who may or may not be like oneself. While Katona left the New School shortly before Schutz arrived, they shared similar life experiences. They both were academics who occupied the liminal space between the academy and the worlds of business and banking just as home economists, trained as economists, resided in an intellectual space that was neither contiguous with the disciplinary borders of economics nor completely engulfed by the sphere of domestic science. There were similarities, too, in the method of analysis and the choice of subject matter that both Katona and Schutz sought to better understand.

Indeed, one of Schutz's contributions to the field of social sciences is the practical application of Max Weber's concept of ideal types (Pietrykowski 1996). The process of ideal typification utilized by Schutz bears more than a passing resemblance to Katona's idea of habitual patterns of behavior reflecting traditional frames of reference and the conditions under which a switch is undertaken. I argue that Schutz began to problematize his concept of ideal typification after he arrived in the US His émigré experience had a lasting effect on his work and set his research in a direction that parallels the work of Katona in laying a foundation for psychological economics. In particular, Schutz's 1946 essay, "The well-informed citizen" demonstrates a close affinity between phenomenological sociology and psychological economic inquiry.

What Schutz begins to analyze is the creative and repressive role played by power. According to Foucault (1980), power is a system of coordination and sense-making. In other words, attempts to objectively understand the world by, for example, collecting data and creating analytical categories are bound up with the deployment of power through the creation of knowledge. Foucault's research illustrated how, for instance, improved knowledge of the self helps to create systems of control, measurement and surveillance.

In "The well-informed citizen" Schutz posits three ideal types, the man on the street, the expert and the well-informed citizen. In seeking to address the social distribution of knowledge, Schutz takes these types as representations of various approaches toward the acquisition of information. The man on the street has a working knowledge, a disparate and often incomplete knowledge, of many things. This is a knowledge of recipes, habits and traditional know-how that prescribe the actions to take in order to achieve one's goals. Much is taken for granted so there is no need to "shift our interest and to make the accepted state of affairs a field of further inquiry" (Schutz 1964: 124). Of course, such an inquiry is always possible. Our plan of action or interest interacts with aspects of the world that are more or less relevant to us. These zones of relevance – Katona's frames of reference – can be either intrinsic or imposed. That which is intrinsically relevant commands our attention as a result of our conscious and spontaneous choice to attend to this or that – not unlike action directed by intuition in Kahneman's framework. On the other hand, imposed relevances appear to us as somewhat incomprehensible and beyond our control. There is no direct corollary to Kahneman because Kahneman proposes a binary model of decision-making: intuition or reasoning. There is, however, a spectrum along which responses are more or less accessible to us. And accessibility can be manipulated by others. Kahneman mentions the example of billboard advertisers who are able to grab attention and draw upon easily accessible elements (symbols and visual associations) that may not normally be accessible when one thinks of the object being displayed. One example would be automobile advertisers who seek to imbue the particular vehicle on display with qualities that may not normally be associated with cars. Emotion then plays a role in determining how we assess the probability of success attached to alternative actions (Kahneman 2003: 1454). So, imposed relevance and the shaping of attention by other actors are recognized as important determinants of how people come to know the world around them in phenomenological sociology. And this resonates with some aspects of behavioral economics.

To continue with Schutz's analysis, the three types – man on the street, expert and well-informed citizen – each act in a world defined by both intrinsic and imposed relevances. The man on the street confronts imposed relevances as mere data and as part and parcel of the world as it appears. The expert, on the other hand, inhabits a world in which action is tightly structured and delimited by the imposed relevances received from her field of endeavor or study. "Or to be more precise, by his decision to become an expert he has accepted the relevances imposed within his field as the intrinsic, relevances of his acting and thinking" (Schutz 1964: 130). Finally, the well-informed citizen inhabits a world without reliable recipes that produce given results. The zone of relevance is more inclusive and constantly open to querying.

To this extent, Schutz is suggesting that the well-informed citizen is the model upon which to base human action in an increasingly de-personalized, sterile and anonymous world. Rather than lauding the process of anonymous social interaction as a type of ideal action, Schutz argues that increasing anonymity increases the role and scope for actions determined by systems of imposed relevance. "We are less and less able to choose our partners in the social world and to share a social life with them. We are, so to speak, potentially subject to everybody's remote control" (Schutz 1964: 129). Schutz conveys the sense of paranoia that describes a panoptic world in which individuals are subject to continual control and observation. To be clear, this is not a deviant situation Schutz is describing. Rather it is the normal state of affairs in the modern world. I argue that Schutz's work foregrounds those cases in which "I *cannot* do it again," instances that stymie reliance on the ideal type, examples that destabilize the discourse of stability and the rough-and-ready predictability of everyday life.

Markets and prices: shifting frames of reference

Indeed, it is this populace of well-informed citizens that Katona wished to cultivate in his recommendation that the government undertake a policy of systematic communication with its citizen consumers about the meaning of price controls in both the wartime and postwar economy. However, in order to gauge the degree to which the man on the street deviates from the well-informed citizen the material conditions, aspirations, and expectations of the populace needed to be measured. For this, the government could undertake to poll its citizenry about their knowledge of the likely effects of proposed government economic policies. By polling, the government can better understand popular misconceptions about economic problems and proposed solutions as well as measure the expectations of various population subgroups concerning economic trends and the effects of particular economic policies (Katona 1942: 173). In addition to large-scale polling using random sampling techniques with standardized multiple-choice answers, governments could use long interviews and open-ended questions. In this situation, participants are presented with lengthy explanations of the situation – a summary of possible determinants of inflation, for instance – after which they are then expected to discuss the persuasiveness or plausibility of each explanation.

> By describing in detail a specific instance and the way it will affect the person interviewed, an attempt is made to find out whether a contemplated measure would be felt as unjust or an uncalled-for-sacrifice, or whether the Government

could rely on voluntary cooperation on the part of the public ... Still more important is the advance determination of the arguments by which the public could be made to understand the necessity and appropriateness of a measure.

(Katona 1942: 180)

Beginning in April of 1942 Katona was able to embark on just such a survey as director of field studies for the Cowles Commission's Committee on Price Control and Rationing. However, for this study "the public" was limited to businesspeople in the Chicago area.

Price Control and Business was the result of two years of survey research conducted among 528 Chicago businessowners in order to make sense of pricing behavior under conditions of wartime regulation and price control. A major focus of the study was to determine the effectiveness of price controls enacted as part of the 1942 General Maximum Price Regulation (GMPR) and, in particular, to examine the responses by sellers at the retail level to the GMPR. The Office of Price Administration (OPA) was charged with administering and regulating prices. The OPA was responsible for enforcing mandatory price controls in some sectors and voluntary controls in others (agricultural products, for example). In addition, the enforcement power of the OPA shifted during the early 1940s from central control to decentralized adjudication of retail prices by some 5,500 local price control boards consisting of 275,000 volunteers and over 63,000 paid staff (Katznelson and Pietrykowski 1991: 324; Bentley 1998: 17). Hazel Kyrk became chair of the Consumer Advisory Committee of the OPA in 1943 (van Velzen 2003: 46). Given its role in the wartime economy as a substitute for the market, OPA incurred the displeasure of both producers and consumers. In the case of food rationing, the homemaker was drawn into the war provisioning effort. Shopping and meal preparation came to be inserted into the public discourse about one's political commitment to win the war. Bentley notes that the discourse narrowly ascribed women's contributions to the war in terms of the private, atomistic household. Aside from a few contrarian voices, like that of Day Monroe, there was no consideration of transforming the world of family provisioning to accommodate the challenges of a wartime economy characterized by labor shortages – production labor in the plants and domestic labor at home – and food rationing. As a result, alternatives like communal kitchens and the concomitant socialization of private domestic tasks were rarely placed on the table for public debate and deliberation (Bentley 1998: 42, 57). This, as Lizabeth Cohen notes, did not mean that the homemaker and consumer were untouched by wartime policies and practices. "Suddenly tasks that had been viewed as private and domestic were brought into the civic arena and granted new political importance" (Cohen 2003: 67). The enormous scale of citizen engagement in recycling, rationing and the vigilant monitoring of price controls helped to create a moral economy in which profits and prices were subject to broader citizen scrutiny and management. And the majority of citizen volunteers working at the state and local were white women (Cohen, 2003: 87).

On the other side of the government-mediated exchange of price-controlled goods for money or ration coupons was the retailer. Given the fragmented structure of price controls in 1942, Katona was able to identify several methods used by business to evade price controls. For instance, uptrading was used to sell higher quality goods that could be sold at a price that yielded a higher profit margin (Katona 1945: 71). The obverse of this technique – lowering the quality of a product yet selling it at the same price – was also used to circumvent price controls. Finally, outright evasion was committed by businesses. Katona discovered notable variations in the behavior of businesspeople by product category. For example, price stability (little or no deviation from the controlled price) was found in the majority of sellers in men's wear (53 per cent) and drugs (54 per cent), whereas liquor dealers were least likely to report that they abided by price controls and were most likely to engage in direct evasion. Sellers of women's wear and general apparel were most likely to utilize indirect methods (lowering quality or uptrading) (1945: 92–94). In addition to indirect price increases, sellers could also limit the size, duration and frequency of special sales and markdowns. What Katona's empirical evidence illustrates is the multiplicity of meanings attached to price controls, and the variety of methods used by sellers to exert their power within a highly regulated marketplace.

Furthermore, price controls at the wholesale and retail level increased the importance of social ties between sellers and buyers. When demand outstripped supply, informal means of rationing goods could take place mainly by reserving products for long-standing customers. Although Katona reports that this situation was rarer at the retail than at the wholesale level, the retail environment within the wartime marketplace valorized the social standing of the loyal customer. This was best illustrated by the success of independent grocers during the war; reversing a trend toward chain stores beginning in the late 1920s (Tedlow 1990). Katona found that most independent grocers favored regular customers. Bentley notes that butchers sometimes sold better quality meat as "preground" hamburger to save their customers' ration stamps (Bentley 1998: 36). This selective treatment led one grocer to claim "People trust chains with their money but not with their stamps" (Katona 1945: 196). In particular, those independent stores offering higher quality merchandise were better off during periods characterized by price controls and rising income. However, to the extent that higher quality stores utilized more personal service (telephone orders, personal delivery) labor shortages curtailed their ability to differentiate themselves from the lower price competitors. This fact, combined with the tendency of manufacturers to turn out more standardized product lines with fewer embellishments intended to signal higher quality, meant that "customers found fewer differences in the merchandise than ... in the price – since the stores added different markups to their buying prices" and, as a result, shopped at the less expensive stores (1945: 201).

Katona endeavors to show that rather than nullifying the actions of businesses or the desires of consumers the regulated marketplace required an alteration in the frame of reference and a subsequent reorientation of behavior. The strategic behavior adopted by businesspeople was heterogeneous and dynamic.

> Since fundamental changes in the business environment, especially in available supplies and consumer demand, were much more frequent in the war

than in the peace economy, it would appear that the former offered more rather than less occasion for new business decisions.

(Katona 1945: 207)

In addition, price controls guided business expectations and lessened the chance that a dynamic environment would become a volatile one.[5]

Although Katona's research project was undertaken under the aegis of the Cowles Commission, it did not fit comfortably within the scope of Cowles. Cowles was interested in developing an econometric model of Walrasian equilibrium. At Cowles, under the leadership of Jacob Marschak, it was understood that a robust econometric model would replace the Walrasian auctioneer (Mirowski and Hands 1998; Mirowski 2002). On the one hand, Katona's characterization of price controls as a qualified success lent credence to the role of the government in allocating goods and services. On the other hand, his acknowledgment that standard economic variables were grossly insufficient at capturing the behavior of business people and consumers pointed out the vulnerability of an econometric fix to the Walrasian model of general equilibrium. Katona's monograph was faintly praised in the Cowles Commission's 1942–46 Five-Year Report: "The study has probably contributed to the fund of experience relating to the use of interview methods for economic research ..." (Cowles Commission 1947: 15).

Surveys of consumer sentiment

After his brief stint at Cowles, Katona fixed his sights squarely on consumer behavior. In 1945 he was hired by Renis Likert to work at the US Agriculture Department's Program Survey Division and to direct its Survey of Consumer Finances. In 1946 the Division moved to the University of Michigan. Katona was director of the Economic Behavior Program at the University of Michigan's Survey Research Center from 1946 until 1972 (Wärneryd 1982). In 1951 a summary measure of "consumer confidence" was constructed and published as the Index of Consumer Sentiment. This project of surveying the economic public had the consequence of constructing a representation of "the consumer." By advocating that economics includes methods of surveying and polling in order to discern motives, expectations and attitudes, Katona was implicitly advocating for a different way of conceptualizing economic agents. However, in place of traditional polling's construction of the political subject, the well-informed citizen, Katona needed to assemble a representative economic actor. The consumer fit the bill as consumption was a necessary economic activity that appeared to transcend class boundaries. Beginning in the 1920s, psychological theories of group behavior – in particular buying behavior – gained currency within business circles as a result of manufacturers' burgeoning interest in marketing new products to a mass of consumers (Igo 2007). As discussed in Chapter 3, the 1935–36 Study of Consumer Spending was one source used by corporations to analyze and then construct their own image of the American consumer. Over time, the actions of the subgroups were less important than the identification of consumers who bore the closest relationship to the statistical average – an ideal typical consumer. In the case of political polling surveyors diligently enumerated responses by race, gender, political affiliation, class and age, but the transformation of the polling data into public statements by Roper and Gallup ignored complex fissures and cleavages in favor of broad patterns. "Social factors and social structures were usually invisible in surveyors' presentation of the results, if not in the making of the polls" (Igo 2007: 140). This was the parlous situation that awaited the University of Michigan's Survey of Consumer Finances and Index of Consumer Sentiment.

A further consequence of Katona's analytical approach was to legitimize the economic knowledge of the "man on the street" as worthy of collection and study. For many economists this would seem to be a startling admission. On methodological grounds there was little reason to spend time and resources ferreting out the banal opinions of individuals. However, the political impact of Keynes' recognition of the productive role played by spending, together with the interest of business leaders in sustaining a postwar system of mass consumption, abetted the effort of Katona and colleagues to chart the hopes and fears of American consumers. A few of the seeds for this project lay in the work of home economists and the recognition that household budget-making was a productive activity. In their own way, both the home economists and Katona wanted to construct a model of an active, productive, complex, and contradictory consumer whose behavior had profound effects on the economy they inhabited. Also, they each wanted to use as data what conventional economists might well refer to as ersatz economic knowledge.

Yet the postwar economy was markedly different from the decades that preceded it. Whether we follow the actors and explore the way in which government resources were allocated in order to maintain and expand wartime interests in operations research (Mirowski 2002), explore the paths leading toward a modernist project involving efforts to represent the national economy as a tractable object of control (Mitchell 2004), or acknowledge the logic of expanded accumulation in the establishment of a Fordist regime (Piore and Sabel 1986; Aglietta 1987), one can identify an overlapping set of interests in depicting economic processes in terms of coordination and control. The roots of this modernist turn can be found in the Lynds' detailed social survey of 1920s life in a typical American town, *Middletown*, Muncie, Indiana. In stark contrast to the Study of Consumer Spending, the Lynds excluded blacks and foreign-born residents from their survey. Igo, poignantly notes that these groups "became hindrances to locating the typical, and the surveyors instead aimed their questions at Muncie's white native-born residents" (2007: 55). The survey process, through means of exclusion, sampling methodology, question format and summary, created new categories, new aggregates and, as a result, new knowledge. As James Morgan, a colleague of Katona's, recalls, the surveys undertaken by the Economic Behavior Program at the University of Michigan eschewed studies of "detailed expenditure allocations" in favor of "mass changes, rather than on cross-section differences" (Morgan 1972: 16–17).

However, as detailed above, Katona's early research conducted during the war more closely reflects his interest in integrating Gestalt psychology with economics.[6] In a 1947 paper presented before the American Statistical Association, he criticized the emerging tendency in economic analysis to gather macrolevel aggregate data. Aggregate data masks the underlying patterns of uneven distribution and dissimilarity. Furthermore, aggregate data is ineffective at capturing expectations, something that Katona sought to redress through the use of survey instruments intended to measure consumer attitudes and sentiments. Keynes' introduction of uncertainty and expectation was a partial remedy at best, according to Katona. The real problem was the exclusion of psychology from economics. Katona attributes this partly to the conflict between nineteenth-century psychology, on which the concepts of utility maximization and rational action are based, and twentieth-century psychology, which portrays human behavior as pliable and flexible (Katona 1947: 452). For Katona, twentieth-century neoclassical economics rested on a foundation of outmoded nineteenth-century psychology. Additionally, he argued that the trend toward macroeconomic aggregates discounted the variation and heterogeneity of individual consumers by assuming that deviations would cancel out (Katona 1947: 454; 1963: 640–3).

A substantial part of Katona's postwar writing and research explicitly acknowledges a new frame of reference shaping consumer behavior, rising incomes and favorable expectations about the future. This new way of framing economic conditions required consumers to adopt a different orientation toward the role of income and saving in their lives. A Gestalt experience was taking place in the postwar period. Katona attempted to make sense of this new behavior that contradicted the Keynesian consumption function linking changes in consumption to changes in income (Katona 1960: 22–3; 1963: 653). Consumption could increase, for example, even if there was no change in current income. One's willingness to buy is distinct from the ability to buy. Friedman (1957), along with the majority of the economics profession, was content to resolve this conundrum by positing that consumers made purchasing decisions today on the basis of their expected lifetime or permanent income. Katona found this to be unsatisfactory for several reasons:

> The emphasis on long-range planning and on definite expectations rules out flexibility and learning as well as uncertainty. It not only relegates current income to a minor position in explaining current saving and consumption but also disregards the probable impact of changes in motives, attitudes, and expectations on expenditures.
>
> (Katona 1960, 151)

In raising this issue, Katona is attempting to carve out a role for uncertainty in consumer spending that is on par with the role of uncertainty played in the Keynesian theory of aggregate demand (Katona 1960: 23). For Katona, rising postwar affluence made spending on mass-produced consumer durables a key aspect of consumers' aspirations, status and spending decisions. He found, for instance, that people with adequate income to afford expensive refrigerators and television sets purchase on credit as a self-control mechanism.

This apparently irrational behavior appears to be due partly to people's awareness of their own savings habits. Some people doubt they would have the fortitude to replenish their depleted bank deposits, while buying on installment necessitates the repayment of the debt and leaves the bank deposits intact.

(Katona 1963: 654)

This, in turn, resonates with contemporary explorations of self-control and commitment devices (Thaler and Shefrin 1981; Starr 2007). For Katona, the postwar economy represented a Gestalt-like experience for consumers formerly habituated to the Depression-era and wartime constraints. His analysis of the active, flexible, creative consumer stood in contrast to an alternative portrayal of postwar consumer society offered up by John Kenneth Galbraith.

Katona versus Galbraith

Katona, in his attempt to apply Gestalt theory to an examination of economic behavior, began his investigation with an examination of the way in which the consumer frames decisions to buy now or later. This focus on the phenomenological dimension of everyday lived experience set the stage upon which the individual acts of consumer purchase were played out. Relevant features of the experience involving consumer purchases were determined by the psychological disposition of the consumer in relation to the social world around her. This was the space between economics and psychology that Katona wished to explain.

This framework rested on an economic system within which the expansion of consumer needs was both recognizable and taken for granted. It was only during the postwar period that the concept of an affluent consumer could be applied to broad portions of the US population. Katona, especially after the 1960 publication of *The Powerful Consumer*, realized that this condition of generalized – but by no means universal – affluence perceptibly changed consumer behavior. Consumption decisions became increasingly loosened from physical needs and could expand the scope of consumer subjectivity. Katona acknowledged that neoclassical theory was incapable of sufficiently taking account of this transformation in the consuming subject. On the other hand, he was critical of the idea that affluent consumers were always susceptible to the manipulations of corporate blandishments and that this necessarily led to waste and ruin. This was the perspective raised by John Kenneth Galbraith.

Galbraith's position, on the role of consumption in modern society is well-known. Perhaps best articulated in the *Affluent Society* (1958), Galbraith maintained that consumers were manipulated into desiring objects unrelated to their needs. Producers, intent on maintaining sales and profit, synthesized wants through the use of advertising and salesmanship. In exploring the dilemmas inherent in the affluent age of postwar capitalism, Galbraith identifies a deep chasm between economic thought and the real manifestations of material abundance. Economists of all ideological persuasions are fixated on increased production as a talisman, the possession of which will secure prosperity. Such fascination was sensible during the time of Smith, Malthus, Ricardo and Marx when wages gravitated toward that sum necessary to maintain physical subsistence. But the economics of scarcity and insecurity for the masses had been surmounted in the postwar United States. Rather, prosperity has been achieved for vast swathes of the developed world and, as a result, the continued pre-occupation with private production is misplaced. This fixation has led to a serious conundrum for modern economies:

> Why is it that as production has increased in modern times concern for production seems also to have increased. Production has become the center of a concern that had hitherto been shared with equality and security. … [I]t has managed to retain the prestige which inevitably it had in the poor world of Ricardo.
>
> (Galbraith 1958: 120)

Interestingly, Galbraith's attack on production as the idée fixe of economists does not exempt Galbraith himself. This is seen in his characterization of consumption as a codicil intended to satisfy the intentions of corporations. The consumer is thereby rendered a powerless entity through which the desires of producers are enacted. Consumption activity, in turn, is reduced to a set of binary impulses shifting from real needs to artificial wants. While Galbraith recognizes problems inherent in the productivist framework he wants to replace it neither with consumption nor with an interest to investigate the line of demarcation between production and consumption. Rather he wants to substitute public, social production in place of private, individual production. By re-allocating the mix of resources given over to public versus private goods and services, he seeks to redress a deeper imbalance in the ability of the economy to deliver the good life. Galbraith rightly points out the inherent power relations involved in mass consumer society but the determination of consumer purchases above a certain standard of living as necessarily artificial and wasteful was contested by Katona.

Katona also adopted a binary formula with which to understand consumption. The consumer was divided in two: a need-based consumer who may well conform to the dictates of marginal utility formulations of consumer demand, and a want-based consumer who can postpone or bunch purchases together. This understanding is summed up in Katona's declaration that "there is a psychological difference between money we *must* spend and expenditures we *like* to make" (1961: 16). The implication is that individuals engage in what Marx refers to as productive consumption – consumption aimed at reproducing the commodity labor power. In addition, however, they also take part in this enjoyable pursuit of material acquisition. This latter pursuit, in turn, stimulates economic growth through the purchase of large-scale, costly consumer durables like houses and cars (Katona 1972). Katona reclassified consumer durables as a type of investment expenditure along with business capital investment and human capital investment.

It is worth exploring Katona's analogy between capital investment and consumer investment. The analogy lies in the categorical similarities rather than in their economic effects. The direct impact of net capital investment on economic growth has no direct corollary in consumer durable investment. Instead, the effect of such purchases on productivity is psychological. "For productivity increases depend, in part at least, on the material standards of the people" (1961: 14). With increasing affluence, tangible increases in one's standard of living are perceived as attainable. This psychological state affects one's willingness to exert effort in production. "When the possibility of improving our standard of living appears doubtful, we don't work as hard as when we are confident of the outcome" (1961: 16). The policy recommendation made by Katona is, therefore, to expand the reach of attainable goods for the broadest segment of the population. Governments could offer consumer tax incentives to purchase automobiles, new houses or home remodeling, thereby raising the standard of living of consumers and increasing the propensity of workers to exert greater effort on the job.

From psychological economics to behavioral economics

In *Psychological Analysis of Economic Behavior* (1951), Katona describes the type of psychology appropriate for economics. He explicitly adopts the framework of Gestalt theory and related work in field theory and abandons rational action as a useful framework within which to begin a study of economic behavior. "Unlike pure theorists, we shall not assume at the outset that rational behavior exists or that rational behavior constitutes the topic of economic analysis" (Katona 1951: 16). Furthermore, he maintains that the concept of a self-regulating market is incapable of describing a postwar economy characterized by both monopoly power on the one side, and dynamic, independent consumers on the other.

The Gestalt perspective is applied to consumer behavior by analyzing the ways in which problems and choices present themselves to consumers, the social psychological environment within which consumers operate and the subject positions that consumers occupy at various points in time. The psychological approach to economics starts from the premise that consumers' perception of the world is organized. Attitudes, motives and emotions all combine to shape perception and all are affected by intervening variables, frames of reference and our own reference group. For Katona, consumer behavior is inherently social and interactive. Perceptions can be shaped and transformed. Even the assumption of a fixed subject position represented by consumers with coherent, stable preferences is challenged by Katona.

> In terms of social psychology, this means that the individual may at certain times of a day be a factory worker or a student, in other words, he may belong to the group of workers or students. At other times, the same individual may be father and husband, his whole situation or group being represented by his family. At still other times, he may be a club member or a member of a political party.
>
> (Katona 1951: 37)

And these multiple identities will shape and influence consumer expenditures.

Much current research in behavioral economics bears the unacknowledged traces of Katona and his adaptation of Gestalt psychology for economic analysis. A few examples will serve to illustrate the connections. First, the identification of "anchoring effects" in studies of consumer behavior demonstrates the severe limits of rational choice models and the need to incorporate psychological concepts and methods of analysis. An anchor takes the form of irrelevant signals provided in advance of consumer choice. The anchor then shapes and directs the consumer choices that follow. So, if consumers' preferences among a given set of goods are affected by trivial, irrelevant signals, each consumer will still display a well-ordered, internal ranking of commodity preferences. This is what Airely, Loewenstein and Prelec (2003) term "coherent arbitrariness."

Briefly, an experiment was designed such that test subjects were asked their willingness to accept (WTA) a certain payment to listen to an annoying sound. The sound is provided ahead of time and the sound is recorded at three different lengths of time (10, 30 and 60 seconds). Individuals are then provided with an anchor price (either a high anchor price or a low anchor price) at which they would indicate their willingness to listen to the sound. Then the individuals were asked to derive their own WTA a monetary payment to hear the sound. They were then provided with a computer-generated payment and, if the computer payment exceeded their WTA, they would listen to the sound and collect that payment for themselves. In a later experiment, the first three digits of the individual's social security number were used in order to more strongly signal the arbitrariness of the initial valuation. In both experiments, the distribution of WTA offers closely resembled the anchor and the two groups' (high anchor versus low anchor) WTA reflected this difference. The internal ordering of WTA per time period of the sound was consistent even though the valuation itself was arbitrary. The upshot is that well-ordered preferences can result from thoroughly random initial valuations.

Airely and colleagues then replicated the structure of the experiment within an auction market setting. Individuals, sorted into groups, would each submit their WTA as a bid. The three lowest bidders would hear the sound and collect the WTA price of the fourth lowest bidder. Once again, a low anchor and a high anchor were used at the start of the experiment. Once again, the anchors had a determinate impact on the distribution of WTA and payouts between the two groups. In addition, there was no tendency for the bids to converge. The results indicated that not only were the results obtained within a market environment, more provocatively, they also go on to say that "markets can strengthen the impact of arbitrary stimuli, such as anchors, on valuation" (Airely *et al.* 2003: 91). This study of preference formation reveals that if consumers' preferences are largely arbitrary, "then the claims of revealed preferences as a guide to public policy and the organization of economic exchanges are weakened. Market institutions that maximize consumer sovereignty need not maximize consumer welfare" (2003: 102). What is left unexplored by this study is an examination of the degree to which anchors reflect random noise or intentional, strategic manipulation. What behavioral economics too often fails to identify are those structural mechanisms and institutions that channel, guide and influence consumer behavior.

In another study, Lee *et al.* (2006), conducted three experimental taste tests of two beers. One sample was an off-the-shelf brand and the other sample was the same beer to which some drops of balsamic vinegar were added. Three experiments were conducted. The first experiment consisted of a blind taste test.

In the second experiment, drinkers were told that the second beer contained vinegar prior to the tasting. In the third experiment, subjects were told that the second beer was vinegar-spiked only after they had tasted it. Surprisingly, the percentage of subjects who preferred the vinegar beer in Experiment Three did not differ much from the blind taste test (Experiment One). There was a statistically significant difference in the results of Experiment Two, with fewer subjects reporting their preference for the beer with vinegar. Providing the information before the taste test affected the taste experience, whereas providing the same information to subjects after they tasted the beer had less of an impact on their reported assessment of the beer. Not only does information matter but also the location of the information in the consumption process matters. Individual taste is malleable and structured through communicative acts.

This is important in a number of ways. First, it supports the idea that tastes and preferences are socially constructed. In addition, the timing of information – its place within the sequence of consumption acts – affects consumer experiences and the evaluation of those experiences. Marketing agents and other hidden persuaders are keenly aware of the power of suggestion and the effectiveness of "buzz" in the creation of consumer desire (Schor 2004). Galbraith's concept of synthetic demand creation indicted Madison Avenue in the creation and expansion of wasteful consumer spending. The tendency in economics has been to maintain a division between those who characterize advertising as an innocuous and generally helpful activity involving the dissemination of product information and those who see advertising as a means to manipulate individuals into purchasing goods and services for which they have no "real" need. McCloskey and Klamer (1995) cleverly argue that a large part of GDP is devoted to sales, marketing, and other such persuasive talk, which enables the facilitation of exchange. Manipulative speech acts occur when one of the parties actively attempts to deceive the other that they are engaged in reaching mutual understanding (Habermas 1984; Pietrykowski 1995a). Consumer education, including the acquisition of negotiating skills, could be made available to offset this imbalance of power between producers and consumers (Earl 1990). Consumers could also enter into a "market for preferences" by seeking out the knowledge and advice of specialist experts to help overcome their own bounded rationality (Earl and Potts 2004).

Communication can also help to frame the motives of other agents in the market. Suppose a store offers a wide variety of low priced goods and markets itself on this basis. Suppose that additional information comes to light about the unfair treatment afforded workers at the store. Individuals might be willing to forego lower prices in order to punish the store's labor policies. This would be a form of reciprocity as it is analyzed in behavioral economics.

> Reciprocity motives manifest themselves not only in people's refusal to cooperate with others, but also in their willingness to sacrifice to hurt others who are being unfair. A consumer may refuse to buy a product sold by a monopolist at an 'unfair' price, even if she hurts herself by foregoing the product.
>
> (Rabin 1998: 22)

The psychological (re)turn in economics broadens the scope of analysis while it rejects key axioms of neoclassical theory. Earl (2005) recently enumerated a set of foundational principles for twenty-first-century behavioral economics: agents' actions are socially conditioned; consumer sentiments are influenced by non-economic variables; agents operate under conditions of bounded rationality; frames of reference and heuristics are often used in decision-making; choice involves an affective dimension; non-selfish behavior is commonplace and consumers make their choices based on aspirations, group norms and lifestyle goals. There are marked similarities between these principles and the research approach taken by home economists and social economists in the early twentieth century, and between these principles and Katona's foray into psychological economics. At the time, these approaches were located far from the mainstream. It is important to note that Katona was often treated as an outsider by his colleagues in economics and his research was increasingly to be found at the margins of the profession. In 1980, Katona, then emeritus professor, protested moves by the University of Michigan Economics Department to eliminate courses in psychological economics and sunder faculty connections to researchers working at the Survey Research Center. In a letter to University President Harold Shapiro, he complained about the sharp disciplinary lines drawn by the Economics faculty:

> The Economics Department has apparently decided to adopt a very restrictive definition of economics, centered on algebra applied to economics and on econometrics. The failings of old economic theory, recently recognized by an ever-increasing number of economists as remote from real-life developments, are disregarded.
>
> (Katona 1980)

James Tobin avers that Katona "annoyed many of the brethren of his adopted scientific community" because he eschewed utility maximizing assumptions and challenged the adequacy of macroeconomic models (1972: 37).

The resurgence of psychology-based research into economic behavior highlights the need to re-examine roads not taken in order to critically examine the history of ideas in economics. I argue that the project of behavioral economics remains open to different approaches. Several questions are left unanswered by the behavioral studies. First, what is the scope of relevant information shaping the consumption experience? If, for example, divulging information about the content of the product being consumed ("This beer has drops of balsamic vinegar in it.") alters the taste experience, would revealing information about the conditions under which the product was produced also affect the taste for products? The usual assumption is that communication has to be top-down from the producer or her agent to the consumer. Yet, it can also be bottom-up, it can be collective and it can involve people not directly involved in the final market exchange. For example, unions can conduct an informational campaign highlighting the social value of buying union-made products. Ethical and fair-trade activists can share information with consumers about the working conditions under which products are made. The value added at each stage of the commodity chain can be shared with consumers. Advertisements can be parodied and corporations mocked for their attempts to sell dangerous products, like cigarettes, or their abusive labor practices. Buyers of locally produced vegetables and meat can interact with direct producers. Such communicative practices can, and do, unsettle the discursive terrain upon which corporate marketing is based. They can also alter the tastes and preferences of consumers. By inserting a political dimension into the discourse of behavioral economics, we can begin to analyze and apply the experimental results in a broader context.

5   Fordism and the social relations of consumption

Many of the postwar consumers that George Katona and his colleagues at the University of Michigan's Survey Research Center interviewed were increasingly able to achieve rising levels of consumption. What was so remarkable about the affluent society that John Kenneth Galbraith wrote about in 1958 was the institutionalization of a system capable of fabricating consumer desire for mass-produced products.

> So great has been the change that many of the desires of the individual are no longer even evident to him. They become so only as they are synthesized, elaborated, and nurtured by advertising and salesmanship, and these, in turn, have become among our most important and talented professions.
>
> (Galbraith 1958: 2)

The roots of postwar consumerism can be traced to the diffusion of a regime of mass production best characterized by the term Fordism. Within economics, the French Regulation School and its US counterpart, the neo-Marxist Social Structure of Accumulation (SSA) School, advanced a thick history of the political economy of twentieth-century capitalism.[1] With its affinity for structure along with agency, its focus on the institutional mechanisms promoting or retarding capital accumulation, and a social conflict account of income distribution, this theory has been largely ignored by mainstream economists.[2]

Fordism and the consumer society

The term "Fordism" was originally used in the United States by workers and union activists as an indictment of machine-paced production and brutal working conditions characteristic of assembly-line production. In the 1910s, workers at Ford's Highland Park plant described their work life as so unremittingly tedious and repetitive that they coined a common nervous condition affecting line workers, "Forditis" (Meyer 1981: 40–1). Ford experimented with job rotation as a method to break up the monotony, only to find that workers resisted changing jobs. Whereas Ford Motor managers believed that this unwillingness on the part of workers to switch jobs signaled their satisfaction with the tasks, workers, by contrast, objected to being moved between equally monotonous and nerve-wracking jobs (Meyer 1981: 42). The Fordist production process emphasized the utilization of unskilled and semi-skilled labor rather than skilled craft labor, although it also relied on the latter to produce and maintain capital equipment (Watkins 1920; Chandler 1964). The emerging trend toward mass production and the need for large numbers of industrial workers previously unfamiliar with the nature of machine-paced production, disturbed the balance of power between labor and management and drove a wedge between craft workers and the new crop of unskilled laborers. The culture of craft-based labor relations was incompatible with the need for a high volume of standardized goods. Difference and heterogeneity of labor practices was being challenged by an influx of unskilled workers charged with performing relatively homogenous tasks. Following Ford Motor, the problem for management in the early twentieth century was no longer one of merely acclimating agricultural labor to the logic of capitalist production. Rather it became a task of carefully designing a staffing policy that would both homogenize job tasks through de-skilling while simultaneously utilizing cultural difference (gender, race and ethnicity) to maintain barriers to collective action and unionization (Gordon *et al.* 1982). A high-wage policy – the five-dollar day – helped to stem the tide of workers quitting their production jobs, often after less than one day (Meyer 1981; Pietrykowski 1995c). The five-dollar day, combined with the internal spatial segregation of workers into ethnic-, gender- and race-typed jobs, helped to forestall strike activity and unionization (Raff 1988; Gordon *et al.* 1982; Pietrykowski 1995b). The production and labor management system at Ford Motor became emblematic of modern industrial production (Hughes 1989; Smith 1994).

One of the earliest analyses of Fordism as a new form of capitalist production was written in the 1930s by the Italian Marxist political theorist Antonio Gramsci. In his essay, "Americanism and Fordism," Gramsci attempted to interpret changes taking place in the social, economic and political landscape of Europe during the 1930s by examining the widespread changes wrought by Ford's system of mass production and Frederick Taylor's system of labor control. Gramsci treats mass production and the routinization of labor as a quintessentially American style of capitalist development. According to Gramsci, the key condition for the successful implementation and subsequent expansion of Fordist production involved the reorientation of the workers' lives outside of the factory gates. In particular, Gramsci argued that Fordism required that individual morality needed to be policed through the close examination and surveillance of consumption behavior. Employees of Ford's Sociological Department were charged with the task of visiting workers' homes in order to examine the outward signs and symbols of what Ford considered to be a lifestyle worthy of the five-dollar day. Saving a portion of one's paycheck was considered to be an important sign of exemplary moral character. Home ownership was encouraged. Learning to identify and acquire the trappings of middle-class respectability – including proper furniture, eating utensils and personal hygiene products – was also expected (Meyer 1981; Hooker 1997). For Gramsci, Fordism provided a viable American alternative to European capitalism without the vestiges of feudal traditions and aristocratic classes:

It seems possible to reply that the Ford method is rational, that it should be generalized; but that a long process is needed for this, during which a change must take place in social conditions and in the way of life and habits of individuals. This, however, cannot take place through coercion alone, but only through tempering compulsion (self-discipline) with persuasion. Persuasion should also take the form of high wages, which offer the possibility of a better standard of living, or more exactly perhaps, the possibility of realising a standard of living which is adequate to the new methods of production and work which demand a particular degree of expenditure of muscular and nervous energy.

(Gramsci 1971, 312)

Fordism was connected to the emergence of a new social type – the modern worker–consumer – who needed to acquire traits and habits necessary for proper behavior at work but also at home and in the marketplace (Pietrykowski 1995c). Fordism requires the synchronicity of mass production and mass consumption. The development of large-scale production processes using expensive, single-purpose machinery together with masses of semi-skilled and unskilled workers resulted in a high volume of standardized consumer goods. The persuasive high-wage strategy that Gramsci refers to not only purchased the consent of workers to labor under harsh conditions, but also provided a means for workers to afford to buy the products that they fabricated. This is the hallmark of the modern era of industrial capitalism. In the event that individual private employers were unwilling to adopt a high-wage strategy, first unionization and then collective bargaining together with the strike threat helped to diffuse the high-wage strategy throughout the US economy.

Throughout the 1930s and 1940s, industrial unions played an important role in the establishment and maintenance of the Fordist regime, although always within the contested spaces of production marked by consent, resistance, revolt and accommodation. They radically changed the rules governing labor market behavior, created new institutional structures and constituted new habitual forms of economic behavior. Collective bargaining substituted the union in place of the individual worker on the supply side of the labor market. This had the profound effect of reducing intra-firm income inequality. Wage increases were provided to workers as a group rather than on the basis of craft affiliation. Grievance procedures, arbitration proceedings and staffing regulations all required new forms of economic behavior and new relations of production between managers and workers and between workers themselves. In particular, the 1948 contract between General Motors and the United Auto Workers institutionalized the practice of tying wage gains to changes in the cost of living. After years of rancorous negotiations and costly strikes, the wage bargain itself came to be re-defined in terms of the real wage. Workers came to see the cost of living adjustment (COLA) as an essential part of the contract. In addition, the 1948 contract also linked wage gains to productivity increases. This contract became the industry standard and the template for union negotiators in other industries. It formed the basis for a "capital-labor accord" through which the interests of labor and capital meshed over the shared goal of increased productivity while denying more militant calls to give labor leverage over the determination of investment and workplace control (Gordon *et al.* 1982; Gartman 1986; Kochan *et al.* 1986). Acknowledging the inherently unstable growth of capitalist market economies, countercyclical fiscal policy and automatic stabilizers, such as unemployment insurance, would stimulate spending and extend consumer purchasing in the absence of income from employment. In this way, Keynesianism came to be another essential component of the Fordist economic regime.

The more contemporary theory of Fordist production and the transition to post-Fordism was first detailed in Michel Aglietta's *The Theory of Capitalist Regulation: The US Experience* (1987). Aglietta laid the theoretical groundwork for the concept of Fordism and the development of the French Regulation School approach to economic theory.[3] For Aglietta, the stability of twentieth-century postwar US capitalism depended on the successful attempt to establish patterns of consumption that harmonized with the production technology being deployed by capital. The technological foundations of mass production – large-scale, single-purpose machinery, automatic assembly lines, semi-skilled labor – needed to find a corollary in consumption technology. This new mode of consumption was one in which: commodity relations usurped space formerly given over to non-commodity relations; a social consumption norm developed for the entire working class; and a design aesthetic compatible with the limits of mass production technology helped to define popular consumption norms. Where it was necessary, household credit and government underwriting of lender risk was instituted in order to sustain the mode of consumption (Aglietta 1987: 81–2).

There is no doubt that an essentialist logic runs through much of Aglietta's analysis of Fordist capital accumulation. The status of consumption activity in Aglietta's account of Fordist regulation appears to be of secondary importance. Consumption is characterized by private activity within the household. As it is removed, spatially and temporally, from relations of production, consumption activity is a site in which the individual is relatively insulated from the economic (production) sphere. The interaction between individuals is thereby governed by relations of status. Status attainment is accomplished through the purchase of commodities. Maintaining one's social status becomes a habit expressed through routine consumption activity (Aglietta 1987: 157). What is gained is a richer, more multi-dimensional consumer no longer focused solely on the satisfaction of physiological needs. The purchase of consumer goods is tied to more than the need to reproduce the worker in a form suitable for the capitalist production process. Although he does not explicitly develop this idea, Aglietta is implying that consumption is predicated on the need to maintain an identity similar to the identity of others in an individual's economic class. To what extent are individuals self-reflective in constituting their status position through consumer purchases? This is not discussed by Aglietta but, as Davis (2003) points out, the constitution of a sense of self through social activities cast within a specific institutional environment allows for these social constraints to be channeled and directed by individual agency.

On the other hand, Aglietta accepts a dualist separation between consumption and production activity, he identifies production as the sphere in which social conflict helps to forge a particular regime of surplus value extraction and relegates consumption to the household sector, where individuality retains the symbolic power that has been lost in the creation of the social division of production labor. Not only does Aglietta ignore the gender division of labor between market and household labor, but also he reduces consumption to the private actions of individual, and presumably cooperative, family members. In this way, the Regulation School assumes that the consumption sphere is merely a necessary concomitant to production labor without scope for the type of conflict and resistance allowed for in the sphere of production. If a crisis in production jeopardizes the ability for expanded accumulation such that the wage relation itself is threatened, then the consumption sphere will likewise manifest a crisis of realization and valorization of commodity values and the state will be called upon to valorize commodity production. Consumption is, therefore, portrayed as an auxiliary and largely passive force. Thus, the social and cultural context within which consumption takes place is largely neglected by Aglietta. Yet, elsewhere he acknowledges that consumption is a material process, a spatial location and a "specific geography and object-network" (Aglietta 1987: 156). This leaves open the possibility of the elaboration of a richer account of consumption practices. This account would, however, need to jettison the unitary conception of the subject as laborer whose consumption is determined solely by the requirements of capital accumulation under a regime of mass production.

A brief account of Gramsci's original attempt to trace out a description of Fordism may provide some direction for an account of consumer behavior under a regime of mass production. One striking aspect of Gramsci's conception of Fordism lies in the way in which he perceived Fordism as a system of social and cultural control marked by political contingency and conflict:

> The fact that a progressive initiative has been set in train by a particular social force is not without fundamental consequences: the 'subaltern' forces, which have to be 'manipulated' and rationalised to serve new ends, naturally put up resistance. But resistance is also offered by certain sectors of the dominant forces, or at least by forces which are allied to those which are dominant.
>
> (Gramsci 1971: 279)

He cites the Prohibition movement and its failure as an example of an alliance forged to help create the new American worker. While Gramsci notes the need to link mass production with mass consumption, he also realizes that mass consumption is not a unitary or fixed set of acts automatically driven by the imperative of capitalist accumulation. Thus, Fordism is linked to a particular regime of accumulation with a particular set of norms tied to the social re-construction of both resistant (deviant) and rationalized (normal) forms of behavior. It is not surprising then that Gramsci links Fordism to the creation of a new ethic of sexual relations based on monogamy and a new "feminine personality" connected, in part, to the need to rationally reproduce labor power (1971: 296). Gramsci's account of Fordism presents us with an anti-essentialist theory of politics – a politics of contingency. Yet, through it all the economy remains an essential determinate of cultural life (Laclau and Mouffe 1985: 70).

However, other researchers within the Regulation School tradition, most notably Alain Lipietz (1988), help to further re-position the work of Gramsci and Aglietta. Lipietz is intent on creating an account of capitalist regulation and structuration that attends to the theoretic and empirical issues of indeterminacy and contingency. Lipietz acknowledges that theoretic explanations are inherently partial and reflect a particular perspective. He goes further to suggest that the very attempt to craft a coherent narrative of a regime of modern capitalist development is illusory:

> In any case, there remains something arbitrary in the identification of rela-
> tions since human beings ceaselessly invent new ways to enter into relations,
> and new occasions or new ways of entering into the same relation. The malle-
> ability of social relations above and beyond their historical permanence is an
> essential property of the concept of relation ... The theoretician can at most
> endeavor to identify types of relations, or rather, typical universal characters
> of a set of social practices, characters which are reproduced regularly enough
> to be identifiable, and to which the less typical are then connected with more
> or less success. This connection is a matter of style, almost a fashion.
>
> (Lipietz 1988: 12)

Lipietz develops a theoretic structure that addresses the characteristic "Regulation School" concern for how social norms are reproduced (forms of regulation such as authority relations are sanctioned by the state, for example). However, he goes on to argue that even authority relations need to be organized and maintained daily through networks of social control and accommodation (1988: 14–15). Thus, institutions of regulation may vary between localities and accumulation crises may be local in nature rather than only occurring at the systemic level. The recognition of the inherent variability and plasticity of social relations sustaining or threatening a regime of capitalist regulation is important in that it allows for a shift in the focus of Fordism away from the speed of diffusion and replication of Fordist practices to non-Fordist firms, industrial sectors and nation-states and toward an examina-tion of local forms of institutional variety (in terms of production technology, consumption practice, gender and culture) in existence under a regime of capital accumulation (Sabel and Zeitlin 1985; Pietrykowski 1995b; Scranton 1997). What this suggests is that the institutional foundation of capitalist accumulation is less homogeneous, and, therefore, crises of capitalism may be much more localized, more prevalent, and the capitalist system much less hegemonic than the traditional meta-narrative of Fordist production would suggest.

From the perspective of gender relations, the framework Lipietz presents allows us to depict a capitalist economy as one in which both commodity production and non-commodity household production exist side by side. "The patriarchal social relation, or domestic mode of production, assures its reproduction by making use of the 'means of production' purchased by a worker's wage" (1988: 23). Lipietz does, however, maintain that consumption norms are intrinsically tied to the wage relation established as the outcome of struggle between capitalists and workers. Yet the Regulation School framework can be re-interpreted, along the lines that Lipietz suggests, to allow for a partial re-construction of the relationship between consumption and production relations within an economy characterized by a gender division of labor.

The framework advanced herein bears some resemblance to the "anti-essentialist" or "overdeterminist" model of political economy developed by Resnick and Wolff (1987; 1988) together with Amariglio (1988). From the overdeterminist perspective, economic life is structured by a multiplicity of factors – so many so that no one factor can be seen to independently determine any other. Culture and politics influence and effect[4] one's class identification, which, in turn, redounds on what is and what is not possible in the realm of politics and culture. The system is so interdetermined it is "over"-determined. For Resnick and Wolff, "Theories are inherently partial, distinct stories or rhetorics about portions of social reality" (1988: 53). So, the concept of class represents an important, albeit partial, understanding of an individual identity (1988: 491). Class locates individual consumers in relation to their position within the production process, but consumer identity is not reducible to class identity. And consumer behavior is not determined solely by the social reproduction needs of the capitalist enterprise. Consumer identity and class identity can, therefore, combine to form a rich self-understanding of one's actions but each represents an intersectional moment for the economic agent.

The contribution of Regulation theories of Fordist production lies in their attempt to identify a middle ground between structural determination and atomistic rational choice. Regulation School proponents introduced institutional and social factors into economic theory at a meso-level and allowed these factors a relative autonomy and evolutionary capacity to alter or reproduce the conditions of expanded capital accumulation (Jessop 1997). On the other hand, there are two major problems with Fordism as a theory of consumption.

First, the establishment of a consumption norm consistent with the production technology of capitalist enterprise and the reproduction needs of labor leaves the interaction between institutions of consumption and consumer acceptance of these norms unexplored. Or, to put it differently, if habits are propensities to act in particular ways or "submerged repertoires of potential behavior," they can be discarded, resisted or ignored in favor of alternative behavioral responses (Hodgson 2003: 164). Institutions can influence the degree to which consumers consent to habitual forms of action but individual behavior can also legitimate or challenge institutional structures. So, rather than seeing consumption norms as relatively stable structures reflecting the current level of social reproduction of labor, consumption standards could be seen as fluid and attached to the various subject positions that individuals occupy. By acknowledging the multiple subject positions of individuals acting in their role as consumers, we can also begin to challenge the dichotomy between a Fordist world of mass production and standardized consumption versus a post-Fordist environment characterized by flexible specialization, and niche consumer markets (Pietrykowski 1994; 1995b). For instance, while many workers aspired to attain the next most prestigious car in the hierarchy of GM products some, especially black workers who saw the capital-labor accord through the dual lens of race and class, resisted and challenged the logic of a consumerism shaped by capitalist industrial production (Boggs 1970; Joseph 2001).

A second shortcoming of the theory of capitalist regulation lies in the lack of attention to the institutional and behavioral mechanisms leading to the establishment and maintenance of a mass consumption society. The ability to buy mass-produced goods is determined in the production process and the labor market. The actual purchase of consumer goods is determined, in turn, by the acquired habits and ways of life passed down from generation to generation. Only changes in capitalist production techniques and profit levels can alter the dominant habits of consumption adopted by the working class (Aglietta 1987: 157). This leaves little room for the exploration of how it is that certain modes of life became widely accepted and how consumer aspirations for particular goods actually come about. Again, the automobile serves as a particularly illustrative case. The Fordist model of mass standardization was soon supplanted by a hierarchical model of automotive desire tied to income and aspiration, namely Sloanism. Alfred Sloan at General Motors sought to create distinctions between classes of cars and operating division (Chevrolet, Pontiac, Oldsmobile, Buick and Cadillac) and to introduce yearly model changes to mimic fashion trends in the clothing industry (Hounshell 1984: 267). So, knowing the incidence of automobile ownership itself was insufficient for understanding the consumption norm in effect at any moment in time as the symbolism attached to model, make and styling were additional cues that needed to be included in the decision to buy. Furthermore, the ability to buy is insufficient if not accompanied by a willingness to buy and it is the latter that was the subject of Katona's brand of psychological economics. The gender division of consumption is also largely neglected by Regulation theory. Once again using the example of the automobile, the functional characteristics of cars were gendered in such a way that certain automotive technologies (electric engine versus internal combustion, for instance) were gender-typed (Scharf 1991). Furthermore, even after the goods are purchased there remains the question of whether they are used in ways that conform or confound the expectations of producers and re-inforce or challenge the institutional framework within which consumption takes place. Historical evidence suggests that the reception on the part of men to the earliest versions of the internal combustion engine was positive because the cars were unreliable and prone to mechanical failure. These features appealed to consumers interested in tinkering, adjusting, fixing and disassembling the automobile as a part of the experience of using the vehicle (Mom 2004). The assertion of male control over the machine through the representation of automobiles as unstable, unpredictable and prone to sudden breakdown also played on gendered stereotypes and practices whereby men were responsible for mechanical repairs (Kline and Pinch 1996). In this case, what would otherwise be seen as flaws in the technological performance of the car were re-defined as a valuable quality. Therefore, user practices and user culture represent important and much neglected facets in economic accounts of consumer behavior.

From social relations of consumption to social practice of consumption

I propose to develop the idea that consumption behavior is constituted through social relations and social practices. To do so, I first explore the contributions and limitations of applying Marx's concept of the *social relations of production* to the realm of consumption. Next, I propose an alternative framework for understanding the institutional context within which consumption takes by building up a theory of social practices.

The notion that there are similarities that can be made between Marx's concept of the social relations of production and what I have termed the social relations of consumption rests on several shared characteristics. First, both production and consumption involve a set of structured social relations. Production relations include interactions between workers and supervisors. These relationships involve the use of language, symbols and material (including means of production in the form of machinery, computers, buildings, break rooms, parking lots). Similarly, the sites of consumption (the family, the marketplace, the retail sector) are also characterized by social relations mediated by language, symbols and material (use-values, means of consumption in the form of shopping carts, circulars, coupons, money and monetary substitutes).

The concept of trans-subjectivity has been used to convey the communicative element involved in identity formation. As meaningful action, one's behavior is understood discursively through social interaction that makes use of signs and symbols to construct meaning. In particular, economic action is open to interpretation and interrogation by others. As such, economic behavior involves a set of social practices which are presented to others and which others interpret as a performance situated within a particular institutional and cultural space (Goffman 1959; Milberg and Pietrykowski 1994; Pietrykowski 2007b). At the most basic level, the goal of such social interaction is to be understood by others. Meaningful actions include, but are not limited to, speech acts. Speech acts are used to perform action through the utterance of words that are understood to effect change in a social situation ("The meeting is adjourned"). Speech acts can also be used to effect a change through the use of other people ("Shut the door") (Austin 1962). But they will be effective only if certain shared understandings and interpretive frameworks hold. The important aspect of this communicative dimension for economics is that speech acts do something other than convey information. To the extent that they bring about the changes expected by the speaker, they constitute the world in which information is evaluated and assessed. Habermas refers to the goal of shared understanding as a specific form of rational action, communicative rationality. This goal is not necessarily always achieved as it depends on a set of validity claims in order to be sustained. These claims include legitimacy, veracity and sincerity. A legitimate statement will be appropriate to the normative situation. For example, asking a nearby shopper in a clothing store to check the stockroom for additional colors of a shirt would violate the normative situation whereby consumer requests are communicated to employees and not to other customers, and where the employment relationship determines that only employees search the stockroom. A truthful statement, the second claim that needs to be met, would convey accurate knowledge on the part of the speaker. In this case, the nearby shopper might inform you that, based on personal experience, the shirt is very well-made and durable. Even though the recommendation of a single individual may well be contrary to the results obtained by a consumer research lab, a personal testimonial carries weight. However, the shopper's recommendation might have been due to the fact that they own the shirt and ownership alone makes the shirt more valuable to them regardless of its actual physical qualities. This variant on the "endowment effect" now enters into the decision-making process of other shoppers. The third validity claim concerns the sincerity of the speaker about what they are saying. Once again, the nearby shopper who recommends the shirt may be heard joking that the owner owes her a commission for talking up the quality of the stock. In this case, the joke may alter the perceived trustworthiness of the recommendation previously given. Although all of the examples of validity claims were applied to consumer experiences in the retail sector, they did not directly involve the buyer and seller interaction. Rather they consisted of social relations between shoppers that may include shopping – browsing – that falls short of actual purchase (Gregson *et al.* 2002). This example highlights the interdependence of consumer choice even where the social situation consists of relative strangers and anonymous others. This communicative background of shared meanings and taken-for-granted rules, institutions, and rituals of consumption often remains unquestioned. However, validity claims can be challenged and contested (Pietrykowski 1995a). This leads to another way in which an exploration of the social relations of consumption expands the scope for political economy as it troubles the sharp analytical divide between production and consumption (Fine 1995; Pietrykowski 2007b).

Regulation School and SSA research into the labor process revealed that commodity production is structured by relations of cooperation and conflict (Gintis 1976; Edwards 1979; Bowles *et al.* 1983; Bowles 1985). This research moved political economics beyond the depiction of production as a black box reflecting the transformation of inputs into saleable outputs. A corresponding analysis of the social structure of consumption would reveal collaboration as well as contestation. For example, the allocation of goods and services within the household involves consultation, coordination and sharing as well as bargaining, threat-making and conflict. In the retail sector, a complex set of social interactions defines the consumer experience. For example, the sales clerk occupies a contested social space as both representative of capital and a customer attendant, accomplice and confidante. Sales clerks are expected to be conversant with the customs, culture, and lifestyles of their clientele. So, in their relations with consumers, clerks variously occupy positions of authority, subordination and deference (Pietrykowski 2007b).

For Marx, the property relations embedded in the system of ownership of the means of production determine the contours and the dynamics of class cohesion and class conflict. Whereas there is a clear distinction in the simplest form of capitalist production between worker and owner, such a classification is more often than not opaque, at best, when applied to the retail sector. Aside from the case of a "moral economy" in which prices are collectively established by recourse to social norms of fairness, the retail sphere appears disconnected from any governing logic of group solidarity and conflict. There are occasions when resistance and conflict on the part of consumers comprises a social movement, but they are sporadic and largely isolated instances.[5] I endeavor to render those moments more tractable in order to identify patterns of similarity across the diverse places of consumption.

Whereas anthropologists, cultural historians and sociologists have explored the way consumer goods are used to construct a material culture of symbols and meaning (Douglas and Isherwood 1979; McCracken 1990; Shields 1992; Lee 1993; Miller 1995; McCracken 2005), for most economists, both mainstream and heterodox, analysis of consumption ends at the marketplace. Yet, the legacy of classical political economy can be read in such a way that the particularity of the commodity, together with its use-value, are part of the consumption process (Fine 1995). Elements of an alternative analytic framework can be found in Marx, for instance. Marx is concerned with the way in which the production process functions to generate surplus value for the capitalist. Capitalists utilize labor together with means of production to create commodities that have both use-value and exchange-value. Exchange-value represents the labor-time embodied in the production of the commodity, whereas use-value refers to those properties that consumers find desirable. Surplus-value – the value added by labor in the production process in excess of the value of the labor power used to produce it – is the source of capitalist profit and is the result of process of commodity production. Marx realizes that expanded production and capitalist profit requires an increase in the scale and scope of consumption.

> [T]he production of *relative surplus-value*, i.e. production of surplus-value based on the increase and development of the productive forces, requires the production of new consumption ... First, quantitative expansion of existing consumption; secondly, creation of new needs by propagating existing ones in a wide circle; thirdly, production of new needs and discovery and creation of new use-values. In other words, so that the surplus labour gained does not remain a merely quantitative surplus, but rather constantly increases the circle of qualitative differences within labour ... makes it more diverse, more internally differentiated.
>
> (Marx 1973: 408) (emphasis in the original)

Marx links the need for increased profitability to expansion of consumption through the extension of markets for existing goods, as well as the creation of new use-values. Interestingly, Marx alludes to the creation of new needs by propagating existing ones in a wide circle. And this is different from the first path toward expansion, namely a quantitative increase in consumption of extant goods. The diffusion of consumer durables consumption in the decades following the Second World War illustrates this extension of consumption to a wider circle. But, for Marx, an additional role played by consumption is to differentiate consumer/workers through the diversification of consumption patterns. Marx identifies individuals as occupying the dual subject positions of worker and consumer. Rather than depicting consumption as a functional requirement for the reproduction of labor power, the consumption of a diverse array of consumer goods has the effect of differentiating the working class. Ironically, some postmodern interpretations of post-Fordism characterize consumption as a process in which agents intentionally use consumer goods to creatively construct and re-construct identity (Pietrykowski 1994). The return to small batch production utilizing flexible capital and multi-skilled labor finds its complement in consumer markets characterized by customization, rapid style changes and an emphasis on design (Murray 1992: 270).

Another dimension of the social relations of consumption is reflected in the material culture of consumption. In capitalist relations of production, workers come to feel alienated – estranged from the products of their labor, the production process and their very identity as creative beings (Marx 1964; Ollman 1971). For consumption, the corollary to alienation in the sphere of production is commodity fetishism. The concept of commodity fetishism is employed by Marx to explain the profound transformation of social life under capitalist commodity production and exchange. The distinctive qualities of the goods to be exchanged, the relationship between commodities and the particular types of laboring skills that were used to produce them, fade from the scene only to be replaced by an objective relation between things (Marx 1973: 157; Marx 1977: 165). Marx argues that exchange is the sphere in which the social laborer and the autonomous individual intersect. Private, independent laborers come into contact with one another in the exchange of commodities. The sphere of commodity exchange is, therefore, where individuals occupy the dual subject positions as workers and consumers. In this way, Marx can be read to suggest that the agent in consumption occupies potentially conflicting subject positions – as the producer of commodities with exchange-value and as the purchaser of commodities with a particular use-value. Furthermore, instead of strictly adhering to a theory of commodity fetishism, wherein human relations become reified, commodities, after they are purchased, can be seen to enter into non-capitalist systems of consumption. "At least where final consumption goods are concerned, the continued success of commodity production therefore depends on successful decommodification by the consumer, usually with a steer by the producer" (Sayer 2003: 346). Therefore, the transition of commodities to the stage of final consumption depends on the practical usefulness and meaningfulness of the commodity consumed. But standards of practicality and symbolic significance are themselves socially and culturally constructed. These user cultures of consumption extend consumer behavior beyond the marketplace and into the spaces where products help us to enact our everyday lives. So, the ways in which consumers make sense of commodities is a key part of consumer behavior that economics has largely neglected. Insights can, however, be gleaned from work in the history of technology and cultural studies.

Consumption as social practice

In the provocative essay "Do Artifacts Have Politics?" (1986), Langdon Winner argues that technology should be investigated in light of the systems of power that it calls forth. Contrary to espousing a sort of technological determinism, he avers that there are times when technology is contingent and can be accommodated to a number of different social and political arrangements. For example, in choices to adopt new production machinery some options may result in the ability of capitalists to employ fewer militant craft laborers. In this way, Winner brings politics to the forefront of technological change.

The analysis of technological change in mainstream economics largely ignores its political aspect. In the 1970s and 1980s, however, radical labor historians and political economists examined the ways in which power and social control were maintained through the adoption of new technology. Even the failure to adopt new technology was examined in light of the relative shift in the balance of power between capital and labor on the shop floor (Marglin 1974; Lazonick 1979; 1990). These studies focused exclusively on production technology in order to highlight the influence of class-based power on decisions usually ascribed to efficiency considerations. Yet, consumer technologies, too, share some of the characteristics of contested technological change. They are open to adoption, resistance and re-interpretation by various factions of manufacturers, marketers, designers, users and non-users. In fact, the self same workers who resist technology in the workplace that limits their autonomy and degrades their skill may embrace technologies at home that facilitate passivity, social isolation or the maintenance of patriarchal power. By contrast, other workers who acquiesce to the use of the same type of workplace technology might resist or re-purpose consumer technology.

Recent research by historians of technology utilizes a key insight, that of the social construction of technology (SCOT). An important principle governing SCOT research is that technological change is not determined through a hermetic process of scientific experimentation and discovery. Rather, technology is subject to an initial period of interpretive flexibility during which the results of scientific research are subject to a variety of interpretations. Over time, economic, cultural, and political interests and resources are deployed to highlight, promote, and sustain a particular set of results or findings. In a similar way, technological artifacts are produced, often in multiple, competing versions. Alterations take place through the interplay of producer knowledge and user experiences. In the process, consumers help to shape the nature of the technological failures and successes. This portrait is quite different from the neoclassical stories of consumer sovereignty. It is also distinct from approaches that ignore the way in which the social meaning of use-values circulates between producers, distributors, and consumers. From the SCOT perspective, consumers are integral players in a field of social relations. Even the universal term "consumer" belies the multiplicity of social groups that participate in interpretive acts of consumption.

Take, for example, the development of the bicycle in the late nineteenth century. Commodities enter the realm of useful objects to the extent that they meet needs or solve problems. This is not to deny the symbolic function of consumer goods but rather to highlight that feature of consumption which deals with the social and material relations of commodities in use. The bicycle can be understood as meeting mobility needs. Additionally, the development of various types of bicycles reflects how needs can be satisfied through an array of technological designs, each of which, in turn, attempts to solve particular problems defined by relevant user and non-user groups. To be more specific, let us consider the issue of safety. Bicycles were originally defined in terms of the safety challenges they presented to both riders (users) and pedestrians (non-users). Anti-cyclists, representing a strategic group interest, depicted the bicycle as an unsafe mode of transportation (Pinch and Bijker 1989: 32; Bijker 1997: 74). Both users and non-users struggled over the place bicycling would occupy within public spaces. For example, a user culture developed around attributes of the bicycle related to recreation. Non-user resistance to technology shifted the discourse toward issues of safety. Gender also played a role in the discussion over what technical features were to matter in the development of bicycle technology. The high front-wheel design of the Ordinary bicycle required the body to be displayed and maneuvered in ways that ran afoul of the prevailing gender codes of the late nineteenth century. The Ordinary was frequently ridden by young men who defined bicycling in terms of speed and physical endurance – bicycling as sport (Pinch and Bijker 1989: 34). These contested interpretations mattered because they were aligned with competing designs and technological emphases (safety versus speed, for example), and because they influenced the further development and design of the artifact (Pinch and Bijker 1989: 40; Bijker 1997: 75–7). Pinch and Bijker argued that these different interpretations did not just result in competing meanings of bicycle usage but went further, to the extent that they helped to shape the content of the technological artifact itself (1989: 41). These differences also mattered because, as gender meanings were re-negotiated, the safety bicycle came to be seen as an acceptable mode of transit for females. And, as a result, the safety bicycle had the material effect of re-defining access to space and modes of travel thereby reflecting "a physical enlargement of where a person could go in a day's travel and also where a woman could go alone" (Lerman *et al.* 2003: 3). This example highlights the interaction between product design and user interests. It also conveys a picture of the contested nature of product use and the heterogeneity of user and non-user groups whose lives are affected by outcome of the contest. "Gender, age, socio-economic and ethnic differences among users may all be relevant. Because of this heterogeneity, not all users will have the same position in relation to a specific technology" (Oudshoorn and Pinch 2003).

In addition to the need to account for the diverse ways consumers make meaning out of consumption goods and shape technology, there is a reciprocal need to develop a detailed analysis of the life histories of specific consumer goods. Fine refers to this as the "vertical approach" and uses it to trace out the systems of provision around food and clothing. The system of provisioning entails an in-depth description of the spheres of production, distribution, retail, and material culture through which consumer goods move (Fine and Leopold 1993; Fine 1995: 142; Fine, Heasman and Wright 1996). This attention to difference and complexity lends itself to some methodological approaches over others. Ragin (2000), for instance, makes a distinction between variable versus case-oriented research. Complex social phenomena contain unique attributes that disqualify the use of statistical variables meant to capture similarities and homogenize discrete phenomena. Instead, complexity is rendered tractable through detailed case study.

Attending to user and relevant non-user cultures in the consumption of particular products avoids the pitfall of describing all consumer choices as revealed preferences and, therefore, as unproblematic acts of consumption. The product, at the point of purchase, represents an unfulfilled set of expectations on the part of both seller and buyer, often mediated by third parties (advertisers, celebrity lifestyles, consumer watchdog groups) and facilitated through access to a technical infrastructure (electrical grids, gas stations, internet service providers) that forms a larger social network or "consumption junction" (Cowan 1987). Analyzed from this perspective, the consumer good embodies the qualities of a script that gets written by producers, edited by mediators and potentially re-written by consumers. Products emerge from the design and production process with a particular end-user (with specific tastes, motivations, aspirations and capacities) in mind. But, rather than ascribing unilateral power to producers to create demand, the user, together with non-users, also emerge as active participants in the consumption process. "[W]e have to go back and forth continually between the designer and the user, between the designer's projected user and the real user, between *the world inscribed in the object and the world described by its displacement*" (emphasis in the original) (Akrich 1992: 208–9). By acknowledging a countervailing power for the consumer, we can begin to identify cases when consumers resisted and transformed the social relations of consumption. Two examples from the history of technology serve to illuminate this process.

The first example considers the different trajectories along which homemakers in the United States and Canada welcomed the automatic washing machine into their homes. In the postwar decades of the 1950s and 1960s, Canadian women, in direct contrast to their US counterparts, shunned the automatic washing machine in favor of the traditional wringer washtub. Why might this be the case? Joy Parr maintains that household appliances had to fit within the frame of reference of what it meant to be a Canadian homemaker. For them, the automatic washer was not part of this identity.

> A discussion of household technological choice must reckon not only how women's technological preferences as users differed from men's technological preferences as makers and sellers, how engineering and commercial priorities came to prevail, but the possibility that men, as makers and sellers, did not always get their way.
>
> (Parr 2003: 332)

Applying a vertical analysis to the provisioning of clean clothes reveals that the two appliances were produced by different technological processes. Wringer washers were made in small volumes using batch-production techniques, whereas automatic washing machines were mass-produced. Yet, even after price differentials narrowed between wringers and automatics, there was no rush to switch to the modern technology. The reason was that the decision to purchase a wringer or an automatic was embedded in an ecological system of family provisioning. Parr explains this in terms of the different ways through which the user engaged these competing consumer technologies. The automatic washer was a closed system that functioned largely independently of the user. On the other hand, the wringer represents technologies that "constantly disclose and allow their operator to monitor the demands of the machine upon the provisioning system of which it is a part" (Parr 2003: 347). As a result, the automatic washer was decried as a profligate waster of resources – particularly water. Additionally, the automatics had considerably shorter warranty periods and were much more liable to mechanical failure, thereby making claims on future household resources. Parr argues that Canadian women resisted the adoption of this domestic "improvement" by asserting an identity of themselves as homemakers that differed drastically from those they received from producers and marketers. "The choice between wringer and automatic machines implicated Canadian homemakers in forming distinctions between consumer and user, between gratification and prudence, between production and conservation, between built to last and built to replace" (2003: 349).

A second example highlights the feedback effect between resistant forces within user cultures on producer designs. Kline (2003), exploring the adoption of electricity among farm families during the 1930s and 1940s, finds a marked lack of receptivity to electrification owing to a variety of reasons ranging from religious objections, fear of a new and curious power source, and satisfaction with the current technology, to mistrust of the New Deal – in the form of the Rural Electrification Administration – and the long-arm of Washington (Kline 2003: 60). Even when electricity was invited into their homes, farm families displayed a marked indifference toward the very same gadgets – toasters and coffee-makers, for example – that fascinated similarly situated urban families. In particular, electric cooking ranges were not well received by farm women. Although urban homemakers were initially reticent to purchase electric ranges, the utility companies enlisted the help of home economists to demonstrate the techniques for safe and healthy cooking (Goldstein 2003). Utility companies, appliance manufacturers and local dealers also re-designed their products and their stores to appeal to female shoppers. A social network of consumption mediators was created to serve the interests of appliance producers. Utility companies established home service departments, model kitchens complete with cooking instructions all coordinated by home economists.[6] The sheer density of urban population suggests that these activities were more common in cities than they were in rural communities, but home economists were also making the rounds among farm wives as well. However, their self-image as "agents of modernity" delivering a clearly superior form of energy to rural folks, met with substantial resistance from farm women. Why?

Kline (1997), following Cowan (1983), notes that the adoption of new household technology did not necessarily reduce the labor time devoted to household tasks if it also resulted in changing expectations about what constituted cleanliness and order. The vacuum cleaner was a prime example and vacuums were low on the list of electric gadgets owned by farm families. Potential changes in the gender division of labor in farm households also affected the willingness to buy these appliances. The electric range, for example, was intended to replace wood-burning stoves. Yet, electric stoves reduced the need for men and boys to cut trees and split wood, thereby lessening their labor requirements (Kline 1997: 250). In addition, in rural farm houses lacking central heating, wood stoves served the dual purpose of cooking and home heating. Therefore, the type of electric cooking appliance that did begin to sell among rural women combined the wood- or coal-burning capacity with an electrical cooking element. These hybrid units bore the appearance of the modern electric stoves. The combination allowed for the adoption of a new technology without abandoning traditional standards and routines that combined cooking and heating, while also introducing new ways of life (summer indoor cooking) not practical with the wood or coal technologies. As with the wringer washer, the dual fuel stove permitted a new technology to be integrated into the lifeworld of rural consumers. As Kline notes, "The invention of the combination stove shows the interactive aspect of the contested urbanization of the family farm" (2003: 64). That the interaction occurred as resistance to a technological design imposed on farm families by utility companies and their agents highlights the idea that power is not always unidirectional but calls forth responses, engages conflict and can take the form of consumer resistance. In addition, resistance to the all-electric stove took place in a specific context of family provisioning activities: cooking and heating. Furthermore, resistance to purchasing electric stoves was linked, in part, to its impact on an always already contested gender division of labor.

These examples also point in the direction of understanding consumer behavior in terms of consumption practices. Practices are conceived as "embodied, materially mediated arrays of human activity centrally organized around shared practical understandings" (Schatzki 2001: 2). This description captures many of the key features of the social relations of consumption. For example, rather than attending to the atomistic individual choosing among different commodities, the focus on consumer practice is the set of social activities, shared meanings and material engagements that are enacted through consumption. Consumption practices transgress the traditional boundaries demarcating production and consumption. Attention to user culture highlights the contest over the use prescribed by producers, inscribed onto products by engineers and designers and then described by users in ways that conform or contest the expectations and interests of producers and their agents (Akrich 1992: 209).

Retail services in which sales staff play a multiplicity of roles that require constant attention to emotion management find that they become not only participants in the market exchange but also are a part of the product sold (Hochschild 1983). Consumers, for their part, are purchasing a product but also consuming the attention, blandishments and recognition of the sales staff (Lowe and Crewe 1996). Retail sales workers are wage laborers. But they are also symbolic representatives of the company. The friendly demeanor, attention and courtesy of the sales staff is "performative labor." Performative labor entails the management and disciplining of the body and the emotions in the service of a customer or client. Emotional labor, a subset of performative labor, takes place when workers are expected to manage their own feelings as well as the emotions of customers/clients (Steinberg and Figart 1999). Retail sales work often involves large expenditures of emotional labor (Hochschild 1983; Lowe and Crewe 1996; England and Folbre 1999). With emotional labor, the commodity sold is often bundled up with the feelings and personality of the worker selling the product. The clerk's labor then becomes an integral component of the service purchased (Leidner 1999). Consumers can also transgress the boundary between consumption and production. For example, shoppers may be encouraged to perform managerial duties for the store. Shop owners may "employ" shoppers as supervisors over their sales force, asking them to report any evidence of less than productive behavior thereby implementing a scheme of "management by customers" (Fuller and Smith 1991). This blurring of the border between production and consumption troubles a distinction that underlies traditional economic theory (Pietrykowski 2007b).

Practices, therefore, are sets of actions recognized as socially meaningful. There are some similarities to the use of the term consumption practices and Fine's conception of systems of provisioning. A primary difference lies with placing more emphasis on the performative dimension of economic life, in contrast to Fine's approach which highlights, and often times privileges, the structural institutional environment out of which consumer goods are derived and around which consumer practices are oriented (Lockie and Kitto 2000). I argue that consumption practices serve to provide additional insight into the dynamics of consumer demand. For instance, practices refer to socially meaningful behavior in the sense that other people can interpret the behavior and perform the same behavior themselves. Reckwitz identifies the following components of practices:

> forms of bodily activities, forms of mental activities, 'things' and their use, a background knowledge in the form of understanding, know-how, states of emotion and motivational knowledge. A practice – a way of cooking, of consuming, of working, of taking care of oneself or of others, etc. – forms so to speak a 'block' whose existence necessarily depends on the existence and specific interconnectedness of these elements and cannot be reduced to any one of these single elements.
>
> (Reckwitz 2002: 249–50)

For Reckwitz, the practice is detached from the social in that practices are enacted without regard to intersubjective justification as is the case with Habermas' validity claims. "In social theory, consequently, practice approaches promulgate a distinct social ontology: the social is a field of embodied, materially interwoven practices centrally organized around shared practical understandings" (Schatzki 2001). In this sense consumption practice, understood as the performance of consumption in which the performance entails material conditions, bodily movement and tacit knowledge, triggers wants and desires on the part of consumers. Shifts in consumer demand can be traced to modifications in practices, transformed practices or development of new practices. Warde (2005) attempts to apply the theory of practices to an understanding of consumption. He argues that consumption activity is a feature of most forms of practice. By contrast, I argue that specific activities engender practices and that those practices incorporate specific combinations of material goods together with bodily movements, emotions and know-how. Different practices can be enacted around the same general activity. For example, driving is a general activity and racing, touring, commuting are all practices that make use of different components of the elements associated with driving. The emotional state of mind associated with the practices differs markedly and the material culture – car culture – with which it is associated will vary with each different driving practice (helmets and roll cages, cup holders and satellite radio, entertainment systems and GPS). Participating in a practice or what Warde calls "enrolment," shapes the form and content of consumption (Warde 2005: 145). The focus on practices shifts our attention to the collective processes of consumption, which may or may not correspond to one's class interest. Class becomes one of several perspectives from which to make sense out of the social context within which one finds oneself. Consumption practices do not a priori reproduce class interest, nor does it necessarily fragment and diffuse class solidarity. It is only potentially disruptive. On the other hand, participation in a variety of different consumption practices may displace essential subject positions without rendering meaningless a sense of identity as the product of intersecting roles, interests and affiliations.

> Sequential and simultaneous engagement in diverse practices, especially when involving people belonging to disparate and heterogeneous social networks, might be a source of the much discussed tendency towards fragmentation of the self. Much depends on the extent to which networks overlap and whether the norms of different practices are consistent with each other.
>
> (Warde 2005: 144)

The theory of consumption practices also provides space for the analysis of user culture to the extent that new practices come about through the adoption or transformation of consumer technologies. Perhaps more interesting are the cases in which different consumer practices develop around competing consumer technologies as illustrated in the case of the bicycle. What remains is to investigate the scope of consumption practices, and, in particular, to look at spaces of non-capitalist consumption practices situated within a broader capitalist economy.

The theory of Fordism provides an analytic account of modern large-scale patterns of capital accumulation. The apparent ubiquity of Fordism made it synonymous with modern capitalism. "Postwar Fordism has to be seen, therefore, less as a mere system of mass production and more as a total way of life" (Harvey 1989: 135). And yet the Fordist economy was a regulated economy that required an active state sector to take up the slack during crisis periods in order to prop up mass consumption, without reducing the disciplinary effect of unemployment (Piven and Cloward 1971). During the 1970s, the crisis of Keynesianism and the attendant attack on the welfare state altered the terrain for Fordist mass production.

Spatial competition intensified between geographically distinct Fordist systems, with the most efficient regimes (such as the Japanese) and lower labour-cost regimes (such as those found in the third world countries where notions of a social contract with labour were either lacking or weakly enforced) driving other centres into paroxysms of devaluation through deindustrialization ... The crisis of Fordism was, therefore, as much a geographical and geopolitical crisis as it was a crisis of indebtedness, class struggle or corporate stagnation within any particular nation state.

(Harvey 1989: 185–6)

Although always present within capitalist economies, what the crisis of Fordism brought into especially stark relief was the pattern of uneven decline and growth. Metropolitan growth obscured steep population declines in the central city off-set by robust growth in the suburban ring. Within the United States, this stark pattern of uneven growth laid bare the destructive forces of capitalist development in places like the industrial Midwest, the heart of Fordist mass production. Geographers have recently begun to argue that a "capitalocentric" perspective has diminished the ability of social scientists to identity and evaluate alternative forms of economic organization for these de-industrialized spaces. "A capitalocentric discourse condenses economic difference, fusing the variety of noncapitalist economic activities into a unity in which meaning is anchored to capitalist identity" (Gibson-Graham 2006: 56). In other words, ways of organizing the economy at odds with capitalist goals and logic are deemed abnormal, deviant and, therefore, deficient.

By analogy, the discursive space open to economists interested in discussing the broad theoretical implications of conflict, gender bias, bounded rationality or even the interpretation of experimental results in behavioral economics is similarly restricted. As Marglin (2008) notes with regard to behavioral economics, it "offers the possibility of a trenchant critique from the inside, but this critique has so far been self-limiting in relation to the normative claims for the market" (Marglin 2008: 287). The two projects – to displace the dominance of capitalism in order to explore non-capitalist alternatives and to de-center the dominant discourse of mainstream economics – are linked. One strategy is to destabilize the discursive terrain upon which discussions and analyses of capitalism take place in order to identify the alternative spaces and the diverse practices at economic sites involving exchange, work opportunities and organizational structures (Gibson-Graham 2006: 60). Examining these alternative economies enables us to explore consumer behavior under different rules, norms and expectations. In the following chapters, I develop three case studies to illustrate how consumption practices, user culture and alternative economies can be applied to green automobility, the slow food movement and alternative/local currency projects.

6 Green consumption and user culture

The case of the Toyota Prius

The rising popularity of hybrid vehicles in the United States signals a dramatic shift in the composition of automobile demand on the part of consumers. World-wide sales have exceeded one million since the car's introduction in 1997 (*Globe and Mail*, May 16, 2008). The Prius appears quite popular in Japan where it was first introduced. Since its entrance into the US market in 2001, the Prius has attracted strong consumer interest. A decline in Japanese sales in 2001 and 2002 can be attributed to the need to ramp up production for the US market. The Prius has less than five per cent Toyota brand vehicle sales in Japan. By contrast, US sales of the Prius expanded more rapidly.

Sales nearly doubled from 53,991 units in 2004 to 106,971 in 2006. Indeed, Prius currently accounts for 10 per cent of Toyota division cars sold in the United States (*Wards Automotive* 2004–7). Prius also dominates the US hybrid market with a nearly 50 per cent share of the market. Rising gasoline prices have no doubt spurred recent sales of the gas–electric hybrid but this alone cannot account for its early growth and popularity. Consumers still must pay a premium for hybrid auto-mobiles and, depending on the model selected and the price of gas, the savings in gasoline may not always be enough to recoup that premium over the life of the car. This suggests that, in addition to their utilitarian and instrumental value, con-sumers may also be selecting the Prius in order to signal their interest in a cleaner environment through reducing the level of greenhouse gases their car produces. Prius is marketed as a "green" consumer product. The goal of this chapter is to provide a deeper understanding of consumer preferences for green automobility[1] through a case study of the Prius.

A portrait of the Prius as a young car

One of the first tasks performed by the Toyota team charged with designing and engineering the Prius – under the project name G21 – was to research and report on key words and phrases that might best be applied to automotive use in the twenty-first century.[2] This process of imagining the future car and future user resulted in phrases relating to increased auto fatalities, rising incidence of women in the workforce, and widespread use of multimedia, among others. They settled on three key words that would best define the G21 automobile: "natural resources" and "environment." As explained by author Hideshi Itazaki, Takeshi Uchiyamada, the leader of the G21 group and later the Chief Engineer of the Prius, recounted how these key words resonated with him after hearing his daughter and wife talking about a school lesson in waste recycling (Itazaki 1999: 47).

The "full" hybrid model – allowing for both joint and independent gas and electric sources of propulsion – took a remarkably short number of years to evolve. The idea that a hybrid engine be added to the Prius was only seriously discussed in late 1994 and early 1995. A separate research team was working on selecting the best engineering model for a hybrid engine. They strongly recommended that it be developed for use with the larger Camry sedan. The Camry's larger size would accommodate the increased space and weight of the batteries and electric motors. Also the improved fuel mileage, measured as the per cent increase in miles per gallon, would look more impressive. But this would run afoul of the space-saving, planet-saving paradigm to be embodied in the car. The recommendation was rejected and the research team set to work with G21 to create a hybrid Prius.

The first Prius concept car – adopting the Latin word for prior, in this case marking the end of the twentieth century as the advent of the twenty-first – debuted at the Tokyo Auto Show in 1995 using continuously variable transmission (CVT) and an electric motor in the powertrain. Eventually this design was replaced by one that made use of an electric generator, electric motor and an electronically controlled planetary gear system that partitioned power between the gasoline engine and the electric engine. The system, whereby both the electric engine and the gasoline engine function together yet are capable of performing independently, works as follows: the electric engine acts to propel the wheels. As the wheels rotate, electrical energy is generated, captured and returned to the electric engine. In addition, the planetary gears distribute power from the gasoline engine to the electric engine, which then charges the battery. Finally, when braking, energy created by applying the brakes is converted to electricity, which is then used to recharge the battery. In this way, the Prius engineers wrote a technological script for the Prius engine. Critics argue that the redundancies embedded in the design – namely the dual engine feature – make the Prius inefficient from an engineering standpoint. Yet, I will later argue that consumers found this apparent technological inefficiency an attractive feature once they re-inscribed or "described" (Akrich 1992) the technology into user culture.

The company then convened a competition involving seven design teams from Japan, California and Europe (Itazaki 1999: 127). The goal was to build a four-door sedan that evoked the feeling of the future *today*. While not nearly as futuristic as Honda's two-seat Insight, introduced in the US in 2000, the Prius has what one journalist refers to as a "geek-chic look – a thick, curved body, a high back end and glittering computer displays on the dashboard" (Schneider 2004). The Prius' revolutionary technology and design aesthetic also captured the attention of the modern art world. In 1999, the Prius, along with the DaimlerChrysler Smart Car, Honda VV (predecessor to the Insight), Ford Ka, BMW/Rover Mini, and Fiat Multipla, was placed on display in the sculpture garden of the Museum of Modern Art as part of the "Different Roads" exhibit. A primary goal of this exhibit was to make the case that the small fuel-efficient car was the future of automobility. Using recycled parts, innovative power sources and low-cost components, these cars addressed the same kind of environmental problems that Toyota's G21 team responded to in designing the Prius. Rather than viewing the car as the materialization of a modern design aesthetic, as was the case in the last MOMA auto exhibit in the 1950s, the emphasis here was on heralding the affordability and the environmentally conscious design principles that these cars epitomized. The exhibit creators understood that access to the automobile should not be limited to users in the industrialized countries alone. Rather, the challenge was to extend the benefits of automotive travel while simultaneously reigning-in its deleterious consequences. Attention from the elite arbiters of taste at the Museum of Modern Art is one indicator of a search for a new aesthetic consistent with a different set of social norms (Pietrykowski 2007a).

It should be noted that the decade of the 1990s witnessed record profits at American automobile companies, based primarily on the production of sport utility vehicles and light trucks. In 1998 alone Ford made $2.4 billion dollars in after-tax profit on its behemoths, the Navigator and the Expedition. Ford workers were paid profit-sharing bonuses of $8,000 apiece (Bradsher 2002: 89). Both the union and the corporation were allied in their efforts to produce and sell more and more of these gigantic vehicles. The MOMA exhibit took place against this backdrop. The timing of the exhibit, on the eve of the new millennium, was also calculated to signify a watershed moment in the history of the automobile (Mount 1999).

Prius consumers, user culture and consumption practices

The Prius was able to combine a green aesthetic with practicality and a seamless technology that mimicked the experience of driving an internal combustion engine – with one notable exception. The most remarked about feature of the Prius, highlighted in early advertisements and reviews, was that the gasoline engine shut off when the car came to a complete stop. The silence that accompanied the experience of driving was both disconcerting and revelatory for many drivers. As a writer for *Mother Earth News* wrote, "The hybrid moment came at a stop sign when the gas engine turned itself off to save a sip of fuel. The Prius idled as silently as an electric clock. 'We haven't stalled,' my friend assured me. 'Just press the gas pedal.' The engine purred again" (Nixon 2003). While the shut-off procedure did not require any change in the bodily movements of the driver, the emotional response to the contrast between a running engine and a quiet engine highlights the affective connotations evoked through this green driving practice (Sheller 2004). The initial anxiety induced by toggling between engine noise/movement and silence/stationarity frames a new automobile user experience that substitutes for the unpleasant expectation of stalling out. Over time, drivers came to expect the silence. Early Prius advertisements attempted to equate this silence with environmental virtue and green technology. For instance, the ad campaign "When It Sees red, it charges" depicts a Prius at a stop sign. The campaign titled "Ever hear the sound a stoplight makes?" can be read as an attempt to make sense out of the dissonance associated with an environmental ethos of automobility. Users are not the only group whose behavior is altered by the hybrid car. The silent car also has an effect on non-user cultures as well. For instance, the National Federation of the Blind established a "quiet cars" committee to investigate how pedestrian safety is being compromised by the proliferation of electric vehicles. Legislation was introduced to require hybrid car manufacturers to install an audible alert mechanism for pedestrians (R. S. Chang 2008).

In terms of practicality, the gas–electric hybrid uses the gasoline engine and regenerative power to charge the battery. As a result, unlike the all-electric vehicle (EV), the Prius does not need to be plugged into an electrical outlet. This eliminates the need for "charging stations." Therefore, the Prius technology presented US consumers with the opportunity to "go green" without additional demands that they change their consumption practices. This is a form of green consumption in which environmentalism is mediated through commodity production where the supplier also happens to be a global transnational corporation. In this sense, many Prius owners can be characterized as "socially acceptable green consumers" whose individual market choices are seen to make a difference in the world through the selection of a vehicle that will allow them to reduce their personal consumption of fossil fuels (Moisander and Pesonen 2002: 331).

Another way of characterizing those who demand the Prius for its green symbolism involves interpreting Prius ownership as a statement against crass materialism and an attempt to live more simply by purchasing a car with a smaller environmental footprint. This conforms closely to the "downshifting" mode of life whereby those, usually upwardly mobile middle-class professionals, choose to scale back their material possessions in order to opt out of the consumerist lifestyle. The Prius thereby symbolizes a "small is beautiful" philosophy, which not only encompasses environmental sensitivity but also extends beyond this to include anti-consumerism. Given the price of the Prius (over $20,000 for the base model) it would be out of reach to those individuals and families adhering to tenants of "voluntary simplicity" (Schor 1998). On the other hand, considering the generally poor state of mass transit in the United States, automobile ownership is often seen as an inescapable evil. As a particular type of consumption practice – green automobility – Prius ownership and use conveys values and motivations that extend beyond symbolic representations of individual identity.

For instance, the Prius has been inserted into debates over consumerism, energy policy, US imperialism and war in the Middle East. Increasingly, the Prius has come to represent the antithesis of the vehicle that has dominated the US landscape since the 1980s – the sport utility vehicle (SUV). Driving a Prius not only signifies the driver as environmentally conscious and willing to do their part to clean up the planet; it also signals its other, namely the ostentatious, resource-wasting SUV. The purchase of the Prius is also a decision not to buy (and buy into) consumption practices engendered by the SUV.

Indeed, anti-consumerist organizations focused on "culture jamming" and "resistance consumption" – such as the Canadian group Adbusters – make it a point to mock and parody both business culture and personal consumer choices that support the interests of the corporate elite (Lasn 2000; Rumbo 2002). For example, Adbusters offers fake parking tickets for placing under the windshield of an SUV. As reported in the *Boston Globe*, "When US troops twice readied to attack Iraq the cry 'No blood for oil!' became the mantra of antiwar activists and tens of thousands of SUV drivers found fake 'conspicuous consumption' tickets under their windshield in cities across North America" (Belkin 2005). Some of these individuals engaged in resistance consumerism find that the Prius fits into their lifestyle.

Recently, an additional voice of protest has been added to the US debate over the morality of automobile ownership. A group of Christian social activists, the Evangelical Environment Network, began a publicity campaign using the slogan "What Would Jesus Drive?"[3] The organization aligns itself with environmentalism as a means to protect "God's creation." Visitors to the group's "What Would Jesus Drive?" website[4] are encouraged to take a pledge that "If I need to purchase a vehicle, I will choose the most fuel efficient and least polluting vehicle available that truly fits my needs." The Reverend Jim Ball conducted a driving tour of the United States to promote the "What Would Jesus Drive?" campaign. Ball drove a Prius. In this example, driving a Prius is explicitly aligned with moral action. This suggests another type of Prius consumer, one who combines evangelical Christianity with an environmental ethic of care. From these accounts, Prius users, and green consumers in general, are a diverse group including the following characteristics:

- Socially acceptable greens – market- and corporate-friendly, minimal alteration in one's lifestyle
- Downshifting greens – voluntary simplicity, de-emphasize participation in corporate-mediated culture
- Religious greens – Christian evangelicals, WWJD (What Would Jesus Drive?)
- Political greens – anti-imperialist, anti-war, anti-corporate, anti-consumerist

Prius consumers represent a heterogeneous group of environmentally conscious drivers who discern a link between their personal consumption practices and larger social movements. So the Prius serves multiple functions, ethical, symbolic as well as material, in the lives of consumers. This diverse group of green automobile users suggests that buying a Prius expresses meta-preferences for enhanced environmental quality, less materialism and human scale (Sen 1977). Is there a larger shift toward a green consumer ethos that is reflected in the growing popularity of the Prius? In other words, is the growing interest in more sustainable consumption a sign of a new form of post-affluence consumerism?

Evidence from some survey data confirms that there is a shift in the value-orientation of individuals, particularly in the United States. The World Values Survey,[5] undertaken by a global network of social scientists led by University of Michigan political scientist Ronald Inglehart, collects responses to a number of different questions related to values and culture. I want to briefly explore answers to five key questions:

1   How often, if at all, do you think about the meaning and purpose of life? (Table 6.1)
2   Would give part of my income for the environment (Table 6.2).

3   I would agree to an increase in taxes if the extra money were used to prevent environmental pollution. Please tell me, if it were to happen, whether you think it would be a good thing, a bad thing, or don't you mind? (Table 6.3)
4   Less emphasis on money and material possessions (Table 6.4).
5   More emphasis on the development of technology (Table 6.5).

How often, if at all, do you think about the meaning and purpose of life?

The survey data reveal that while there is an increase across all of the selected countries in the proportion of respondents engaging in frequent periods of reflection, people in the United States are, surprisingly, most apt to reflect on life's meaning. In 1999, nearly 90 per cent of United States respondents thought about the meaning and purpose of life sometimes or often. Italians were somewhat less introspective and the British were least prone to ponder these existential questions.

Would give part of my income for the environment

With the exception of Japan, the responses to this survey question show a decline over the course of the 1990s in those who would strongly agree to pay for supporting the environment. But the smallest decline over the two periods is reported for US respondents. By 1999, those who at least agree to give a portion of their income for environmental improvement still comprise roughly 70 per cent or more of survey respondents in Denmark, the Netherlands, Japan and the United States.

I would agree to an increase in taxes if the extra money were used to prevent environmental pollution

In response to this question, the United States stands out as the only country of those selected to report an increase in the proportion who strongly agree with this statement from 1990 to 1999. The results for 1999 alone show that Denmark, Japan and the United States report the highest proportion of individuals who agree or strongly agree to a tax increase.

Less emphasis on money and material possessions

Interestingly, this question reveals that the United States showed the largest decline in those who feel that this state of affairs would be a good thing. On the other hand, the US also witnessed the largest decline among those who felt that declining significance of material goods and money would be a bad thing. Only 6 per cent of US respondents in 1999 felt that a less material-focused world would be bad.

More emphasis on the development of technology

The results to this question are the most disparate across countries and over time. France, together with the United States, reports the largest declines among those

Table 6.1 Question: How often, if at all, do you think about the meaning and purpose of life?

	TOTAL	Denmark [1990]	Denmark [1999]	France [1990]	France [1999]	Italy [1990]	Italy [1999]	Japan [1990]	Japan [2000]	Netherlands [1990]	Netherlands [1999]
Often	37.7	29.1	36.5	39.2	0.0	47.2	50.3	21.3	25.8	30.6	0.0
Sometimes	41.5	42.3	40.5	43.6	0.0	36.8	36.7	57.9	60.5	50.1	0.0
Rarely	15.6	20.7	18.8	10.7	0.0	11.3	8.8	18.9	13.0	14.9	0.0
Never	5.1	7.9	4.2	6.5	0.0	4.7	4.2	1.9	0.7	4.3	0.0
Total	22495 (100%)	1024 (100%)	1013 (100%)	988 (100%)	0 (100%)	2004 (100%)	1986 (100%)	976 (100%)	1316 (100%)	1010 (100%)	0 (100%)

	Great Britain [1990]	Great Britain [1999]	United States [1990]	United States [1999]	Germany West [1990]	Germany West [1999]	Germany East [1990]	Germany East [1999]
Often	36.1	24.4	50.6	58.1	30.4	21.4	37.9	24.5
Sometimes	33.9	36.5	35.3	31.1	45.0	46.0	42.1	44.8
Rarely	19.7	22.2	11.3	9.0	19.8	24.5	17.1	23.8
Never	10.2	16.9	2.8	1.8	4.8	8.1	3.0	6.9
Total	1479 (100%)	981 (100%)	3094 (100%)	1194 (100%)	2081 (100%)	1032 (100%)	1320 (100%)	997 (100%)

Source: www.worldvaluessurvey.org

Table 6.2 Question: Would give part of my income for the environment

	TOTAL	Denmark [1990]	Denmark [1999]	France [1990]	France [1999]	Italy [1990]	Italy [1999]	Japan [1990]	Japan [2000]	Netherlands [1990]	Netherlands [1999]
Strongly agree	15.4	39.0	29.8	17.1	13.5	16.2	10.8	9.7	10.6	28.4	16.1
Agree	48.2	45.3	49.0	44.2	32.7	51.3	54.0	58.3	59.6	53.0	58.5
Disagree	25.3	13.0	15.2	24.4	26.1	25.3	28.0	27.4	26.6	14.2	20.1
Strongly disagree	11.1	2.7	5.9	14.2	27.7	7.2	7.2	4.6	3.2	4.3	5.3
Total	23926 (100%)	1007 (100%)	979 (100%)	963 (100%)	1572 (100%)	1951 (100%)	1892 (100%)	784 (100%)	1094 (100%)	1009 (100%)	997 (100%)

	Great Britain [1990]	Great Britain [1999]	United States [1990]	United States [1999]	Germany West [1990]	Germany West [1999]	Germany East [1990]	Germany East [1999]
Strongly agree	14.8	7.9	17.6	16.6	10.9	4.4	12.2	4.8
Agree	52.7	40.9	56.2	52.7	41.6	29.6	49.2	25.0
Disagree	25.7	38.9	20.7	24.4	34.7	32.0	29.2	27.5
Strongly disagree	6.7	12.4	5.6	6.2	12.9	33.9	9.4	42.7
Total	1417 (100%)	903 (100%)	3034 (100%)	1189 (100%)	1913 (100%)	1000 (100%)	1270 (100%)	953 (100%)

Source: www.worldvaluessurvey.org

Table 6.3 Question: I would agree to an increase in taxes if the extra money were used to prevent environmental pollution

	TOTAL	Denmark [1990]	Denmark [1999]	France [1990]	France [1999]	Germany West [1990]	Germany West [1999]	Italy [1990]	Italy [1999]	Japan [1990]	Japan [2000]	Netherlands [1990]	Netherlands [1999]
Strongly agree	10.5	26.9	22.1	11.5	9.0	7.5	4.0	9.8	6.5	5.4	6.9	19.4	10.3
Agree	43.7	42.6	43.0	42.9	27.6	41.7	25.7	43.9	37.1	45.6	55.3	48.5	44.6
Disagree	31.6	24.0	24.2	26.3	28.0	34.8	32.3	35.1	42.9	42.6	31.3	25.9	37.4
Strongly disagree	14.2	6.5	10.6	19.2	35.4	16.0	37.9	11.2	13.5	6.5	6.5	6.2	7.7
Total	24105 (100%)	1003 (100%)	986 (100%)	957 (100%)	1575 (100%)	1943 (100%)	1002 (100%)	1966 (100%)	1922 (100%)	836 (100%)	1147 (100%)	999 (100%)	996 (100%)

	Great Britain [1990]	Great Britain [1999]	United States [1990]	United States [1999]	Germany West [1990]	Germany West [1999]	Germany East [1990]	Germany East [1999]
Strongly agree	11.1	6.4	11.1	12.7	7.5	4.0	10.1	3.1
Agree	58.7	43.5	51.8	48.2	41.7	25.7	53.1	22.5
Disagree	23.3	37.5	30.0	29.6	34.8	32.3	29.5	29.4
Strongly disagree	7.0	12.7	7.2	9.6	16.0	37.9	7.3	45.1
Total	1420 (100%)	910 (100%)	3034 (100%)	1189 (100%)	1943 (100%)	1002 (100%)	1262 (100%)	957 (100%)

Source: www.worldvaluessurvey.org

Table 6.4 Question: Please tell me, if it were to happen, whether you think it would be a good thing, a bad thing, or don't you mind? Less emphasis on money and material possessions

	TOTAL	Denmark [1990]	Denmark [1999]	France [1990]	France [1999]	Germany West [1990]	Germany West [1999]	Italy [1990]	Italy [1999]	Japan [1990]	Japan [2000]	Netherlands [1990]	Netherlands [1999]
Good thing	62.3	77.7	70.0	70.6	70.9	50.6	53.7	71.9	70.6	41.1	39.0	62.1	60.1
Don't mind	20.5	10.6	15.6	17.2	16.8	19.8	17.6	17.7	20.0	29.5	38.4	28.4	29.8
Bad thing	17.2	11.6	14.4	12.2	12.3	29.6	28.7	10.5	9.3	29.5	22.6	9.5	10.1
Total	24848 (100%)	1005 (100%)	943 (100%)	950 (100%)	1578 (100%)	2093 (100%)	995 (100%)	2016 (100%)	1938 (100%)	988 (100%)	1303 (100%)	1015 (100%)	996 (100%)

	Great Britain [1990]	Great Britain [1999]	United States [1990]	United States [1999]	Germany West [1990]	Germany West [1999]	Germany East [1990]	Germany East [1999]
Good thing	63.9	65.7	71.1	65.2	50.6	53.7	46.9	52.7
Don't mind	26.2	27.5	11.3	29.1	19.8	17.6	14.7	15.6
Bad thing	9.8	6.7	17.6	5.7	29.6	28.7	38.4	31.8
Total	1483 (100%)	960 (100%)	3087 (100%)	1198 (100%)	2093 (100%)	995 (100%)	1336 (100%)	963 (100%)

Source: www.worldvaluessurvey.org

Table 6.5 Question: Please tell me, if it were to happen, whether you think it would be a good thing, a bad thing, or don't you mind? More emphasis on the development of technology

	TOTAL	Denmark [1990]	Denmark [1999]	France [1990]	France [1999]	Germany West [1990]	Italy [1990]	Italy [1999]	Japan [1990]	Japan [2000]	Netherlands [1990]	Netherlands [1999]
Good thing	62.6	58.9	61.9	76.4	58.3	52.2	60.3	64.5	64.9	60.5	49.5	48.2
Don't mind	21.7	15.8	11.4	15.5	23.9	25.6	26.4	21.9	27.4	31.9	23.3	25.1
Bad thing	15.7	25.3	26.7	8.1	17.8	22.2	13.3	13.6	7.8	7.6	27.2	26.7
Total	24620 (100%)	983 (100%)	898 (100%)	922 (100%)	1554 (100%)	2087 (100%)	2013 (100%)	1905 (100%)	979 (100%)	1292 (100%)	1012 (100%)	990 (100%)

	Great Britain [1990]	Great Britain [1999]	United States [1990]	United States [1999]	Germany West [1999]	Germany East [1990]	Germany East [1999]
Good thing	64.1	69.9	68.6	56.8	63.1	83.1	62.7
Don't mind	21.4	23.9	10.4	34.6	23.3	11.3	26.8
Bad thing	14.5	6.3	21.0	8.7	13.5	5.6	10.4
Total	1483 (100%)	955 (100%)	3078 (100%)	1194 (100%)	982 (100%)	1336 (100%)	958 (100%)

Source: www.worldvaluessurvey.org

who feel that an increased emphasis on technology would be a good thing. The Netherlands is the only country in which less than half of those surveyed had a positive view of technological development. Among the countries selected, by 1999 the United States was the second lowest in terms of pro-technology sentiment.

These survey results indicate that, contrary to popular belief, when compared to European countries and Japan, individuals in the United States can be characterized by espousing a concern for the environment and one's purpose in life together with heightened skepticism toward materialism and technology. The popularity of the Prius in the United States[6] is a reflection of this broader set of socio-cultural values. A clear trend toward post-materialist values over the period 1970–2006 is observed by Inglehart (2008) as well. His comparative survey reveals that beginning in 1970:

> In the six Western European countries as a whole,[7] materialists were four times as numerous as post-materialists ... Similarly in the US materialists were three times as numerous as post-materialists. During the next 35 years a major shift occurred. By 2006, post-materialists were slightly more numerous than materialists in Western Europe and post-materialists were twice as numerous as materialists in the US.
>
> (Inglehart 2008: 136)

Does purchase and use of the Prius bring about a change in social and cultural values? In the words of Langdon Winner (1986), do artifacts have a politics? I think that the Prius is a material representative of green values both as a symbol and expression of identity (Dolfsma 1999), as well as a vehicle for instituting and inscribing an alternative user culture and driving practice. As the composition of Prius ownership broadens to include those who, first and foremost, want an economy car, the degree to which the use alters frames of reference, ethical commitments and the willingness to support pro-environment policy is worth further investigation.

Prius marketing and celebrity culture

The idea that owning certain consumer goods is a form of emulation and status-display places the consumer in relation to a world of others (Veblen 1953). The example of the Prius illustrates multiple contradictory layers of symbolism and status. The Prius incongruously marries environmental consciousness, and its associated meanings of conservation and frugality, to celebrity lifestyle, usually aligned with images of lavish excess. Here, Galbraith's (1958) view of the corporate creation of consumer desire takes center stage.

Starting with the 2003 Oscar award show, four award nominees arrived in Prius automobiles. By 2006, 25 film stars were driving up to the red carpet in a Prius (Taylor III 2006). The cars are provided through the efforts of Global Green USA, in cooperation with Toyota. The international organization, Global Green, is an environmental group founded by former Soviet president Mikhail Gorbachev. The utilitarian Prius that was once exhibited at the Museum of Modern Art now came to be associated with the film and glamour of Hollywood. The Toyota corporation fuels consumers' desires to emulate the stars by driving a car that is driven by movie celebrities. The Oscars are also broadcast on nationwide television and so the arrival of stars in a Prius helps create a "buzz" – talk, excitement, energy – around the product. This informal talk has itself become a strategic form of commercial marketing. "Buzz marketing" is a clandestine form of product advertisement. Unlike traditional advertising, with buzz marketing the product is located in a natural, everyday setting. For example, a book publisher could enlist the help of individuals to create buzz for a novel. These individuals (often unpaid volunteers) are asked to lounge in coffee shops or other public spaces reading a recently published novel. The confidante is encouraged to naturally and casually strike up a conversation with random strangers in which positive endorsements of the book eventually figure into the discussion (Walker 2004).

A frequently used type of underground product advertising is the placement of products in television shows. For example, the Prius is featured prominently in the cable television comedy *Curb Your Enthusiasm*. Larry David, creator of the immensely popular US television comedy *Seinfeld*, plays the character Larry David and drives a Prius. The Prius is featured in numerous episodes of the show. The car even generated buzz beyond the television show when MTV U – the music video television station's website aimed at college students – featured Larry David and Laurie David, an environmental activist and producer of the global warming documentary *An Inconvenient Truth*, making a surprise appearance in a University of Southern California class ("Effective Methods of Social Change") to give away his Prius to a lucky student.[8] This effectively illustrates the way in which buzz marketing of a "green" car can be used to capture the imagination of automobile consumers. So, while the advertisers' attempts to stimulate consumer desire have not disappeared, they have become more discrete and multi-layered. Corporate attempts at demand creation are pervasive, to be sure. The emulation of the lifestyles of the elite, the symbolic use of functional goods and the desire to claim status to norms and values through the ownership and use of the Prius is an example of the multi-dimensional character of consumer choice. However, an adequate account of consumption practices cannot end with an explanation of corporate imagery and persuasion. The next step is to illustrate how hybrid technology can be used by consumers.

Prius technology and user culture

By and large, the green consumers described above appear to have a relatively passive relationship to hybrid technology. But it would be a mistake to assume that the user culture of Prius drivers is no different from the automotive technology encountered by any other car driver. Although the Prius was intended to look identical to an internal combustion car, the driving experience can be adjusted to the type of user. For instance, a group of Prius users in California combine the desire to free themselves from reliance on gasoline with an avid hobbyist's interest in exploring the technological capacity of the Prius' electric engine. The California Cars Initiative (CalCars), an informal collaboration between hybrid enthusiasts, entrepreneurs and engineers, outfitted the Prius with a larger battery that allows it to charge from the electrical grid (plug-in hybrid or PHEV) and power the car exclusively by electricity (CalCars 2008).[9] There are also kits on the market that allow consumers to convert their hybrid into a plug-in all-electric automobile (A. Chang 2008). Here, the Prius becomes an ongoing experiment in maximizing gasoline fuel economy. The various user identities that have developed around the Prius help us to better understand the sources of demand for the hybrid automobile. In addition to technologically sophisticated users like CalCars members, the hybrid engine and regenerative braking system creates the possibility for development of green driving practices. The purported inefficiency of the dual engine structure of Prius technology plays a significant role in user technology.

As an electric car, the Prius shares many of the same advantages as the early twentieth-century electric vehicle; namely, it is quiet, efficient and simple to own and to operate. However, these are also some of the same characteristics that symbolized the electric car as a "woman's car." Indeed, the gendering of the electric car has been usefully explored by automotive historians (Scharf 1991; Mom 2004). Curiously, the Prius seems to have been able to bridge the gender gap. One reason might have to do with the way in which the driver interacts with the hybrid technology.

While the user's experience of driving the Prius is quite similar to the experience of driving a traditional gas-powered vehicle, there are some differences. First, with earlier models, the process of starting the car involved turning the key in the ignition. Yet, instead of initiating the starting of the gasoline engine, the act of turning the key starts the electric motor. Later models of the Prius did away with the key altogether and use a push button ignition instead. The other major difference between the Prius and most gas-powered automobiles lies in the instrumentation. The Prius makes use of touch-screen technology to display basic controls for audio options and climate control. However, the unique function of the Prius touch-screen monitors is to provide the driver with two displays: "Energy" and "Consumption." The energy display illustrates the source of power (electric motor, gasoline engine) and the flow of energy to/from the battery. The consumption display shows the driver the fuel consumption (miles per gallon) in time intervals (Figures 6.1 and 6.2). The consumption screen divides time into discrete units – six five-minute intervals per screen. This allows drivers to adjust their driving behavior in order to alter the miles per gallon consumed by the Prius. Unlike the gas-powered engine, the Prius' fuel consumption is dependent on many variables that lie within the control of the driver. While drivers of traditional gas-powered vehicles can improve mileage by keeping tires inflated properly, carrying less weight in the car, idling less and driving more slowly, only one of these tasks, slowing down, actually involves changing one's driving behavior. By contrast, the Prius – because of the continuous re-assignment of power to the gas or the electric motor – responds to changes in driver behavior such as: coasting on slight descents, gradual increases in acceleration on ascents, strategic braking and coasting in slow traffic to engage the electric motor. As gas prices climb, the quest to increase mileage through changing driving behavior has spawned a new cohort of "hypermilers" who share information, gadgetry and driving tips in order to boost Prius mileage from 47 miles per gallon (mpg) to 60, 70 and even 80 mpg (Clayton 2008). Websites oriented to hybrid car users collect reports from Prius drivers detailing strategies used to achieve high mileage:

There are two schools of thought about using the Prius's display to maximum effect:

Simple: Watch the instantaneous mileage numbers. Learn what produces the best results by watching the effects of your experimentations. Don't worry about the arrows that appear on the "Energy" display.

Advanced: Use the Energy display to watch the direction of the arrows. Drivers getting the best mileage are able to use split-hair changes in how they press on the accelerator and brakes to move energy from the gasoline engine to the wheels and/or the batteries – or to get all arrows to disappear completely from the screen, in what is referred to as "glide mode."

(Berman 2006)

The consumption screen acts as a feedback mechanism providing the driver with information that is then used to adjust driving behavior. The bars display the miles per gallon, and so the taller the bar the more positive re-inforcement the driver receives. For more advanced drivers, the energy screen informs the driver about the conditions under which power is switched to the electric motor. The object is to drive in such a way that the automotive powertrain engages the electric motor. In this sense, driving is a game in which high fuel economy – measured in mpg – is the goal. Winning involves getting as far as possible on a gallon of gas.

The analogy between Prius driving and gaming is not inconsequential, I argue. The activity of video-gaming is an appealing and challenging form of recreation

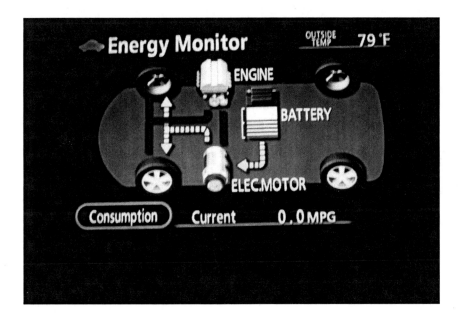

Figure 6.1 Toyota Prius energy monitor.

Source: Photo by author.

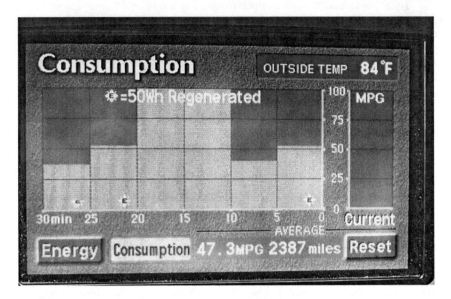

Figure 6.2 Toyota Prius consumption monitor (miles per gallon).

Source: Photo by author.

especially among young people, somewhat more prevalent among young males (Ogletree and Drake 2007). Gaming requires focus, quick response time and dexterity. It contains some of the elements identified with "flow" experiences. Flow represents a mental state in which difficult tasks appear almost effortless and enjoyable. The key components of a flow experience that are relevant to the gaming activity are that: (1) the task is difficult enough to be challenging but not so difficult that success is out of reach; (2) the activity requires some skills that can be honed and improved over successive plays of the game; and (3) there are clear objectives, performance is measureable and feedback is provided (Csikszentmihalyi 1990). Video-games contain these elements. Prius drivers can experience driving as a gaming activity. It is, therefore, possible to add "video-game" onto the characteristics that define the Prius. This suggests that driving practices in which a "passive" driver is attended to by automatic technologies (automatic transmission, power windows) and consumer comforts (cup holders, heated seats) are now joined by an alternative set of practices around the image of the "gaming" driver. Additionally, the use of video-displays and game-like, interactive technology in the Prius might help to account for a shift in the gender signification of the electric car. Finally, this feature of Prius technology also allows for feedback between human and machine thereby drawing them closer together in the pursuit of environmental conservation.

7 Slow Food

The politics and pleasure of consumption

If we conceptualize a social practice as an ensemble of relationships, emotional states and material artifacts constrained by structures of power and reproduced as a familiar routine, we can see that practices combine to form a way of life, a structure of activity and attitudes akin to Bourdieu's notion of *habitus* (Bourdieu 1977). But practices are contingent and open to disruption, questioning, challenge, and reform. The structures that both shape, and are shaped by, the habits of mind that enact *habitus* are capable of being re-interpreted and transformed. For example, the practice of factory production not only patterns the behavior and disposition of labor and capital but it also carries in it, as Marx noted, the possibility for transformation. "Structures, then, are sets of mutually sustaining schemes and resources that empower and constrain social action. But their reproduction is never automatic" (Sewell 1992: 19). The social practice of food consumption is the subject of the present chapter.

Food consumption offers a particularly rich case for studying consumer behavior from a political economy standpoint. Food involves multiple sites of economic activity, from the commodity chain getting food from farm (or laboratory) to plate, to spaces of buying and selling (supermarkets, produce stalls, pick-your-own), to the home kitchen or restaurant. In particular, I will explore the development of a set of practices situated around food purchasing and preparation that explicitly politicize the activity of eating: the Slow Food movement.

The origins of Slow Food can be found in Italy during the late 1980s. The name "Slow Food" was intentionally selected in order to contrast it with fast food and, in particular, to critically engage in political discourse about the dominant role of McDonald's in producing high volume, standardized food at low cost. The mass-production technique perfected by McDonald's for use in the food service industry was a source of protest (Schlosser 2005). Finally, the earlier link made by Gramsci between Fordism and Americanism was further applied to McDonald's, the world's foremost corporate purveyor of American values (Jenkins 1994). The particular flash point for the Slow Food movement occurred when McDonald's announced it was planning to open an outlet near Rome's historic Piazza di Spagna. This spurred widespread public opposition and discussion about the local, national and global forces affecting consumption (Kummer 2002; Pollan 2003). In December of 1989, Slow Food was officially born as an international organization dedicated to preserving a world of unique flavors, local food customs, and quality food and wine. Today the organization boasts a membership of over 85,000 individuals in 132 countries. Although susceptible to the charge of romanticizing an authentic, pre-capitalist agrarian lifestyle, Slow Food fomented a battle for control over culinary culture and food consumption practices by choosing to fight within the structure of a global, market-based system of provisioning.

The opposition to fast food is directly connected to a critique of the lifestyle emblematic of fast-paced society. As one declaration of the "Slow Food Manifesto" reads: "We are enslaved by speed and have all succumbed to the same insidious virus: Fast Life, which disrupts our habits, pervades the privacy of our homes and forces us to eat Fast Foods" (Petrini 2001b: xxiii). But the pace of consumption promoted by fast food establishments is not the only criticism leveled by Slow Food adherents. Advocates of Slow Food are worried that fast food endangers the very survival of "local osterie and trattorie, the kinds of places that serve local dishes and which have traditionally been frequented by people of all classes" (Miele and Murdoch 2002: 317). Proponents of Slow Food are keen to focus on the place-based nature of foodways and agricultural resources. Preserving and strengthening local food cultures, it is argued, has the effect of maintaining community cohesion and local producer–consumer networks.

Yet another signal feature of the Slow Food Movement is its self-consciously celebratory and sensuous engagement with gastronomy. It would not be an exaggeration to say that the movement wishes to embrace a social ethic of hedonism. The purpose of eating should be enjoyment, pleasure and conviviality. Rather than depicting food consumption as a means to an end, the "pleasures of the table" are meant to be savored for their own sake. But for the ability to savor and appreciate fully, one needs to educate one's taste. Part of the education process includes understanding the conditions and the techniques that brought your food to the table.

Slow Food: the politics of pleasure

The movement's founder, Carlo Petrini was born in Bra in the Piedmont region of northern Italy. In the 1970s, as a sociology student, Petrini became involved in radical politics. A guiding principle for Petrini and his associates was to imbue political action with song and pleasure. Eating was a communal activity and a way to combine education with sensory pleasure. In 1980, he helped open a restaurant in the northern Italian town of Bra that served local "peasant" foods at reasonable prices (Kummer 2002). The Praiseworthy Friends of Barolo, as they called themselves, organized tasting courses, classes and social events centered around food and wine. This then sparked a broader interest to discover local and regional foods, wine, and cuisines throughout Italy (Petrini 2001b). In 1987, Petrini helped publish a guide to Italian wine, *Gambero Rosso* (Red Prawn), as a supplement to the Communist newspaper *Il Manifesto* (Stille 2001: 21). Now Italy's authoritative food and wine guide, *Gambero Rosso* is published under the auspices of the Slow Food movement. The guide rates wineries and restaurants and, as such, has become a valued arbiter of gastronomic quality in Italy. It serves as an institutional embodiment of socio-cultural values (Dolfsma 2002) surrounding the production and consumption of food and wine. It not only reflects but also helps to constitute individual taste and culinary preferences.

The hedonistic edge of Slow Food created a wedge between its members and those of the left-wing of Italian politics. The group was undeterred and, in 1987, managed to create a competition among the restaurants participating in the huge "Feasts of Unity" sponsored by the Communist Party. "We were convinced that to raise the quality of the food and drink served at the festival was a fit goal, as a matter of both politics and civility" (Petrini 2001b: 11). But the desire to create a social movement centered on the pleasures of the table and the education of taste needed to be combined with an awareness of the conditions of production that sustain Slow Food consumption practices. Therefore, in 1994, the organization initiated an ecological mission – the Ark of Taste – to preserve the increasingly endangered tastes and flavors of the world.

In economics, as opposed to anthropology, the role of food in maintaining the productive classes and providing subsistence to the poor overshadows the alternative functions it plays. Food reproduces labor to be sure. But food consumption also communicates ethnicity, regional affiliation, values, aspirations, gender, and care. According to Slow Food principles, the production and consumption of food involves choices that have significant consequences for individuals, communities, and the environment. "The movement understands that every set of genes on its Ark of Taste encodes not only a set of biological traits but a set of cultural practices, as well, and in some cases a way of life" (Pollan 2003: 76).

The practice of buying, cooking, and eating food is a feature of everyday life that reproduces bodies and identities. Food purchases, cooking and eating form part of our everyday mode of life. Yet it is these taken-for-granted practices that help us make sense of our world and ourselves.[1] Slow Food practices entail material, cultural and social reproduction. Identity-formation is one part of this process. Identity is complex, multi-faceted and can be used to describe the relation between food consumption and class, ethnicity, culture, or nation (Wilk 2002). Cuisine, as Fischler notes, "transfers nutritional raw materials from the state of Nature to the state of Culture" (1988: 284). For instance, traditional foods are treasured by immigrant groups. National identity is linked to specific foods and drink (Gabaccia 1998). The specialty products of a nation are, in turn, associated with the geology, soil, culture or some intangible attribute of the local geography and local artisanal practices (Guy 2002; Petrini 2001b). Local cuisine, ethnic foods and foods associated with certain classes are produced within both local and global networks. Fischler (1988) notes that agricultural industrialization threatens traditional cultural linkages between consumers and their meals by increasing the physical and social distance between producers and consumers. "Quite literally, we know less and less what we are really eating and this increased uncertainty has an effect on consumer identity" (Fischler 1988: 289). The rise of the Slow Food movement can be understood in light of this increasing sense of unease over the system of food production. In this sense, Slow Food practices are intended to increase information about the origins and quality of food, and, therefore, reduce risk of food consumption.

In addition, preserving local foods, craft techniques and traditions serves as a bulwark against standardization and mass production. Similarities between Fordism and post-Fordism in manufacturing are clearly repeated in the system of food provisioning. For example, the artisanal cheesemaker is highly skilled, often preparing for her job by apprenticing with a master for a number of years. Only small batches of output are made under relatively labor-intensive production methods. Rather than homogenization of the final product, the goal is to imbue each batch with its own unique characteristics (Kupiec and Revell 1998). Overall, the Slow Food Movement has developed along three dimensions: (1) education of taste; (2) defending the right to material pleasure and conviviality; and (3) preserving the survival of endangered agricultural products and practices through the Ark of Taste.

Learning to eat differently

Slow Food promotes local and regional cuisines through the encouragement of what could be called "global grazing." Travel exposes individuals to indigenous culture and food is an inherent part of the culture. As Petrini declares:

> Being part of an international movement makes it possible to create gastronomic identities that are not the result of ignorant fantasy or a media campaign; to practice cultural relativism in a sound way, learning and teaching that taste and distaste are the result of historical processes and cultural sedimentation; to overcome gastronomic chauvinism by incorporating diversities. Tradition, as a cultural goal, can only be recovered with a polycentric and multicultural approach of this kind.
>
> (Petrini 2001b: 19)

Assuming that not everyone has the wherewithal to travel the globe in search of authentic local street food, the Slow Food Movement has explicitly embraced the global commodity chain.

> Globalization is absolutely desirable when it creates networks of communication among diverse realities instead of leveling them. It offers real advantages to poorer countries as long as they can escape the logic of 'conquest' that only creates wealth in the colonizing countries by exploiting the resources of those they colonize.
>
> (Petrini 2001b: 28)

Efforts like fair-trade, especially prominent in the coffee sector (Fridell, Hudson and Hudson 2008) would fall into this category. So, too, would campaigns to license the naming of food based on their country and region of origin. For example, Parma ham was granted Protected Designation of Origin (PDO) status in 1996. The European Council of Justice investigated a case involving the proper way to slice and sell Parma ham in accordance with Italian rules and regulations (Mohammed 2004). As de Grazia observes,

Slow Food would treat agricultural commodities much like cultural goods, reviving the occasions of their production and use, lobbying for their protection as if they were cultural goods protected by a form of intellectual property rights, their geographical names or indications, or GI in trade parlance, becoming the exclusive property of the villages, regions, or countries where they originate.

(de Grazia 2005: 473)

Both restrictions on naming and guidelines on the handling of food products illustrate the way in which a particular place, its conditions of production and the practices – understood as a set of dispositions, bodily movements, material objects, practical knowledge (Reckwitz 2002) – governing the transformation of products into means of consumption can be embedded in global chains of commodity production.

The Slow Food focus on cultivating taste can be read as conveying an elite sensibility. For example, as the 1989 Manifesto declares, "May suitable doses of guaranteed sensual pleasure and slow, long-lasting enjoyment preserve us from the contagion of the multitude who mistake frenzy for efficiency" (Petrini 2005: 76). The attitude that Slow Food practices are an antidote to the "contagion of the multitude" does not readily admit strategies to broaden participation in the movement. Allen argues, "Without an explicit focus on justice, we may be ushering in this type of two-tiered food system, based on a politics of complacency among the privileged who benefit from the alternative agrifood system" (Allen 2008: 159). But, as we have seen, Slow Food's role as a standard-bearer for taste has its roots in radical politics. Therefore, the acknowledged challenge for Slow Food lies in taking the notion that taste is constructed, learned and fluid, and framing it within a discourse of economic and social justice.

Learning to eat slow: taste education

In terms of taste education, the movement conceives of individual taste as a manifestation of culture and society. The sensory experience of taste is embedded within a social and cultural milieu involving habits, norms, rituals, and taboos. This is not to deny that the sensation of taste involves both physiological and social dimensions. For example, the intensity with which people taste certain foods differs. Korsmeyer notes that,

> While it is true that humans eat radically different foods, of equal interest is the ability to craft one's taste preferences away from the habitual. We can and often do expand our tastes, and we learn to make subtle discriminations among foods that once seemed all alike … The ability to educate one's palate is an almost uniquely human trait.
>
> (Korsmeyer 1999: 93)

The objective of the Slow Food movement is to educate taste through exposure to local and regional foodstuffs and through an appreciation of the linkage between food choices and biodiversity. There is a tendency for proponents of Slow Food to convey an impression that the local is the repository of some authentic essence. Yet, the authentic is also socially and culturally constructed. Whose authenticity sets the standard for cuisine in a region, like most large metropolitan regions in the United States, marked by successive waves of immigration and dislocation? So far, the conclusion seems to be that discovering regional cuisine involves a bit of culinary anthropology, unearthing traditional cuisines and heirloom varieties of produce, poultry and livestock. The US branch of Slow Food International organized a multi-dimensional version of the Ark of Taste named Restore America's Food Traditions (RAFT). The RAFT project seeks to document, catalogue, and perform the tasks of sourcing, cooking and eating "traditional" regional foods. For instance, a picnic in Madison, Wisconsin hosted by the local Slow Food chapter (called a convivium – "to live with hence to feast with") included slow-roasted American Plains Bison over Carolina Gold Rice grits and a Sorghum BBQ Mule-foot pork shoulder sandwich (Slow Food 2008). Emphasis is placed on educating consumers and chefs about the existence of local foods and their suppliers. By reaching out to both home cooks and professional chefs, the intent is to promote regional food communities of producers and consumers. The Slow Food movement depends on a variety of different diffusion mechanisms. If private restaurants were the only sites available for taste education this would interpose the demands of a profitable restaurant (e.g. that the local organic food look aesthetically pleasing using the highest quality ingredients) onto the process of taste education and confine the hedonistic pleasures of leisurely dining to a separate sphere abetted by low-wage service labor (Guthman 2003; Restaurant Opportunities Center 2005; Soper and Thomas 2006).

The education of taste also takes place through meetings of local chapters of the movement where capacities to distinguish between foods, wine varietals and cuisines are developed. A form of cultural capital is being acquired in these settings devoted to Slow Food principles. Bourdieu (1984) refers to cultural capital as the knowledge, practices and familiarity with the rules and norms governing everyday life – including consumption behavior – within a given social class. Taste, therefore, is an expression of one's group affiliation as well as an individual predilection (Lupton 1996; Akerlof 2007). Bourdieu examines the ways in which individuals acquire and display material goods as part of their frame of reference, classificatory scheme or *habitus* (Lee 1993: 32). Food consumption practices signal class and group identification. This is no less the case with Slow Food. The desire to resist the dominant culture of fast food, and the quest for obscure local and regional foods and cuisines that evoke a cultural heritage are part of the constitution of *habitus*. The cultural capital acquired by participants in the Slow Food movement signals that one has a rather sophisticated palate, a love of food, and a respect for local cultures and farming techniques that are light on the earth. Yet, by adopting cultural capital normally associated with upper-income or highly educated individuals, the movement conveys a sense of elitism and has been criticized for displaying an overly aesthetic sensibility that privileges symbolic use-value over material use-value (Guthman 2002: 300). Neither does the Slow Food movement explicitly challenge the gender divisions of labor within the household. It is women who traditionally labor to transform food into cuisine (Bourdieu 1984: 185). To date, there has been a general neglect of the gendered spaces occupied by those who enjoy the pleasures of the table versus those who still traditionally produce these sensory delights.[2] Furthermore, the quest for artisan-produced, regional foods and support for antique varieties of corn, apples, turkeys and other products can easily slip into a discourse of authenticity bent on preserving an idealized past. The romanticization of rural life raises problems for the movement (Lauden 2001).[3]

Bourdieu provides us with a useful set of concepts – cultural capital in particular – but his insistence that food choices primarily reflect class affiliation appears too restrictive to account for the multiplicity of forces that shape identity. Southerton (2001) proposes that Simmel's notion "taste communities" be used to supplement Bourdieu. Taste communities reflect the local, personal expression of food preferences and desires that may deviate from class-based norms. Cultural capital is developed as a way of understanding and appreciating certain foods, cuisines and local production methods, without reducing culture to class. A Slow Food convivium can therefore be characterized as a taste community in which individual taste is socially recognized and validated. However much taste communities in the United States, at least, tend to be disproportionately represented by more highly educated and wealthy individuals, this does not negate the possibility that taste education could influence the dispositions of less wealthy consumers by reworking the meanings and practices associated with meal preparation (Lockie 2002). Petrini seems to think as much when he argues that the percentage of income spent on food has fallen since the end of the Second World War so individuals at every level of the income ladder could adjust their spending toward higher quality food (Petrini 2001b: 50). Admittedly the case of the US is more challenging; one reason is differential access to locally produced foods by income and race. Many neighborhoods in the US and UK are without convenient access to purveyors of healthy, let alone locally grown, foods (Zenk *et al.* 2005; Shaw 2006). These "food deserts" are one problem of relying on the capitalist marketplace to distribute Slow Food products. Another difficulty lies in the disproportionate share of poor families' income going toward housing (Duly 2003). Increasing the availability of affordable housing would allow more opportunities for poor families to diversify their food purchases and join in the Slow Food movement.[4]

One novel program supported by Slow Food organizers involves integrating small-scale farming and cooking into the elementary school curriculum. The "Edible Schoolyard" program is the brainchild of Alice Waters, chef and owner of the Berkeley, California restaurant Chez Panisse. Martin Luther King, Jr. Middle School in Berkeley was the site for the first project in tilling, planting, harvesting, cooking and eating food grown on school property (Orenstein 2004; Winokur 2008). Slow Food USA has used the Edible Schoolyard program as a model in over two dozen local schools throughout the country.[5] At the level of the political economy, what these projects intend to accomplish is an institutional re-structuring – in this case the elementary school curriculum. Rather than isolating food production from consumption, the Edible Schoolyard blurs the distinction between the two by integrating farming activity and the technologies of agricultural production with kitchen technologies to create a user culture around food provisioning.[6] In addition, the project involves appropriating space on school grounds for use as gardens. This rearrangement of institutional structures and spaces has an effect on the habits and dispositions of the actors themselves. As Hodgson argues, "Instead of merely enabling individual action, the hidden and most penetrating feature of institutions is their capacity to mould and change individual dispositions and aspirations" (2003: 164). The restructured curriculum at Martin Luther King, Jr. Middle School includes training in tasks of food preparation. This was formerly the purview of home economists (Babbitt 1997). So, in this way, the Edible Schoolyard might re-legitimate home economics as a stock of knowledge, practical techniques and user culture surrounding food consumption.[7]

Another formal manifestation of the Slow Food commitment to taste education is the creation of a university dedicated to developing the academic field of "eco-gastronomy." The University of Gastronomic Sciences, opened in the fall of 2004, trains approximately 60 professionals in the fields of gastronomy and agro-ecology. Both undergraduate- and graduate-level degrees are awarded. The three-year undergraduate program, for example, includes courses in history of cuisine and gastronomy, marketing, food communication, economics and statistics, history of agriculture, sensory analysis, anthropology of food, nutrition and dietetics, food policy and food and wine tourism. Participating faculty include feminist philosopher and scientist Vandana Shiva and chef Alice Waters.

The intent of the University is to diffuse knowledge of local and regional cuisine, ecology, and sustainable agricultural practices through formal training and education, including training for agricultural and gastronomic tourism. Formal education will result in the creation of knowledge experts able to influence the direction of food trends, especially in the restaurant and food marketing sectors of the economy. In this way, the movement seeks to develop stocks of human capital through the creation of specific skills and knowledge about sustainable agriculture, sources of artisanal production, and marketing and distribution practices relevant to craft-based agriculture. The development of sensory capabilities combined with a deeper understanding of the unique attributes – including the conditions of production – of local and regional food add to stocks of cultural capital as well. As a producer of human and cultural capital the Slow Food movement presents us with a way of thinking about how consumption choices made by individuals are both shaped by, and form part of, an interdependent network within a social economy.[8]

Conviviality and the pleasures of Slow Food

A key element of Slow Food consumption practice rests upon the interpretation of the modifier slow. For Slow Food proponents, modern industrialization harbors a dark side: the insidious nature of "time–space compression" (Harvey: 1989). Technological advances in transport allow commodities to circulate at a much greater speed over much greater distances. In the commodity chain of foodstuffs this allows for the virtual elimination of seasonal produce. Food buying and consuming can then be released from its dependence on seasonality. This triumph of modern transport over nature not only disconnects consumers from the local conditions of agricultural production, but also affects the way in which resources are allocated. The lengthening supply chain – defined both in terms of the number of intermediaries between the grower and the consumer and the amount of physical distance of "food miles" traveled by the product from farm to plate – between producers to consumers is an outcome of this process.[9]

In opposition to this trend, Slow Food philosophy focuses on the pleasures of the table. The table represents both material culture – the culture of kitchens and food – and serves as a metaphor for shared community. The emphasis on the leisurely, conscious enjoyment of food and drink expands the concept of consumption beyond that of physiological reproduction. For instance, Bourdieu finds that food consumption "remains one of the few areas in which the working classes explicitly challenge the legitimate art of living" (Bourdieu 1984: 179). For Slow Food proponents, the pleasure of the table is seen as a key element in cultural reproduction. This extends to the pleasure of the commercial table as well as the pleasure of the private table. The emphasis on pleasure also presents a stark alternative to the more ascetic lifestyles associated with downshifting (Schor 1998) and the "left's self-denying culture of consumption" (de Grazia 2005: 467).

Furthermore, Slow Food proponents argue that the commercial provision of food is governed by the need to increase turnover and serve more customers per unit of time. As a result, pleasure and hospitality are compromised. Their goal is to challenge the practices upon which fast food culture is constructed. For instance, the passive consumer is one trope that Slow Food resists. Petrini resists using the term consumer to describe the participants in Slow Food convivia, opting instead to call them "co-producers" (Petrini 2005: 184). Nevertheless, this radical re-positioning of the customer as co-producer, while blurring the lines between production and consumption, is hard to imagine in a world of private ownership of the means of consumption – the private restaurant setting. Slow Food advocates do not go as far as Jane Addams and Charlotte Perkins Gilman in the late nineteenth and early twentieth centuries in advocating for collective kitchens and kitchenless homes (Addams 1896; Hayden 1978). However, attention to the spaces in which consumers and producers have an opportunity to interact and learn from one another highlights the potential for developing an awareness on the part of consumers of the material and social conditions under which food is produced (Holloway *et al.* 2007). The two goals of Slow Food, education of taste and defense of pleasure, are joined to an ecological imperative: the preservation of biodiversity through the support of sustainable agricultural practices. This goal is embodied in the movement's project to construct an Ark of Taste.

Ecological agriculture and the activist consumer

In 1996, Slow Food organized a conference in Turin, Italy entitled "An Ark of Taste to Save the Universe of Savors." The object was to find a way to systematically catalogue cheeses, meats, fish, poultry, fruits, grains, and herbs threatened with extinction due to consumer substitution with lower priced, standardized products. The Ark is a direct challenge to the neutrality of the marketplace. Slow Food president Petrini declares that, "It is our view that, rather than pay homage to the logic of macroeconomics, we should operate within a regional framework and promote new forms of 'slow' production and supply" (2001a: 2). Yet, elsewhere Petrini hews to a more market-driven criterion for determining which products should be admitted onto the Ark, "The Ark is a place for products with commercial potential, for which consumers will pay premium prices because of their superior flavor" (2001b: 92). But this does not mean that the market is a neutral arbiter. The demand for products with a deep local meaning and historical significance can be developed through the education of taste, and the price paid can be ascribed to the additional knowledge gained about the personal and professional qualities of the producer and the conditions of production.

So, the movement attempts to create a market for the preservation of food as both a bearer of cultural heritage and an embodiment of material pleasure. In order to facilitate this project, a databank of information about local food products, producers, recipes and restaurants is compiled. From this data endangered products can be identified and their consumption promoted. A presidium – a strategic support group within the movement – provides resources to assist with publicity, marketing, technical support, apprenticeship training, and assistance in navigating governmental regulatory systems (Kummer 2002).

One goal is to create regional networks of agricultural production and consumption. Steady, predictable local demand would allow small-scale producers to continue to maintain traditional production methods, methods that would otherwise be seen as antiquated and inefficient. In fact, one could advance the argument that heritage foods, farmed using traditional methods at odds with the standards of efficient manufacturing imbue the product with additional value. This, like the Prius dual-engine hybrid, illustrates the social construction of useful qualities that may be in conflict with standard norms of economic efficiency.

The regional network envisioned by Slow Food International based upon local produce and regional cuisine constitutes a variation on the concept of the "industrial district." The Emilia-Romagna region of Italy was one of the prime examples of the successful industrial district (Brusco 1982; Piore and Sabel 1984; Sabel and Zeitlin 1997). Within each district, interdependent small batch producers or large mass producers that have developed strong ties with small-scale producers engage in the production of regionally specific goods. Resource inputs of labor and capital are often flexibly deployed and the primary contractor on one job may be a secondary supplier in another. Sharing of labor and technical know-how is commonplace within the district. To be effective, the participating firms and employees develop large stocks of trust and loyalty. The districts are often comprised of members of extended families or long traditions of cooperation fostered by loyalty to one's community and region (Pietrykowski 1999; Portes and Mooney 2002). Some of the same characteristics define the type of social economy envisioned by the Slow Food movement. Take, for example, the need to develop trust as an element in the successful establishment of local markets for endangered products. A vexing problem for small-scale agriculture is the need to conform to national health and sanitation regulations. Often, food safety regulations were written with large-scale producers in mind. The cost of meeting national standards often imposes a large financial burden on small producers. Slow Food opposes food regulations that favor large industrial producers. Yet, this introduces an added element of risk into food consumption. To ameliorate the risk, the Slow Food movement needs to build up trust between consumers and producers. By promoting social contact between producers and consumers and making knowledge of the producer and production process as important as knowledge of the food itself, the Slow Food movement seeks to establish a connection between buying food and understanding and valuing the conditions under which it was made. It is important to remember, however, that these spaces of social contact are not devoid of power and contestation (Goodman and Dupuis 2002; Goodman 2004). An intriguing example is the case of raw milk cheese. The health risks associated with raw milk cheese are subject to debate and interpretation. For instance, soft cheeses are most likely to harbor harmful bacteria but the appellation soft cheese is not standardized at all. Slow Food USA teamed up with the Raw Milk Cheese Makers Association to draft a set of guidelines for cheese producers in order to pre-empt more stringent government regulations. The growing presence of artisanal cheese producers in dairy farming regions has the additional benefit of offering small dairy farmers in depressed rural economies an alternative market that does not require the need to purchase pasteurization equipment (Paxson 2008: 35).

Another attribute of the Slow Food economy or "consumption district" is the use of loyalty as a buffer against vacillations in price and supply. Consumers who are committed to the preservation of a local product or traditional cuisine are less likely to decrease their demand when prices rise. In this sense, there is a form of gift exchange between buyer and seller (Akerlof 1982). Similarly, the producer will not likely switch production or adopt industrial production techniques if either of these strategies will adversely affect the quality of the food being produced and, therefore, their reputation within the local Slow Food convivium. But more than reputation may be involved. A desire to maintain relationships based on mutual commitment and loyalty may also be at work. Commitment and loyalty decrease the probability of exit, the primary response to an unsatisfactory exchange as depicted in standard utility maximization theories (Hirschman 1970; Etzioni 1986; Minkler 1999). This new "moral economy" (Sayer 2004) relies on trust as well as bonds of community, commitment, and solidarity. These are hallmarks of social capital (Putnam 1993; Schuller *et al.* 2000; Killerby and Wallis 2002) that could make the movement less susceptible than the countercultural food movements of the 1970s (Belasco 1989) or the organic milk sector today (Dupuis 2000) to cooptation by industrial producers.

Performing the economy differently

By encouraging producers and consumers to interact and support one another's ways of life, consuming Slow Food can be interpreted as a process of socializing economic agents in performing new roles as buyers and sellers. To the extent that economics is performative, we can all be said to act out our roles within the economic spaces of markets, workplaces, social institutions and families. Now, our performances differ from those choreographed movements that appear in economics textbooks. This activity forms the raw material upon which some of the research in behavioral economics is based (Thaler 1992). It also constitutes a stock of knowledge that people make reference to in conjuring up their own explanations of the economy. It is the ersatz economic knowledge that is often in stark opposition to the scientific knowledge espoused by academic economists (Ruccio and Amariglio 2003).

Recently, Michel Callon and colleagues have begun to note moments of convergence between textbook economics and economic performances "in the wild." The wilds of economics consist of sites where economics intermingles with engineering, life sciences and management science to actively create markets (Callon 2007: 338). At other times, the wild spaces appear to incorporate everyday, popular representations of economics (Callon *et al.* 2002: 195–6). Callon posits that economics is being performed on the ground as it were; that neoclassical economic theories of rational calculation and self-interested behavior are coming into being through real-world technologies. One of the best examples for this performativity thesis is the fishing industry. Due to depleted stocks of fish, governments, in partnership with the private fleet owners, establish a quota system for each vessel. These quotas are randomly assigned as tradable rights to a subset of fisherman who can choose to fish their quota, buy additional quota rights or sell their rights to others. The fish then become transformed into a stock of private property and fishermen into investors. Some vessel owner–managers will prosper, but many will fail and either leave the industry or be forced to work as hired hands.

> The fish, which previously was regarded as a common heritage of the coastal people, is expropriated, without compensation, and given free of charge, as private property to a small elite. These fisherman–owners now get to decide whether to fish the quota or to sell it, without the communities that depend on such decisions for their survival having any say in the matter.
>
> (Holm 2007: 236–7)

The argument that neoclassical theory has leaped out of the textbook and made markets in its own image has been criticized for mistaking economic ideology (virtual reality) with everyday economic practice (Miller 2002), missing the contingent nature of market outcomes because they are embedded in cultural frames (Slater 2002), and misreading neoclassical price theory (Mirowski and Nik-Khah 2007). But the fishing quota case does highlight the linkage between economic theory and practice. The point here is that these links are contingent and contested and the economy can be performed differently. The counterexample of Slow Food illustrates that the qualities of food can be re-positioned to include the conditions under which food was produced, the values of the producer, the chef, and the community of others in whose presence the food is consumed, thereby re-investing food with properties that may overflow even those neoclassical accounts that bother to attend to the vector of attributes associated with a given commodity (Lancaster 1971). Food choices then become more than discrete decisions about commodity preferences between substitutes. Choices may be non-compensatory in the sense that there are no acceptable trade-offs available (Earl 1986). Therefore, the purchase and use of Slow Food commodities enmeshes consumers in a set of food practices linked to a community based on affinity and necessity; affinity because of the shared norms and values, necessity because of continued survival of small, local craft producers depends on consumer loyalty and commitments to purchase in the future (Pietrykowski 2004; Marglin 2008).

If the case of the quota trading in the fisheries industry turns fishermen into investors and fish into stocks of capital to be managed so as to guarantee a future stream of returns, we can also think about how a heterodox economics can be applied to perform the economy differently. The case of Slow Food is one example. It shares similarities with the fair-trade coffee and anti-sweat shop clothing campaigns to the extent that all of these grass roots social movements attempt to establish a just price, living wages and decent working conditions for the direct producers and the communities in which they live (Miller 2003; Wilkinson 2007). The effect of these social movements is to re-connect consumers with producers and re-animate the social conditions of production that are reflected in the commodities exchanged in the market. The social theorist Jurgen Habermas (1985) puts forth a theory of capitalist modernization whereby the steering mechanisms of instrumental rationality – money (economic system) and bureaucratic power (administrative system) – come to colonize the non-instrumental spaces of social and private life. The Slow Food, anti-sweatshop and fair-trade movements are forms of post-colonial resistance to the incursions of instrumental rationality. However, the risk is to assume that the lifeworld itself is free of contested meanings and power formations (Foucault 1980). For example, the Slow Food discourse of heritage foods, traditional foodways and authentic, rustic cuisine needs to be critically explored in order to identify whose heritage and authenticity are presented and which frames of reference are used to construct slow cuisine (Cook and Crang 1996; Bryant and Goodman 2004).

The importance of Marx's concept of commodity fetishism can also be used to highlight the move from performing the neoclassical economy to performing the social economy. Marx offered a critique of economists' view that market prices determined the value of commodities. The exchange of money for commodities masked the underlying social relations of production that endowed the commodities with value (Marx 1977: 168–9). By creating bonds of personal knowledge, affiliation and commitment between producers and consumers, the fetish character of commodity exchange – defined as a relation between things – is re-framed as a relation of solidarity and support (Hudson and Hudson 2003). As Marglin describes the motivations behind consumers engaged in fair-trade purchases:

> There is more than one way to understand the willingness of (some) consumers to pay more for coffee or bananas or athletic shoes when these commodities

are produced in conditions that provide something approaching a decent standard of living for the producers themselves. It is possible, for example, to
cast the argument in more or less individualistic terms, in language of human
rights to which nobody steeped in Immanuel Kant's individualism could
object. But I believe the motivations underlying consumers' participation in
fair trade efforts go beyond the individualistic. If the motivation were simply
one of abstract human rights, there would be no reason or need to personalize
the producers. But, in point of fact, promoters of fair trade and the like go
to considerable efforts to make the producers and their communities real to
consumers, to foster a sense of relationship between consumer and producer.

(Marglin 2008: 234).

Particularly noteworthy is that the Slow Food movement has been able to take an
attribute normally associated with cultural capital – culinary taste – and insert it
into an economy built around the preservation of unique food, local cuisine, and
cultural heritage. Taste then comes to encompass more than a signaling device
for social status and individual identity. It is effectively transformed into a form
of social solidarity. Knowledge and appreciation of food can be used to engage
in consumption practices that promote sustainable local, small batch, craft-based
production within a consumption district representing a unique cultural heritage.
As Hendrickson and Heffernan (2002) note in their case study of a local food network, "Embedding food production and consumption in community means that
eaters respect that process as much as the food that they eat ... Thus food becomes
the expression of relationships that are much more than exchange relationships"
(364). By inserting taste education into a social movement aimed at creating
local and regional networks of mutually sustaining producers and consumers the
pleasures of the table become a form of resistance to corporate, standardized,
mass-produced foods.

8 Consuming with alternative currency

Within capitalist market economies, access to the world of consumption is open to those members of society who possess the means to purchase goods and services. In the two cases analyzed so far – green automobility and Slow Food – the material goods and services were obtained primarily through market exchange. Even after the initial car purchase, driving practices commit drivers to a series of marketed services and supplies that enable the driving experience to continue into the future. Drivers can also purchase optional equipment – like Global Positioning Systems (GPS) – that can alter the quality of human–machine interaction and driving practices. In the case of the Slow Food movement, participants attempt to re-work the processes of globalization in order to preserve local agriculture and culinary heritage by expanding the geographic market for endangered foods, venerable recipes and threatened cuisines. Here, the market implies capitalist, profit-centered market exchange. However, the spaces of consumption are not co-extant with the capitalist market nor are consumption practices always mediated through this form of market exchange. The spaces that lie outside of the main currents of the capitalist economy are the focus of this final case study. In particular, the participation of economic agents in the local currency movement is examined for its role in facilitating and constituting a set of alternative consumption practices.

Circulating goods and services

Rather than depicting money as inherently corrosive of social relations colonizing the lifeworld through the logic of instrumental rationality (Habermas 1985), recent research by sociologists and geographers abjures and instead maintains that money is plural, variegated and invested with a range of meanings. Zelizer (1994) lists over ten separate social functions served by the earmarking of money for special uses. The social relations effected through the use of earmarking monies include: dealing with risk, managing intimacy, breaking or maintaining social ties, control over others and promoting group or individual identity (1994: 26). Contrary to predictions that the widespread use of money leads ineluctably to modernization characterized by impersonal, instrumental relations between individuals, money itself can act as social glue, preserving relations where norms of reciprocity are stronger than expected acts of reciprocity (Williams 2005). Zelizer defines as "social money" all objects that are recognized and habitually used in exchange (1994: 21). These can include items as diverse as postage stamps, subway tokens, casino gaming chips, gift certificates or food stamps. However, the ability to use these objects as one would use money requires that they be incorporated into a series of diverse social relationships involving interpretive skills, trust, intimacy, and cooperation. Even government-issued currencies are treated differently depending on whether they are acquired as wages, lottery winnings, bequests or court settlements. For most people, the level of risk they are willing to take with gambling winnings would be greater than for an equivalent amount of weekly earnings (Thaler and Johnson 1991). To say that money is social in this sense is to say that it is socially constructed via the processes through which it is received and the meanings attached to its intended use. Zelizer intentionally focuses her study on the ways in which people earmarked government-issued (fiat) money for specific uses. She did this in order to confront head-on the claim that fiat money necessarily dissolves distinctions between buyers and sellers, universalizes the experience of the market economy and commodifies personal relations (Zelizer 1994: 34–5).

Variously referred to as alternative, local, social, community or complementary currencies and functionally related to local exchange trading systems (LETS), the use of alternative currency expands the scope of economic activity to individuals with limited access to the world of commodity exchange. Contemporary models of alternative currency can be traced back to Vancouver Island's Comax Valley where, in 1983, Michael Linton established a computerized system of accounting for the debits and credits that represented exchanges of goods and services. The LETS system is primarily an accounting framework that does not need to print and circulate physical currency notes. Especially popular in Britain, the LETS system functions by maintaining a centralized, computerized account, revised periodically, that tallies credits earned against payments out for each member (Greco 2001; Seyfang 2001; Ingham 2004). More generally, "LETS are local systems of production, multilateral exchange, and consumption, articulated through a local currency – a single-purpose money – independent of, but often related to, the prevailing national currency" (Lee 1996: 1377–8). By contrast, local currency systems issue geographically limited, community-defined monetary units, and, so, divisibility of currency and intermixing national and local currency becomes an additional part of the exchange process (Maurer 2003). In Ithaca, New York for example, many local businesses will accept the local currency – Ithaca HOURS – for a percentage (up to one hundred per cent) of the purchase price.

There are several types of alternative currencies in use today (North 2007). The three main types are scrip subject to demurrage (Blanc 1998), LETS, and time dollars not subject to demurrage. Demurrage involves the assessment of a fee meant as a penalty for not throwing money back into circulation after a fixed period of time. The goal of demurrage is to speed up the circulation of currency through the local or regional economy. In this sense, there is an opportunity cost associated with holding this form of currency. On the one hand while this may boost spending in the short-term, over time monies that pay a positive real rate of interest would be preferred to long-term holding of demurrage scrip (Rösl 2006). The result of demurrage is that this form of alternative currency would depreciate over time. Silvio Gesell, a late nineteenth-century socialist, is cited as the source of this alternative money system, which formed the basis for proposals during the 1930s by Irving Fisher and California gubernatorial candidate and novelist Upton Sinclair. Gesell linked monetary flows directly to the sustenance of consumer demand. His form of money – consumption money or "free" money – would earn no interest. But consumption money held two meanings: first, as a channel through which to facilitate exchange, and, second, as a way to tether spending to the locality in which labor income was paid out.

In practice, local currency systems extend the world of consumption and production beyond the capitalist exchange economy. Local exchange trading systems and local currencies have been taken up quite readily in low-income communities and neighborhoods (Williams 1996; Seyfang 2001). Local exchange trading systems are a grassroots response to the disappearance of waged labor in industrialized economies (Gorz 1999: 104). For example, unemployed individuals can use the system to locate other people willing to make use of their skills in exchange for either a product or service of their own or local currency. Sekine envisions local currency as a resurgent form of cooperative exchange set against the capitalist market.

> When the general-purpose money issued by the state is usurped by large corporations and international speculators and fails to function as people's means of exchange, the natural reaction on the part of the local community is to issue its own special-purpose money with limited circulation and limited functions.
>
> (Sekine 2004: 237)

In addition, variation exists as to the source of local currency's value. In some cases, like Linton's Canadian LETS program, the value of local currency is tied to the value of the national currency. However, in other cases, the currency is de-linked from standard money values and is instead defined in terms of the particular quality and quantity of labor being offered, the local cost of living (living wage) or on other social norms of fair and just compensation. For example, the members of the Manchester LETS, begun in 1992, consciously established a fluid value for the "bobbin" – the name of the local currency unit. In routine business exchanges the bobbin was valued at one pound sterling. The typical LETS member came to value their labor at 6 bobbins per hour. Yet, there was no set exchange rate and for some individuals for whom the social interaction provided by their services was valuable to the service provider a single bobbin might be sufficient compensation (North 2007: 81–3). In this last example, the social context in which the transactions are embedded becomes valued for its own sake and this, in turn, affects the currency value. The particular social practice of the exchange becomes part of the value of the good or service being exchanged. This adheres closely to the concept of endogenous preferences. Research by economists into the effect of the changing social structure of exchange on bargaining behavior supports this claim (Bowles 1998; Carpenter 2005).

Local currency systems support a community of individuals interested in forging new economic spaces outside of the mainstream. Just as a social networking site is intended to link individuals who share common interests, the local currency network is useful in identifying those marginalized from the capitalist market economy or those looking to support alternatives to global corporate buying and selling (Pacione 1997).

Alternative currency and local economies

Within the local economic development literature, economic base theory represents the local economy as if it were a nation-state. The economic base is defined as that part of the local or regional economy serving the external (non-local) economy. In terms of exchange, basic sectors of the local economy serve to export goods. Non-basic sectors, on the other hand, directly serve the local community. The traditional approach toward economic growth has been to focus on promoting the expansion of basic industries largely at the expense of non-basic sectors of the local economy (Persky *et al.* 1993). This export-led growth model is markedly different from the functions performed by alternative currency. Compared to export-led growth, alternative currency works to enhance the non-basic (community-serving) sector. The goal is not to promote exports in an attempt to extend the market beyond the locale. Rather, this view of exchange shifts the frame of reference by re-orienting the objective of production away from expansion and growth for its own sake and toward consumer purchases and production decisions that result in domesticating rather than internationalizing the market.

The battle between export-led growth and import substitution characterizes the traditional discourse. Whereas import substitution strategies can be used to promote the local purchase of supplies, alternative currency, with its focus on developing a parallel social economy shifts the discourse away from the metaphor of competing nation-states in search of comparative advantage. Instead, the alternative discourse revolves around the activities of provisioning, sustaining and improving the quality of life for members of the community through the creation of local interdependencies.[1] By shifting the perspective, the objective of maximizing external income flowing into a locality or region is supplemented by the goal of raising net income by maximizing the local spending multiplier (Williams 1996).

To highlight one example, in 2002 Britain's New Economics Foundation (NEF) launched a series of community development workshops aimed at enhancing the size of the local multiplier within high-poverty areas. The goal of these strategies was to highlight the necessity of combining local purchasing networks with programs to secure outside investment. As the author of a NEF handbook for community organizers put it, "And it is only if inward investment is really embedded, with a thick web of local linkages and ties, that it can secure a long-term future for your community" (Sacks 2002: 10). The NEF "plugging the leaks" workshops teach participants first how to identify the flows of money leaking out of the local economy and then how to propose new social enterprises that would provide the same services locally (Ward and Lewis 2002).

The advantages of alternative currency systems are several:

1   Local currencies expand the circulation of goods and services by introducing an additional medium of exchange into the local/regional economy.
2   Lack of interest payment for holding alternative currency excludes its functioning as a store of value, therefore increasing its use value as a means of exchange. In other words, used as a means of exchange, alternative currency is far less likely to be "saved," thereby increasing the absolute size of the local multiplier effect.
3   The limited geographic range of community currency eliminates leakages out of the local stream of spending, thereby increasing the local multiplier effect.
4   The general lack of acceptance of alternative currency by local representatives of national chains and global corporations who rely primarily on supplies imported from outside of the local economy creates competitive advantages for locally owned businesses that use locally sourced products and suppliers (Williams, 1996).
5   As a measure of value independent of national currency systems, community currency re-constructs the social and economic value associated with goods and services. For example, work that is undervalued or marginalized in the conventional capitalist labor market can be re-valued through the use of community currency (Pearson 2003).
6   While an advantage over barter systems to the extent that a coincidence of wants is no longer necessary to complete a sale and purchase, community currency systems often rely on personal knowledge, trust and conviviality. Consumers of goods and services purchased with local currency are more likely to know the conditions under which their purchases were produced.

Responding to economic crisis: local currency in Argentina

The 2001 economic crisis in Argentina can be seen as a large-scale currency crisis premised, in part, on an economic policy that tied the value of the national currency to the US dollar in lockstep fashion. The problem with this convertibility plan was that it left Argentina at a disadvantage in trade with other countries. The debt burden financed through loans from the IMF required Argentina to enact austerity budgets, including both cuts in public services and worker pensions as well as efforts to privatize public services. The cost-cutting measures had the effect of decreasing employment and reducing wages. In response to ever-increasing demands for budget cuts and privatization as a pre-condition for continued loan support from the IMF, the national government froze bank accounts and limited withdraws to a mere 250 pesos (Lloyd and Weissman 2001; Hershberg 2002). In addition, the internationalization of Argentina's banking system increased its dependence on global financial institutions with diversified portfolios that left them less open to single-country risk and did nothing to forestall, and may well have exacerbated, the collapse (Del Negro and Stephen 2002). In 2001 the alternative currency movement in Argentina was already well established, but the collapse of the national financial system presented both an opportunity as well as a challenge to adapt a small, local system based on solidarity and trust into a large-scale organization.

In 1995 a barter club (also called a "node") was organized by urban ecologists working for an NGO charged with promoting sustainable resource utilization. The club experimented with the use of alternative currency, first through a systemized barter system of debits and credits premised on the LETS in Britain. Eventually, the system evolved toward the use of local currency – originally named the "nodine" (*no dinero*) to symbolize that the currency was the antithesis of traditional money to the extent that the purpose was limited to meeting needs and circulating goods rather than earning and interest and profiting from speculation (Demeulenaere 2000). Eventually, the clubs expanded into the Red Global de Trueque (RGT) global barter network with 450 clubs in Argentina and others in Brazil, Uruguay, Chile and Spain. The unit of currency within the RGT was the credito (Pearson 2003). In the case of Argentina, individuals were initially provided with a loan of 50 creditos. In this way individuals become members of the RGT. This permitted them to participate in the barter markets. Creditos, not pesos, were the only currency accepted in Argentina's barter markets. In order to obtain more creditos, individuals were expected to provide something of use to others in the market. In this way the market was constituted by subjects who continuously moved between the roles of producer and consumer. The RGT refers to participants as "prosumers."[2] As the economy in Argentina worsened through the 1990s, more and more people began to participate in the RGT as a buffer against falling real wages and rising unemployment. The 2001–2 economic crisis left most working and middle-class Argentines without access to cash. Mandatory restrictions placed on bank withdrawals (*corralito*) propelled the RGT into printing increasingly large volumes of creditos in order to enact a grassroots expansionary policy (Cato 2006).[3]

The Argentine response to economic crisis involved more than creating an alternative currency to keep exchange functioning. It required the development of new types of capacities or the re-deployment of existing stocks of social capital. For example, the majority of the active participants in the RGT were women. The economic activities of the prosumer seemed to match up with the informal economy of household production and provisioning (Pearson 2003). Pereyra (2007) found that most of the Argentine barter network participants were women whose participation often consisted of socializing the production of goods and services normally produced in the household (baking and food preparation, for example). In addition, the social networks that extended beyond the household became the basis for economic arrangements that facilitated the cooperative production and sale of goods and services. The widespread economic dislocation caused by the collapse pushed more and more middle-class families into poverty and many of them found their way to a neighborhood fair, the exchange markets run by RGT (Cato 2006; Pereyra 2007). For many of the newer participants in this form of barter exchange, new consumption practices needed to be learned. Some exchange clubs designated individuals to monitor prices with the intent of discouraging and shaming those sellers charging exorbitant prices. This form of citizen price control constituted a moral economy of a just price. New participants were taught how to effectively negotiate and how to anticipate the needs of others in order to produce goods and services to offer in the neighborhood fair (Demeulenaere 2000; North 2007).

However, as the crisis persisted and many more individuals were brought into the network of the RGT the increasing scale of participants militated against the operational principles of trust, solidarity and reputation. The ideal of a prosumer buying the raw materials for baked goods with creditos and baking cakes to sell for more creditos within an environment of mutual solidarity and trust broke down under the strains of having to cope with an influx of new participants who had little interest in communitarian principles. As Peter North observes:

> Given the depth of the crisis key activists saw it less as an alternative to capitalism than a way to help the middle classes, not used to fending for themselves, to survive the crisis and generate new forms of livelihood. Barter was almost a game, a trial run for a market-based economy of microtraders, but one that focused on need, not capital accumulation.
>
> (North 2007: 162)

It was estimated that by 2002 the local currency/barter system had approximately 2.5 million participants (Pereyra 2007). With the growing scale of exchange and heightened levels of anonymity, it became increasingly common to buy something at a low price at one fair and then move it to another fair in order to sell it at a higher price. Men often participated in this scheme. Men also functioned as agents who navigated between the barter markets and the informal street markets to re-sell items purchased with creditos at the barter fairs (Pereyra 2007: 104). So, whereas the Argentine case illustrates the potential for creating and sustaining alternative spaces for production and consumption outside of the orbit of profit-based commodity production, the economic collapse of the national economy put pressure on the local currency nodes to expand beyond the point at which bonds of personal knowledge, trust and solidarity could function.

Alternative currency and non-capitalist spaces of exchange

Alternative currencies and LETS function as alternative economies premised not on profit-making but rather on the satisfaction of social and material needs. In addition, in the process of shopping, the local consumer makes a conscious decision to patronize shops and services that accept the local currency. Local currency schemes involve the issuance of local unit of currency. The value of the currency is sometimes benchmarked against the government-issued currency. In other cases the local currency reflects a unit of labor. For example, the Ithaca HOURS system of Ithaca, New York, founded in 1991 and the oldest continuous alternative currency system in the United States, equates an hour of labor with one unit of local currency (hence the name Ithaca "HOURS"). This, in turn, is pegged at $10, an approximation of the living wage for a worker in the upstate New York region where Ithaca is located (Alternatives Federal Credit Union 2007; Burke 2007).

Collom (2005) identified 80 local currency systems in the United States between 1991 and 2004, of which about 17 were still in existence by the end of 2004. He found that the average household income was lower and poverty rates higher in cities whose residents adopted community currency systems. Furthermore, a heterogeneous population including large numbers of young and highly educated individuals distinguished those cities with long-lived local currency systems. Ithaca, New York shares these characteristics. Ithaca is a community of approximately 30,000 residents in rural upstate New York. It is the home to both Cornell University and Ithaca College. Ithaca's population is both highly educated – 58 per cent of the adults hold a Bachelor's degree compared with 27 per cent for the United States as a whole – and poor – 42 per cent of its residents live in poverty compared with under 15 per cent for the nation as a whole (US Census Bureau 2008). The goal of the local currency movement in Ithaca is to develop an economy that is "village based: shop keepers, café owners, craftspersons and alternative health therapists" (Jacob *et al.* 2004a: 31). By facilitating exchanges between individuals marginalized by commodity production, local currencies allow activities that are useful and socially valued to be carried on and supported.

At first blush the use of money in exchange represents an advance over barter systems. In barter the search for a buyer is restricted to the subset of those buyers who are selling what you wish to buy. Money, a commodity whose useful quality is its universal acceptance in exchange, widens the sphere of exchange to include buyers who have nothing in particular to sell in exchange. The resulting circulation of commodities exudes a dynamic and uncontrollable chain of sale and purchase.

> We see here, on the one hand, how the exchange of commodities breaks through all the individual and local limitations of the direct exchange of products, and develops the metabolic process of human labour. On the other hand, there develops a whole network of social connections of natural origin, entirely beyond the control of the human agents.
>
> (Marx 1977: 207)

This rupture of the local terrain upon which the direct exchange of products is predicated depends on the intervention of money. Money serves to flatten the relationship between seller and buyer by overcoming the privileged position of local, individual buyers. As such, local needs and individual knowledge of products and their origin is no longer a constraint on the full development of the division of labor and trade (Helleiner 2000). The social connections Marx refers to are the relations cemented through exchange and the mutual occurrence of sale and purchase. The unregulated or natural rhythm of sale and purchase is also liable to rupture if the use-value produced is no longer able to attract a buyer.

> Circulation bursts through all the temporal, spatial and personal barriers imposed on the direct exchange of products, and it does this by splitting up the direct identity present in this case between the exchange of one's own product

and the acquisition of someone else's into the two antithetical segments of sale and purchase.

(Marx 1977: 209)

So, the use of money as the primary means of circulating commodities revolutionizes the nature of exchange. It becomes a pre-requisite for both the rise of merchant capital and the subsequent dominance of industrial capital. For capitalists engaged in trade, merchant capital, the purpose of buying is selling. The goal of the capitalist merchant is not to sell for its own sake but to sell at a price that exceeds the price she originally paid for the product (Marx 1977: 250–1). As the buying and selling process is a two-sided exchange, unless the buyer of the merchant's commodity is yet another merchant, the commodity reaches its final destination as an object of consumption.

Now, for the industrial capitalist, money acts as the means of exchange for the purchase of commodities (labor, machinery, raw materials), which are then used to produce commodities that exceed the value of the commodities used to produce them. The produced commodity, when sold, realizes an additional or surplus value. In both cases, in order for profit to be made, the commodities produced by the industrial capitalist and sold by the merchant capitalist have to have use-value for some substantial number of buyers in society, but the particular use-value and the qualitative character of that use-value is inconsequential to the capitalist.

So Marx presents us with several scenarios: one in which commodities exchange for one another through barter, another situation established through the use of money where money acts as the universal equivalent in order to facilitate exchange across a wider range of participants, still another in which money is used to purchase goods which are then re-sold at a higher price,[4] and finally the "modern" capitalist scenario wherein money is advanced to purchase commodities that are transformed into products containing surplus value. The alternative currency movement fits none of these scenarios completely; however, it does match up most closely with the second, perhaps evanescent or merely heuristic[5] state where money functions as a lubricant that permits the exchange process to function more effectively.

Indeed the benefits Marx identifies with universal money are precisely the problems that local currency movements intend to address: namely, the ease with which universal money escapes the particularities of place creates problems for communities seeking to regulate the flow of economic activity generated through monetary exchange. In the local currency model, the social acceptance of money is limited by the local knowledge and geographic range of participation. For example, in Ithaca, New York the range of Ithaca HOURS is approximately 20 miles (Beesten 1998). This restriction on the effective range of circulation permits successive rounds of spending and re-spending to take place within the local community. One of the signal features of contemporary local currency movements that set them apart from their historical predecessors (e.g. Owen and Proudhon) is the attempt to create parallel systems of local currency alongside of national and supra-national currencies rather than as autarkic responses. In this parallel system, individuals can adjust the degree to which they make use of alternative currencies. The effect of such fluidity is to increase the diversity of economic lifestyles available. The founder of the Ithaca HOURS, Paul Glover, claimed that he was able to provide for 95 per cent of his needs by using the local currency (Jacob *et al.* 2004a). One local Ithaca restaurant, the cooperatively run Apple Blossom Café, allows their employees the choice to be paid in HOURS or dollars (Burke 2007). Over 500 local goods and services are listed in the 2007 Ithaca HOURS directory used to locate businesses that accept local currency, and, although most do not accept full payment in HOURS, the scope of acceptance by local businesses suggests that negotiating a dual economy of local and national currency has become part of the repertoire of market exchange in this community. In this community, capitalist and non-capitalist enterprises and circuits of exchange dot the landscape. The hegemonic role of capitalist economic lifestyles is offset by other logics and other practices (Gibson-Graham 2006).

The contemporary use of local currency bears a close resemblance to the early American system of non-capitalist household production. Within the context of an eighteenth- and early nineteenth-century subsistence farming community, exchange often took the form of labor services credited to one farm family's account and debited to the account of the family receiving the service. Reciprocity governed the system of exchanges whereby services rendered today would be re-paid at a later date by labor, goods or cash. The need to equate debts through the use of a strict monetary yardstick was not necessary in a non-capitalist system where the labor services and products exchanged were not commodities and were, therefore, not intended to yield a surplus. "In the household mode of production a person can remain continually indebted to some persons as long as others are indebted to him in an equivalent amount ... They [debts] served not to separate the community into classes so much as to bind it together" (Merrill 1976: 63). This approach is mirrored in the LETS and the community currency system. Both schemes allow members to incur debts to others. As the LETS system provides a central clearinghouse for the accounting of debts and credits, the debt can be paid off to someone else. In this way the debt is socialized and becomes part of a system of personal obligation to others in the community (Schraven 2000).

In both the eighteenth-century New England household and present-day local currency system, money is merely one among several handy use-values. New England farmers often swapped work with one another instead of paying for services in cash. Similarly, the exchanges facilitated by contemporary local currency circulate goods and services – primarily personal services – among community members. This corresponds to the situation faced by subsistence farmers studied by historian Michael Merrill:

> A household produces use-values for itself, and use-values for others. But unlike the situation in capitalist or simple commodity production, the use-values-for-others are not use-values in general which become use-values for no one if the supply turns out to be greater than the demand. Instead, the use-values for others in household production are use-values for someone, produced for specific persons to meet their specific needs.
>
> (Merrill 1976: 63)

The relationship between New England household production and capitalist commodity production over the course of the eighteenth and nineteenth centuries can be characterized in terms of resistance. Farmers were defending a form of life rooted in communal values and norms of reciprocity. "The only secure basis for opposition to capitalist forms of production in the nineteenth century was a non-commodity form of production" (Merrill 1976: 62). This economy of personal obligation and customized production lies in contrast to the instrumental rationality ensconced in capitalist commodity production.[6] However, it would be incorrect to suggest that pre-capitalist forms of production are being reconstructed *tout court* through local currency movements. Offe and Heinze, acknowledging the late twentieth-century trend toward increasing unemployment, under-employment and intermittent employment spells, assert that:

> endeavours to dispatch those sections of the population that are affected by the crisis symptoms of the labour market and the welfare state to look for ways out of their difficulties in family, neighbourhood, community and relationship circles, and to conjure up the charms and effectiveness of precapitalist ways of life with the conservative-romanticizing outlook of many protagonists of "new subsidiarity" are likely to prove fruitless and misleading.
>
> (Offe and Heinze 1992: 41)

Instead, they argue in favor of a parallel economy constituted by those individuals excluded from the capitalist market economy. Trades would be consummated with currency denominated in units of time applied equally to labor performed in all services. No price mechanism would function because all services would carry the same price and any imbalance between supply and demand would be addressed through social mechanisms of information-sharing, persuasion and the enforcement of social norms that assign services on the basis of "urgency of need" (Offe and Heinze 1992: 207–9).

> To the extent that market equilibration through communication is achieved, the "pessimistic" assumptions of the analysis of the economic model predicting a breakdown of such exchange systems might very well be falsified by human capacities for communicating, agreement and evaluation of social relationships.
>
> (Offe and Heinze 1992: 209)

This bears a striking resemblance to the mechanisms put into place during wartime rationing in the United States when market signals were abandoned in favor of collective enforcement of fair pricing and purchasing behavior.

Contemporary neoclassical theory has little to say about the economic impact of local or complementary currencies. This is largely due to the assumption that all currencies will share the same set of economic functions: store of value, medium of exchange and measure of value. Currencies that share these characteristics and are available for use in the same markets are understood to be competitors. In global currency markets the exchange rate is determined by the relative attractiveness of holding one currency against another. For example, one investigation of multiple currencies focused on the impact of the Euro as a substitute to dollarization within weak national economies (Müller 1999). But what of currencies that do not evince all the features of traditional money and have a more delimited sphere of usage? These non-competing currencies generally fall outside the mainstream sphere of analysis.

Alternative consumption behavior

If the prototypical market exchange is one in which an individual buyer interacts momentarily with an individual seller (spot market exchange) then the degree of social interaction is indeed limited. This is not to say that the interaction is completely devoid of communication and mutually accepted rules of behavior (Pietrykowski 1995a; 1996). Spot markets involve relative anonymity between buyers and sellers and the exchange itself is an ephemeral event. If anything, the use of money reinforces these characteristics of exchange. Following Bowles (1998), we can argue that competitive market exchange of this type tends also to frame the choices people make. Equally important, market exchange may influence the acquisition of social capital and cultural knowledge useful in facilitating exchange. Or, to put it another way, market exchange may thwart the development of traits unrelated to successful competitive market exchange. "Markets thus affect not only the demand for, but also the supply of cultural traits. Among these are reputations for trustworthiness, generosity and vengefulness" (Bowles 1998: 92). In a world in which market exchange is not complete at the moment of sale (contingent claims) or where information is unequally distributed (information asymmetry), reputation, honesty and generosity (as well as the ability to retaliate) are important traits.

Furthermore, in a world where exchange is local, personal and continuous – as opposed to transient, anonymous and ephemeral – the development and maintenance of social networks, loyalty and solidarity is essential for the success of exchange. For example, individual efforts to establish and maintain a good reputation matter in these exchange arrangements. Bowles maintains that segmentation of members of a population into sub-groups in which individuals of a given type are able to interact repeatedly with like-minded others will result in the overproduction of the traits associated with that type (e.g. trustworthiness, fairness, empathy) (Bowles 1998: 93). This seems to be borne out by several case studies of local currency. Participants in local currency exchange rarely, if ever, enter into complete contracts whereby the entire range of possible outcomes is specified ahead of time. Instead, exchanges are personal and often governed by trust and the willingness of the parties to re-negotiate and enter into dialogue in order to reach a consensual result. Surveys of members of various LETS and HOURS systems seem to reinforce this viewpoint.

One study of LETS members in Britain (Aldbridge *et al.* 2001) uses in-depth surveys to investigate several claims regularly attributable to local currency systems. (1) It is often said that LETS reduce "social exclusion" by incorporating individuals into worlds of meaningful work. The interview results suggest that individual participants value LETS because it allows access to the world of goods without relying on the formal wage-labor market. (2) LETS mitigate the negative effects of labor market flexibility where flexibility is imposed on workers through increasing use of part-time, seasonal or temporary staffing strategies and the expansion of jobs that de-skill workers and segment tasks. At its best, LETS, understood as a complementary currency system functioning within a parallel economy, supplements part-time work by allowing people to blend together a number of part-time jobs and ways of making a living through the performance of a range of services based on their talents, and skills and through the acquisition of new skills (Gorz 1999: 106). At a more basic level LETS is a survival strategy in the face of labor market informalization. (3) LETS allows for control over work. In cases where self-employed individuals offer goods or services, the work relations, hours and working conditions are more directly under control of the worker. This is not to say that power relations are non-existent. For example, the possibility exists for self-employed producers to command the labor of family members to assist in the production of craft-produced items. Or a sudden or unexpected increase in the popularity of a particular item may place pressure on individual producers to ramp up production so as not to disappoint customers who are no longer anonymous others but friends and neighbors. Self-employment has positive and negative dimensions associated with the increased scope for labor control. (4) LETS provide space to develop alternative conceptions of paid work. For example, participants in local currency can forge heterogeneous identities distinct from their traditional roles in the formal labor force. Alternatively, individuals can retain the creative and pleasurable components of a hobby by voluntarily restricting the hours devoted to producing hobby-related products in exchange for local currency.[7] (5) LETS create the possibility for the social revaluation of skills. In this case the market determination of the wage differs from the LETS or local currency practice of making an exchange. While the possibility for restructuring compensation exists, it was discovered that the negotiation of a fair payment was colored by one's position within the formal economy as well as the level of confidence and self-esteem one had about the quality of one's work (Aldridge *et al.* 2001: 576). In another survey, this time involving 42 Ithaca HOURS participants, it was found that over one-third of the respondents indicated that their activities with HOURS increased their self-confidence (Jacob *et al.* 2004b). So, it might be the case that the very process of having to establish the value of one's labor helps to increase feelings of self-worth and create capacities for improved negotiation and communication in situations involving exchange.

In addition, the Ithaca HOURS survey found that the greatest number of participants agreed that HOURS was important to them because it allowed them to help others. The authors speculate, "Perhaps it is this perceived ability to help others that is one of the major contributors to the feeling that Ithaca HOURS increases one's quality of life" (Jacob *et al.* 2004b: 50). A majority of respondents also agreed that their participation in HOURS helps to establish trust and increase their circle of friends. In addition, there was near total agreement with the statement "I consciously try to shop or purchase services at stores of practitioners who accept local currency" (Jacob *et al.* 2004b: 52). Based on this sample of participants in a long-running US alternative currency movement, it would appear that the use of locally issued money has an effect on participants' perception of themselves, their community and the consumer purchases they make. This suggests that money itself and the social practices within which it is integrated have an endogenous effect on consumer preferences.

9 Consuming for social change
Ethical and political consumption

In areas of social science that lie outside the borders of economics, the study of consumer behavior reveals a complex web of social, material, political and cultural relationships. For example, the purchase of a house involves preferences, price[1] and income, to be sure. But housing is simultaneously a consumption good and an investment with an expectation of future returns. This dual characteristic of housing – that it provides a haven in a heartless world and an asset with which to build up one's retirement savings – plays upon cross-cutting sets of value orientations that may affect decisions to relocate, remodel and redecorate. Acknowledging that home remodeling returns less than its full value upon resale, McCracken notes, "We invest in our homes ... because they are transformation opportunities. We make them to make ourselves ... It does not fit very well with our notions of economic man, of ourselves as rational creatures who invest for future profit" (2005: 21). The goal of preserving hearth and home may run afoul of retaining asset value. From the standpoint of economic behavior, home ownership acts as a form of self-imposed liquidity constraint and mortgage payments as a form of forced saving (Thaler 1992). However, beginning in the 1980s, the proliferation of home equity loans helped to re-cast the home as a fungible source of wealth, an asset whose value can be more easily converted into money, which often was not used to improve the value of the asset. Redmond (2007) notes that a shift in value orientation toward a more instrumental view of home ownership accompanied the diffusion of financial instruments, notably home equity financing. But, as Katona might say, the ability to borrow required a willingness to borrow. In this case, the commodity (housing) takes on multiple and, at times, conflicting meanings. The result of this conflict over the meaning of housing has material consequences both for homeowners and financial institutions as well as for neighborhoods and communities, especially dire consequences when asset values are on the decline. Yet, seen from another angle, a house is also a site in which contested gender roles are played out. The home is a primary locus for the provision of, usually unpaid, caring labor (Folbre 1994; 2001). By casting the consumer in the role of an undifferentiated, universal agent responding to a limited set of stimuli in a world of anonymous others, mainstream economics is ill-equipped to provide a satisfactory account of these types of behavior that have had a profound effect on local communities, economies and the environment.

Once we abandon the idealized sphere of exchange between self-interested individuals we can begin to identify forms of contested consumption. The first approach is to look at the "citizen-consumer" whose consumption choices are linked to the requirements for social, environmental and economic justice within a civil society broadly conceived to include local farmers as well as sweatshop workers in the global South and animals, plants and the atmosphere itself. At one level, twentieth-century consumerism consisted of citizen-consumer action in the realm of local, state and federal legislation to improve working conditions, extend civil rights and, later on, improve environmental standards (Tiemstra 1992; Gabriel and Lang 1995; Cohen 2003). However, the idea of citizenship in the citizen-consumer model changed during what Gabriel and Lang call the fourth wave of consumerism in the 1970s and 1980s to embrace a more "communal" vision of citizen action aimed initially at curbing industrial pollution and corporate disregard for the protection of environmental resources (1995: 182), which later expanded to include human rights, labor rights, fair trade, sustainability and global social justice. In the fourth wave, state regulation is replaced by consumer choices made directly in the marketplace. The consumer goods featured most prominently in these movements include clothing, coffee and food.

For example, Johnston, in an analysis of the corporate grocery chain Whole Foods Market, observes, "The fourth wave of ethical consumer activism has used these everyday foods as leverage points to generate reflexivity, encouraging consumers to think critically, buy more selectively, and seek out information on the environmental and social costs involved in their daily meals" (2008: 239). The citizen-consumer is often characterized as a lone individual navigating grocery store aisles, gleaning references and cues to social justice and environmental sustainability from labels and informational displays. The problem, as Johnston notes, is that the focus on voluntary, individualistic choice within the citizen-consumer framework can then form the basis for corporate scripts that accommodate both the desire to consume wisely, ethically and sustainably, and the imperative to profit from consumer choices by eliding issues of unequal access to the means to undertake ethical shopping while simultaneously masking the ecological contradictions involved in conserving resources through purchasing products. The impulse to be other-centered by engaging in ethical consumption is somewhat diminished if labor rights are perceived as a bonus that accompanies the purchase of a stylish t-shirt. The problem can be framed through the following question: "What kind of shopping spaces encourage the abnegation of self-interest, and what shopping spaces create an appearance of beneficence while reinforcing the hegemonic ideals of self-interest and unlimited consumer choice?" (Johnston 2008: 245). The contradiction lies, in large part, with the control over those private spaces of consumption and the limited role of consumers, as individual agents, to effect social change. Kate Soper suggests a way out of the contradiction if we identify points of intersection between the hedonistic interests of consumers and their desires for social justice and environmental sustainability – what she refers to as alternative hedonism. "To act in the spirit of 'alternative hedonism' is in this sense to acknowledge how minimal one's power is as an individual consumer – and then to use it nonetheless" (Soper and Thomas 2006: 215). Alternative hedonism provides one conceptual tool with which to explore the construction of a political self through the consumption of goods and services.

The theory of alternative hedonism grew out of a 2004–6 Economic and Social Research Council (ESRC) project headed by Soper and Lyn Thomas at the Institute for the Study of European Transformations at London Metropolitan University.[2] They proposed this concept in order to map out the development of new, ethically directed forms of consumption that attempt to re-capture that which modern capitalist consumer society has made scarce:

> The examples here might be more or less tangible, more or less retrospective and nostalgic, more or less utopian. It may be nostalgia for certain kinds of material, or objects or practices or forms of human interaction that no longer figure in everyday life as they once did; it may be a case of missing the experience of certain kinds of landscape, or spaces (to play or talk or loiter or meditate or commune with nature); it may be a sense that possibilities of erotic contact or conviviality have been closed down that might otherwise have opened up; or a sense that were it not for the dominance of the car, there would be an altogether different system of provision for other modes of transport, and both rural and city areas would look and feel and smell and sound entirely different.
>
> (Soper and Thomas 2006: 4–5)

This yearning to recover a past represents a reaction against the dominant forms of consumerism. What makes Soper and Thomas' argument compelling is their recognition that alternatives need to be framed through a "more seductive aesthetic" than is usually the case with appeals to downshifting and voluntary simplicity. However, endeavors to return to a romanticized past are neither sufficient nor desirable. Rather, they argue that the goal should be to reflexively construct consumption practices by rehabilitating norms, traditions and institutional foundations of a moral economy.

As for the moral economy, Andrew Sayer (2000) maintains that the economy has always contained a moral dimension. Indeed, Deirdre McCloskey (2006) makes a case for the rediscovery and nurturance of "bourgeois" virtues – for example, temperance (saving) and justice (payment for property and services rendered) – that characterized small-scale competitive capitalism. So, in this sense, McCloskey endeavors to recover a moral edifice upon which an idealized form of Jeffersonian capitalism could be built. However, a moral economy is always based on contested norms and definitions about what counts as virtuous behavior and, within the ambit of the capitalist economy, the bourgeoisie have the upper hand. For example, the historian E. P. Thompson chronicles the process whereby classical political economy came to expunge popular conceptions of moral behavior from economic analysis.

> It is not easy for us to conceive that there may have been a time, within a smaller and more integrated community, when it appeared to be 'unnatural'

that any man should profit from the necessities of others, and when it was assumed that, in time of dearth, prices of 'necessities' should remain at a customary level, even though there might be less all round.

(Thompson 1993: 252–3)

Similarly, alternative consumption practices signal attempts to forge moral identities, take responsibility for others and overlay a system of social norms of fair and just treatment towards participants in the production and consumption of goods and services.

Heterodox economics appears well-positioned to advance interdisciplinary research in the moral economy of alternative forms of consumer behavior. To date, heterodox economists have tended to shy away from engaging with sociologists and cultural studies theorists. This may have something to do with a reluctance to countenance the notion that consumption is a vital activity, which incorporates needs but also desire, fantasy, symbolic display and identity formation. The "pleasure of the table" embraced by the founders of Slow Food was a direct response to those on the Left whose commitment to political stoicism excluded the capacity for epicurean delight. As a result, there is a tendency to depict consumption as either the functional complement to production, in need of assistance when aggregate demand falls short, or as a by-product of some combination of need-based demand and wasteful extravagance intended to promote conspicuous consumption. But, objections to the politically enfeebling and materially wasteful effects of consumerism run the risk of espousing a discourse of paternalism by implicitly associating the consumer sector of the economy with feminine qualities that are contrasted to masculinist characteristics associated with production. As Craig Thompson argues:

The Victorian 'cult of domesticity,' which fostered the cultural link between consumption and femininity, was widely criticized as emasculating, and thus threatening the moral fiber (as well as the bodies) of the next generation of patriarchs. The contemporary manifestation of this historical legacy is the view of consumption as a wanton and scandalously profane activity that impedes the attainment of a higher moral-spiritual plane.

(Thompson 2000: 72)

By refraining from characterizing consumption as a universal set of behaviors and practices and highlighting the scope for difference and heterogeneity of consumers and consumption practices, we leave open the potential for identifying a connection between consumption and resistance to dominant norms and economic logics, on the one hand, and the creation of an alternative "moral economy" on the other.

A heterodox political economy of consumption should acknowledge the pleasure and enjoyment associated with many forms of consumption practice (eating and travel, for example). For many people, the impulse and the desire to care for oneself and to develop capacities for self-expression is part of the process of creating a sense of personal worth and well-being (Matthaei 2001). Furthermore, economists have begun to recognize the importance of the emotional self in decision-making (Kaufman 2006). Passion is not separable from reason in the construction of consumer choice. Marketing professionals have well understood the role of emotion in triggering purchasing decisions (O'Shaughnessy and O'Shaughnessy 2003). As the marketing consultant Paco Underhill observes:

> Clearly, possession is an emotional and spiritual process, not a technical one. Possession begins when the shopper's senses start to latch onto the object. It begins in the eyes and then in the touch. Once the thing is in your hand, or on your back, or in your mouth, you can be said to have begun the process of taking it. Paying for it is a mere technicality, so the sooner the thing is placed in the shopper's hand, or the easier it is for the shopper to try it or sip it or drive it around the block, the more easily it will change ownership, from the seller to the buyer.
>
> (Underhill 1999: 168)

Yet there is a dark side to hedonistic pleasure-seeking, and this can be seen in the often tenuous connection between consumer spending and measures of subjective well-being or happiness (Lane 2000). The market display of dozens of different brands of the same type of product imposes a tyranny of choice on consumers (Schwartz 2004). In a post-affluent[3] society, the motivations for consuming involve care of the self, social interaction, social observation and social recognition from peers and social control of subordinates (Pietrykowski 2007b). This description of consumption as a set of social acts should not obscure the material processes through which consumption also constructs us as social and economic subjects. As David Levine argues, "Our use of objects incorporates them into our life projects. They help us express our sense of self and realize those plans that arise out of the idea we have of who we are" (1998: 103). In addition, these objects are incorporated into our life in order to maintain, develop, sustain or create connections with others. The attempt to combine pleasure-seeking with other-regarding behavior lies at the heart of ethical consumerism and the concept of alternative hedonism.

To date, the terms ethical consumption and citizen-consumer have been used interchangeably to refer to purchasing decisions that are based on more than the individual use-value (including personal status-signaling value) of the product. In fact, the activist consumer is not a new type of individual appearing fresh on the scene of neoliberal global capitalism. An uneasy relationship between the dual roles of worker-consumer marks the history of labor struggles in the United States throughout the twentieth century. Early twentieth-century debates over the value of supporting "union label" campaigns turned on competing definitions of consumers and markets. These debates were linked to demands for a shorter work week, which would allow workers time to enjoy leisure and consumption. Support for union label garments injected an ethical component into market transactions (Glickman 1997). By 1899 the National Consumers' League (NCL) was established with the intent of evaluating working conditions and promoting products deemed worthy of receiving the White Label designation. Kathryn Kish Sklar notes that the League's activities made demands of consumers as well "to recognize her direct relationship with the producer, to learn about the producer's working conditions, and to limit her purchases to goods made under moral conditions" (1998: 28). As a participant in the White Label campaign, the consumer chose to belong to a broader social movement for economic justice. The NCL, in turn, represented an institutional mechanism linking consumers and producers and informing consumers of the conditions under which their clothes were made. Consumers were part of a political movement, the labor movement, which sought to shift the balance of power between capital and labor. In contrast to an ethical commitment to lead a "good life" and shop responsibly, this form of activist consumerism involved a political commitment to bring about large-scale social and economic change. Therefore, political consumption can be seen as distinct from ethical consumption to the extent that participants' purchasing activity is part of a larger strategy to shift the balance of power within the economy. Ethical consumption, by contrast, can be seen as a practice that enacts one's social, environmental values as a by-product of commodity exchange. Ethical consumption need not challenge the institutional framework within which exchange and production take place.

Green automobility is an example of ethical consumption. The purchase and use of a Prius helps to diminish the rate of environmental degradation by limiting the output of carbon emissions. Such purchases help to sustain one's identity as someone who cares about the environment. This can lead to an extension of ethical consumption to the purchase of other commodities. In this way, one can say that "... ethical consumption does not simply bring to light already existing ethical dispositions, but it might well invent new ones" (Barnett *et al.* 2005: 32). However, it also leaves the existing institutional structures and relations of power between consumers and producers intact. In the case of the Prius, environmental values are weighed against personal convenience and norms of social conformity. The Prius remains a form of private transportation produced for profit by a major transnational corporation. Drivers participate in and benefit from the existing transportation infrastructure that, in turn, reflects the Fordist postwar pattern of land and housing development known as urban sprawl. This is not to say that a consumer's commitment to green automobility is incapable of instigating the development of more disruptive consumption behavior – especially in the case of downshifting greens and political greens discussed in Chapter 6 – but it does highlight the way in which some green consumers' – those we termed "socially acceptable greens" – ethical commitments are made to accommodate existing commodity relations.

As ethical consumers are primarily consumers acting within existing institutional structures and norms associated with profitable market exchange, they are required to assess competing claims made by corporations about the company's green credibility. Corporations are capable of fabricating a commitment to green policies and production techniques – a strategy known as "greenwashing" – in order to create an image that runs counter to their actual practices (Laufer 2003).

Furthermore, products that were once bound up with an intersecting set of socially desirable characteristics (sustainable, organic, fair-trade, local) can be transformed into a "product line" offered for sale by a transnational corporation. Both sustainable, fair-trade coffee and organic produce are examples of the contested meanings of ethical consumption (Guthman 2003; Hudson and Hudson 2003). Fair-trade coffee reveals the complexity of ethical and political consumption, as the product can represent sustainable methods of production and/or fair prices and a living wage (Fridell, Hudson and Hudson 2008). In such cases, consumers might have to weigh competing values and assess their own relationship to different reference groups with whom they identify. Different groups will frame the purchase differently and this then enmeshes consumers in a process of negotiating their own sense of who they are and who they want to be through their ethical commitments and consumer purchases.

A political economy of consumer behavior extends the range of activities that count as consumption, even to the point of troubling the division between production and consumption. The anti-sweatshop movement, for example, requires that, in order to avoid sanctions, transnational advocacy networks implement monitoring systems to assess the labor conditions under which clothing is made. Threats of consumer boycotts are a potent enforcement mechanism (Rodríguez-Garavito 2005). The politicized consumer is also represented through the growing interest in green consumption as was discussed with the example of the Toyota Prius hybrid automobile. In particular, this case study of the green consumer movement highlights the ways in which concepts and symbols associated with scarcity, sacrifice, austerity and restraint are negotiated by consumers inhabiting a culture of automobility. Green automobility also displays the contingent nature of political consumption. While the Prius is a super-ultra-low-emission-vehicle (SULEV), it is embedded within a Fordist system of mass production within a global neoliberal economic system. As such, the labor practices of Prius production are subject to scrutiny similar to that applied to sweatshop clothing manufacturers. The National Labor Committee, a formidable proponent of worker rights issued a scathing report on the working conditions at Toyota manufacturers and their supplier plants. The Prius was singled out for special attention as being produced with low-paid part-time workers forced to work 14-hour shifts (National Labor Committee 2008). This suggests the possibility that some consumers will manifest cognitive dissonance over their decision to purchase a Prius. For many US consumers, Toyota Motors, a prototypical Japanese automobile manufacturer, has long been portrayed in the popular imagination as a company intent on supporting humane, if paternalistic, labor relations systems through the use of quality circles, team production and strict limits on the compensation of executives relative to shop floor workers (Womack *et al.* 1991).[4] To now be confronted with evidence that it treats workers unjustly, introduces a dissonant note that conflicts with the ethical choice of Prius ownership. The dissonance reflects a deeper political rift in the economic landscape between the demands of workers for manufacturing jobs and the call for greater environmental protections. Setting aside a discussion of the validity of this trade-off, the question is how do consumers manage competing ethical and political claims?

Within behavioral economics, Akerlof and Dickens (1982) and Rabin (1994) develop a rational choice model of cognitive dissonance. In their models, beliefs are chosen by actors in such a way so as to maximize utility, minus the psychic cost of acting in a way that violates beliefs (fur is cruel) and the cost of changing beliefs so as to align beliefs (wearing fur is acceptable) to one's actions (buying a fur coat). Rabin extends the model to include a social dimension whereby society's moral assessment of an act affects an individual's belief.[5] The assumption that individuals can rationally choose their beliefs and that ethical values can be modeled as inputs into a utility maximization scenario, renders ethical values akin to tastes and preferences. Although the concept of cognitive dissonance is important for our attempt to understand the social construction of ethical and political consumption, the reliance on individual rational choice obscures the way in which people engage in consumption in order to construct a political subjectivity and how, in turn, political values shape moral dispositions, including the ability to resist dominant social norms or to develop connections with others whose frame of reference is at odds with the dominant group. For example, Ettlinger (2004) argues that cognitive dissonance, in which contradictory thoughts and feelings co-exist, can be seen as a micro-motive for social action. Rather than something that imposes a disutility on individuals, Ettlinger understands dissonance as a routine emotional state that reflects both conformist and non-conformist consumption practices and dispositions. In this way, she argues, "conflictive thoughts and feelings can be tapped and used to construct alternatives to community practices" (2004: 35).

The alternative currency movement – taking the form of either local exchange trading system (LETS) or time dollars (HOURS) – provides a useful illustration of how this dissonance can be harnessed for social change. Alternative currencies are locally issued and circulate within a community or region. While the primary goal of local currency movements is to bolster the standard of living for those individuals marginalized by the capitalist sector – unemployed, underemployed, artisans, and independent service providers – it also has the effect of building networks of interdependent consumers and producers outside of the traditional economy. This, in turn, has the effect of creating local knowledge about the conditions of production and the lifeworld of individuals participating in local exchange. Furthermore, people act not just on the basis of the outcome of their actions but are also concerned about the quality of the process and the well-being of others with whom they interact (Bowles and Gintis 2008). If, in addition, alternative currency exchanges reward forms of social interaction – for example, interaction based on trust, reciprocity, empathy, generosity, fairness – different from the system of capitalist commodity exchange, individuals may come to value the system of alternative currency which can then signal their resistance to competitive, profit-centered exchange and their desire to support others who are located at the margins of the formal capitalist labor market. This corresponds to the research of behavioral economists who found that the structure of exchange affects the behavior and other-regarding feelings of the participants (Fehr and Schmidt 1999; Fehr and Fischbacher 2002). For example, success in an alternative currency moral economy can be achieved through including the value of the exchange, the quality of the social relationship, into the price of the service and thereby determining the "just price" for the product or service.[6]

Finally, the connection between Slow Food as a pleasure-producing set of social activities together with its imperative to preserve biodiversity through the Ark of Taste is an example of alternative hedonism and ethical consumption. It also contains elements of political consumption in its embrace of small-scale, local, less efficient, non-commercialized foodways and consumption practices. The Slow Food movement was examined as an alternative form of consumption that contested both the mass production and standardization of foodstuffs and discourses of resistance predicated on asceticism and self-denial. Advocates of Slow Food pursue an ethos of consumption that is directly at odds with trends toward homogenization and the flattening of difference between the particular places of food consumption. Practitioners of Slow Food also seek to redefine the social relations of consumption by integrating food consumption into community practices that sustain and support local agricultural economies. In this way, consumption becomes a deeply political act aimed at re-orienting consumer decisions by attending to the conditions under which commodities are produced.

Several of the Slow Food objectives are intertwined. The diffusion of cultural capital and the acquisition of human capital through formal and informal education are linked to one another (Bourdieu 1984). Taste education that takes place informally through convivia, workshops, and in Slow Food restaurants imparts knowledge of cuisine, local production techniques, local producers, and unique, sometimes endangered, foods. Human capital and social capital are also connected through the interplay between education, employment, heritage preservation and local/regional economic development (Pietrykowski 2004).

The Slow Food movement seeks the preservation of local foods and cuisines by creating and strengthening networks of social relations between consumers and producers. Slow Food production is aligned with the values of a civic agriculture that rejects fast-paced standardized food production embedded in systems of large-scale, capital-intensive industrial agriculture (Lyson 2004). The movement advances a claim to material pleasure through consumption while simultaneously advocating a politics of eco-agriculture. It offers a way to think about the dual role that both desire and resistance can play in creating political consumption practices. Through a case study of the Slow Food movement, I argued that this dual process of pleasure-seeking and politicization attempts to democratize a cultural disposition toward food consumption typically associated with a particular class and status position. As de Grazia argues, "It [Slow Food movement] sought a third way between the superficial sociability promoted by brand recognition and the defensive solidarities favored by closed communities of traditional protest movements" (2005: 459).

The worlds of consumption, including the fluid borders that demarcate production from consumption, are composed of diverse arrays of human beings and social groups performing the economy in ways that extend beyond the limits of the traditional frames of economic analysis. Consumption involves more than the sale and purchase of commodities within the sphere of capitalist exchange. There is a rich legacy of interdisciplinary economic analysis that challenged the mainstream view of consumption and that should be rediscovered. The variety of consumption practices and the ways through which people interact with material artifacts helps to inscribe meaning to the objects of consumption, which may conflict with the traditional meaning and use for which the object was produced. In addition, consumption is more than a process of acquiring objects to meet a physiological need, convey one's status or fulfill a fantasy. In fact, the institutional form and social structure within which consumption takes place has an effect on our social behavior. Consumption practices can also express moral values and political commitments and can be analyzed as arenas of contest and conflict, cooperation and solidarity. Exploring the ethical and political dimension of consumer behavior can help us to better understand economics as inextricably bound up with social, cultural and political modes of inquiry.

Notes

1 Consumption matters

1 And this applies equally to the case where goods are represented by a vector of characteristics associated with the product (Lancaster 1971).
2 Small but growing, it should be added. As of 2004, net exports accounted for over a 5 per cent drain on annual GDP.
3 I acknowledge that gender is but one point of entry into this analysis. Gender, race, class and place and their intersections each comprise key dimensions of consumer practice.

2 Economic knowledge: boundary-keeping and border crossing

1 The best-known example of the application of "expert knowledge" to urban development in the United States was Robert Moses (Caro 1974; Jackson and Ballon 2007). For a brief history of the role of the comprehensive plan in planning practice see Neuman (1998).
2 That economic practice is simultaneously political action is probably hard for most economists to swallow. But if by political we refer to the processes by which power is assembled and deployed in the interests of maintaining dominance over the legitimate forms of discourse and techniques of investigation then the economics discipline can be described as inherently politicized. A few examples of the political dimension of economic practice would include the alignment of economics with operations research and cybernetics (Mirowski 2002) and the strategic deployment of neoclassical economists and economic literature to European nations, particularly Germany, Italy and Japan after World War II (Bernstein 1999). In the case of Japan, the Americanization of the economics curriculum took a bit longer than in Western Europe. Japanese universities maintained a wide-ranging course of study that included Marx along with Marshall and Pigou after the war. If anything, cultural and political resistance to US occupation burnished the reputation of Marxist economists in Japan (Bernstein 1999, 106–7).
3 Note that in order to bias the results against the hypothesis of increasing social preferences, Competitive individuals were dropped from analyses of orientation change as Competitors, as the least social individuals, would only be possible to change their orientation in the direction of increasing regard for others.
4 In the interest of disclosure, and in order to locate my own standpoint, readers should know that the author serves on the editorial board of the *Review of Radical Political Economics*.
5 These popular sources of economic knowledge form the basis of what Amariglio and Ruccio (1999) refer to as "ersatz economics."
6 Earlier in their report they state that economics, circa 1986, lagged behind physics, engineering and mathematics on the quantitative portion of the GRE. Revealingly, they

find that economics students also lagged behind those in physics and mathematics on the *verbal* portion of the GRE as well (Krueger 1991: 1042).

7 "By almost any market test, economics is the premier social science," begins Lazear. He goes on to say that the abstract, spare nature of economic prose is its great strength. "The language permits economists to strip away complexity. Complexity may add to the richness of description, but it prevents the analyst from seeing what is essential" (99–100).

3 Economic knowledge and consumer behavior: home economics and feminist analysis

1 For an account of the creation and maintenance of a gendered laboratory for women researchers in the biological sciences at Cambridge University see Richmond (1997).

2 While Yonay (1998) offers up an often useful and enlightening treatment of the rise and fall of institutional economics over roughly the first half of the twentieth century, the approach tends to reify the struggle between a broad but self-identified institutionalist economics and a self-consciously "neoclassical" opponent. This allows him to create binary classifications such as inductive versus deductive, empirical versus mathematical and pragmatic versus positivistic. By contrast, I adopt the perspective that the discourse of economics during this period was best characterized as a shifting terrain of techniques and alliances.

3 Institutionalist economists as a whole were familiar with Dewey's work during this period (Yonay 1994: 51; 1998: 104–5). Dewey, in his effort to draw close ties between democratic institutions and scientific practice, opposed a naturalistic portrayal of individuals outfitted with fully formed wants (Mirowski 2005: 151). Furthermore, Kyrk shared the institutionalists' desire to build economics on the foundation of a new psychology of economic behavior (Rutherford 2000: 297–8).

4 This last case corresponds to Veblen's (1953 [1899]) notion of conspicuous consumption, to Hirsch's (1976) concept of "positional goods," to Schor's (1998) analysis of "competitive consumption" and to Frank's (1999) account of "luxury fever."

5 Kyrk resists using the female pronoun when describing the consumer until the very end of *A Theory of Consumption* when she acknowledges household spending and the management of consumption is "usually the function of the woman at its head" (1923: 292).

6 The term overdetermination is meant to convey a sense that no single determinant or set of determinants has analytical priority (Resnick and Wolff 1987). Overdetermination is used to stake out methodological ground between essentialist explanations of phenomena and relativist perspectives.

7 George F. Warren was a professor of agricultural economics and farm management whose 1903 dissertation employed tabular data and statistical correlation to identify the determinants of farm income (Banzhaf 2006).

8 In a revealing exchange of letters written in 1929 between Canon and her colleague Faith Williams, then employed at the Bureau of Labor Statistics, Williams congratulates Canon upon receiving her doctorate and making "such a good impression on the department of economics." Canon replies, "Don't think there has been any impression made on the Economics Dept.! There hasn't been nor am I especially concerned about impressing them! I count my 16 hrs. with [Herbert] Davenport as one of the highlights of my life. But he is not the Economics Department (more's the pity – for them)" (Canon 1929a). Herbert Davenport received his Ph.D. in economics in 1898 from the University of Chicago and taught at Chicago, Cornell and Missouri. Davenport represented well the amorphous character of economic research during the interwar period by his "combination of orthodoxy and skepticism" (Dorfman 1959: 468). Canon's personal copy of Davenport's unpublished lectures on the "Economics of Feminism" shows handwritten notes identifying the influence of Veblen on Davenport. (New York State College of Home Economics Records, Division of Rare and Manuscript Collections, Cornell University Library, Papers of Herbert J. Davenport, Accession #14/10/1166).

9 A letter from Louise Stanley to W. Frank Persons, January 11, 1936, puts the cost at 2.3 million dollars (Stanley 1936). Stapleford estimates that the WPA spent nearly 6 million to complete the study (Stapleford 2007: 430).

10 Hildegarde Kneeland folder, General Records, Subject Correspondence of the Bureau of Nutrition and Home Economics 1923–32, Record Group 176, National Archives and Records Administration, College Park, MD.

11 Pearson correlation coefficients were computed by the author using data presented in Dickens (1949: 429). Using analysis of variance to test for between group differences in foods consumed, the p-value is 0.074, statistically significant at the 10 per cent level.

12 Sterner (1943: 103) notes that while farm families could grow some of their own food, based on the 1935–36 data, black farm families (sharecroppers and operators) allocated 45 per cent of their purchases toward food. For white farm families the figure was about 38 per cent.

13 Olney (1998: 409) refers to this as a well-known, perplexing historical fact.

14 Much later research (Olney 1998) on the topic identified two distinct credit markets at work. One market was meant to enable consumers to purchase expensive durable goods on installment. Installment credit, as it involved collateral that could be recouped in the case of default, was more readily extended to African Americans. The other credit market was the less formal credit extended by merchants to their customers. Merchant credit was less likely to be extended to African American families. Even in the presence of racial segregation it would be exceedingly difficult for blacks to avoid patronizing white-owned businesses. If white-owned businesses engaged in outright racial discrimination, credit would not be extended to blacks. If merchants assessed blacks to be more of a credit risk – due to racial stereotypes applied in lieu of perfect information about the actual credit-worthiness of every customer ("statistical discrimination") – they would also reject requests on the part of blacks for store credit. Therefore, savings rates among black families would need to be higher in order to maintain their purchasing ability in case of an unanticipated family financial crisis.

15 Ironically, Samuelson, in a 1948 article reprising the theory of revealed preferences, refers casually to Gestalt psychology in order to move from discrete choices (represented as coordinates on a graph) between goods toward an indifference curve (244–5). As Davis (2003) argues, the effect of revealed preference theory was to banish mental states from consideration by defining them as products of the unconscious mind. This, as we shall see in the next chapter, is at odds with the approach of Gestalt psychology.

16 As an example of the logical positivist turn in economics, Lewin (1996: 1306) notes the willingness of some institutionalist economists to make use of the behaviorist psychology of John B. Watson.

4 Psychology and economics: Max Wertheimer, Gestalt theory and George Katona

1 This problem predates Maier in the form of a popular puzzle at least as early as the second decade of the twentieth century. More recently, it has been utilized by management consultants as an exhortation to think "outside the box."

2 Kahneman's 2003 article was a revised version of his Nobel Prize acceptance speech. It was published in the *American Economic Review*. A similar version was published in the *American Psychologist*.

3 While he does not comment on it, the survey question appears to lead to "framing effects." Namely, the informality associated with the phrase "won't make any difference" may bias respondents away from this choice and toward the more scientific (A will affect B) outcome.

4 A few years later Richard Lester's challenge to marginal productivity theory of wage determination relied upon a survey of employers that Fritz Machlup characterized as "worthless" (Lester 1946; Machlup 1946: 544). As Prasch (2007) argues, subsequent discussions of the celebrated debate cast it in terms of empirical analysis versus theory.

This elides the theoretical implications of survey research methods for economic analysis. Indeed, Machlup's response to Lester includes a supportive reference to Katona's *Price Control and Business* (1945) because it made use of detailed interview techniques (Machlup 1946: 538).

5 Theien (2006) discusses the political discourse surrounding debates over the imposition of price controls in Norway during the first two decades after the Second World War. She notes that the viability of price controls was directly tied to a shift away from a producer-orientation and toward the recognition of the vital role that consumers were playing through their purchases of consumer durables. Over time, the discourse moved even further toward legitimating government intervention in price-setting by linking such efforts to policies aimed at improving the lives of women citizens.

6 Interestingly, Elizabeth Hoyt, whose research crossed the borderlands between home economics and economics, also attempted to apply Gestalt theory to consumer behavior by analyzing the way in which separate consumer goods are perceived as parts of a whole ensemble that, when used collectively, complete the consumption experience (Hoyt 1944).

5 Fordism and the social relations of consumption

1 Gordon, Edwards and Reich (1982) set forth a re-interpretation of Marx that seeks to integrate class conflict into theories of long waves of capital accumulation by articulating the institutional forces that promote and then constrain opportunities for expanded profitability. While the SSA approach has been extensively applied to problems in sociology, within economics, since the early 1990s, there "has been little innovation or development of the basic concepts of SSA theory ..." (McDonough 2008: 160).

2 The major exception is the convergence in the 1980s between neo-Marxist and neoclassical theories of labor market structure and performance. Nevertheless, the similarity between efficiency wage theory, shirking and principal-agent models of unemployment on the one hand, and neo-Marxist measures of the "cost of job loss" and the intensity of supervision on the other, could not erase the fundamental differences between methodologic individualism in which work intensity was freely chosen versus a class-based model of conflict and power (Weisskopf *et al.* 1983; Bowles 1985).

3 Robert Boyer is the most well-known current proponent of the Regulation School (Boyer 1990). Compared to the fields of sociology and geography, economic applications of Fordism are scarce outside of its home in France (Boyer and Saillard 2002).

4 Since Resnick and Wolff (1987: 2) take "effect" to mean "to constitute" and because they claim overdetermination can be understood as a process of mutual and contradictory constitution, the term "effect" was used here.

5 A twentieth-century exception is the strategic re-interpretation of consumer rights as civil rights by African Americans in the postwar US boycotts, protests and demands for equality of treatment in the retail sphere framed political discourse in such a way that consumption became a right of citizenship (Cohen 2003).

6 The profession of home economist was broad enough to include both home demonstration agents acting as promoters of modern consumerism as well as social economists assessing the situation in a more critical light.

6 Green consumption and user culture: the case of the Toyota Prius

1 By automobility I refer to the system of movement – including the infrastructure, fuel sources, driving cultures, rules of the road, resource flows, political coalitions – constructed around the car and the individuals that operate it. See Urry (2005) for a discussion of automobility and the prospects for postcar mobility.

2 An in-depth account of the planning history, engineering difficulties, and product development cycle surrounding the Prius launch was written by Hideshi Itazaki (1999).

3 This is an adaptation of the acronym WWJD (What Would Jesus Do) that has become popular in the Bible belt and other sites of fundamentalist Christianity in the United States.
4 http://whatwouldjesusdrive.org/action/pledge.php
5 www.worldvaluessurvey.org. Comparisons are made in responses between 1990 and 1999. 1999 also marks the year that the Prius was introduced to the Japanese market.
6 The Prius is not nearly so popular in Europe where the more environmentally friendly diesel automobile is the choice of European consumers (Pietrykowski 2008).
7 West Germany, France, Britain, Italy, the Netherlands, Belgium
8 A video of the event can be found at: http://www.mtvu.com/on_mtvu/stand_in/larry_david.jhtml
9 The environmental gains are modified by the need to rely on electricity from electric power plants, the operation of which releases pollution into the atmosphere.

7 Slow Food: the politics and pleasure of consumption

1 This is not meant to deny the power of producers to constrain consumer choices (Fine and Leopold 1993) but the intent of this book is to foreground the consumer as the active agent.
2 In the larger realm of agrifood activism, women play a leading role but this activism "rarely takes an explicitly feminist approach" (Allen and Sachs 2007: 14).
3 Some proponents of Slow Food emphasize the use of fresh foods and distance themselves from romanticizing peasant cuisine (Montanari 2001).
4 Stewart and Blisard (2008), using the Consumer Expenditure Survey broken out by income group, report that small increases in income among the poorest (up to 130 per cent of the poverty line) Americans had no discernable impact on fruit and vegetable purchases. Instead, greater income transfers or a reduction in the price of non-food costs (e.g. housing) could better help to diversify food purchases.
5 http://slowfoodusa.org/education/g2t3.html
6 This characteristic makes the Edible Schoolyard different from Farm-to-School programs that attempt to connect local growers to school districts in order to shorten the supply chain and provide healthy choices in the school cafeteria. Farm-to-School programs are often inadequately funded and, yet, are expected to succeed as profit centers offering more choices to child consumers. The Edible Schoolyard also confronts a neoliberal discourse linking programs to measureable outcomes that may well compromise the less tangible goals of the Slow Food movement (Allen and Guthman 2006).
7 There is, as of yet, no indication whether traditional gender divisions of labor materialize in the tasks associated with farming and meal preparation at the Edible Schoolyard.
8 While every market economy is understood to have a social dimension, I use the term "social economy" in order to foreground those exchanges and forms of consumption that enhance and reward other-oriented behavior. There is a growing body of literature, for example in experimental labor market analysis, which finds that when agents are permitted to act upon norms and reciprocity of fairness markets do not converge on equilibrium and that the particular distribution of preferences (social versus selfish) has a determinate effect on individual behavior and economic outcomes (Fehr *et al.* 1993; Fehr *et al.* 1998; Fehr and Schmidt 1999). Norms of reciprocity entail cooperation, of course, but they also require effective means of punishing those who act in a purely self-interested way (Bowles and Gintis 2002). For example, corporate organic producers (Guthman 2002) could be understood as "free-riders" seeking to gain a share of the Slow Food market without investing in local, sustainable production methods.
9 Borge (2001) finds that from 1970 to 1990 the German economy witnessed a doubling of the distance over which food is shipped with no appreciable rise in food consumption.

8 Consuming with alternative currency

1 There is, admittedly, a risk of idealizing the local and care must be taken to examine the ways in which propinquity inhibits as well as expands the quality of life, economic opportunities and options for creating diverse modes of provisioning.

2 The term "prosumer" is taken from Alvin Toffler's *Third Wave* (1981).

3 For a detailed discussion of the internal struggles over local barter networks in Argentina see North (2007).

4 In his discussion of commodity circulation, Marx refers to prices as "those wooing glances cast at money by commodities" (1977: 205).

5 Here money functions as a medium of exchange and not as a store of value. On theoretical grounds this resembles Irving Fisher's (1912) monetary system and is subject to some of the same criticisms leveled against it by the Cambridge approach to money that recognized the important role of money as a store of value (Pigou 1917). Note that the criticisms apply most forcefully if the alternative currency was introduced as a complete substitute for, rather than a complement to, already circulating currencies.

6 Note that Lamoreaux (2003) criticizes this "moral economy" depiction of New England by first maintaining that eighteenth-century New England merchants were not especially capitalistic in their accounting practices and business decisions. Community and family mattered for merchants, often at the expense of business. Yet, rather than arguing that the moral economy impinged on the actions of business people, she attributes the inattention to accounting to satisficing behavior and the employment of often unqualified relatives as a rational response to the moral hazard resulting from contracting with strangers. As for farmers, Lamoreaux first characterizes the household as a sphere of shared values and cooperation and conflates the family with the community. Merrill, on the other, notes that households are themselves sites of exploitation. Lamoreaux goes on to argue that if, indeed, farmers were more reluctant than merchants to embrace commodity production and commodity exchange it was probably due to differential capacities toward instrumentality. In short, farmers may well have been disproportionately other-oriented whereas merchants had more autonomous personalities (Lamoreaux 2003: 456–58). This, however, does not seem at odds with Merrill's point regarding the persistence of cooperative economic organization in the farms of New England.

7 Offe and Heinze (1992: 67) maintain that the characteristics that inhere in a hobby – namely the absence of standards of efficiency and idiosyncratic quality of the resulting product – do not translate into work. Nevertheless, we can imagine a range of hobbies for which the quality of the product has sufficient general social appeal or that the product could be customized to meet the desires of the purchaser.

9 Consuming for social change: ethical and political consumption

1 In the case of housing, economists estimate prices in terms of an array of characteristics associated with the particular commodity (rooms, lot size, school quality, etc.) (Kain and Quigley 1970). The method is known as hedonic pricing (Goodman 1998).

2 http://www.consume.bbk.ac.uk/research/soper.html

3 The term post-affluent refers to a related set of issues: (a) the finding that high living standards are correlated with high levels of dissatisfaction with one's life situation; (b) that the proliferation of choices interfere with our capacity to choose; and (c) that we make use of goods and services to explore and expand our wants and desires (Gabriel and Lang 1995; Lane 2000; Etzioni 2004; Offer 2006). It is not intended to deny the gross inequalities in income distribution that leave many trapped in poverty.

4 For the lesser known description of the dark side of team production, described as "management by stress" see Parker and Slaughter (1988) and Moody (1997).

5 Rabin is able to formally demonstrate a counterintuitive outcome: increasing the level of cognitive dissonance has the effect of changing societal perceptions about

the immorality of the action. As a result, this change in beliefs will make the activity socially acceptable and will therefore encourage more of it (1994: 185).

6 Thompson, criticizing the tendency for historians to fast forward from the seventeenth-century traditions of a moral economy to the nineteenth-century free market economy, remarks, "But the death of the old moral economy of provision was as long-drawn-out as the death of paternalist intervention in industry and trade. The consumer defended his old notions of right as stubbornly as (perhaps the same man in another role) he defended his craft status as an artisan" (1993: 253).

References

NA (2008) Toyota says Prius sales hit one million worldwide. *The Globe and Mail (Canada)*. Toronto.

Addams, J. (1896) "A belated industry", *The American Journal of Sociology*, 1, 536–50.

Agarwal, B. (1997) "'Bargaining' and gender relations: within and beyond the household", *Feminist Economics*, 3, 1–51.

Aglietta, M. (1987) *A Theory of Capitalist Regulation: The U.S. Experience*, New York, Verso.

Airely, D., Loewenstein, G. and Prelec, D. (2003) "'Coherent arbitrariness': stable demand curves without stable preferences", *Quarterly Journal of Economics*, 118, 73–105.

Akerlof, G. (1982) "Labor contracts as partial gift exchange", *Quarterly Journal of Economics*, 97, 543–69.

—— (2007) "The missing motivation in macroeconomics", *American Economic Review*, 97, 5–36.

Akerlof, G. A. and Dickens, W. T. (1982) "The economic consequences of cognitive dissonance", *The American Economic Review*, 72, 307–19.

Akrich, M. (1992) "The de-scription of technical objects", in Bijker, W. E. and Law, J. (eds) *Shaping Technology/Building Society*. Cambridge, MIT Press.

Albelda, R. (1997) *Economics and Feminism: Disturbances in the Field*, New York, Twayne Publishers.

Aldridge, T., Tooke, J., Lee, R., Leyshon, A., Thrift, N. and Williams, C. (2001) "Recasting work: the example of local exchange trading schemes", *Work Employment Society*, 15, 565–79.

Allen, P. (2008) "Mining for justice in the food system: perceptions, practices, and possibilities", *Agriculture and Human Values*, 25, 157–61.

Allen, P. and Guthman, J. (2006) "From 'old school' to 'farm-to-school': neoliberalism from the ground up", *Agriculture and Human Values*, 23, 401–15.

Allen, P. and Sachs, C. (2007) "Women and food chains: the gendered politics of food", *International Journal of Sociology of Food and Agriculture*, 15, 1–23.

Alternatives Federal Credit Union (2007) *Livable Wage Study*. Ithaca, New York.

Amarigilio, J. and Ruccio, D. F. (1999) "The transgressive knowledge of ersatz economics", in Robert, F. and Garnett, J. (eds) *What do Economists Know?* London, Routledge.

Amariglio, J. (1988) "The body, economic discourse, and power: an economist's introduction to Foucault", *History of Political Economy* 20, 583–613.

Anderson, B. (1991) *Imagined Communities: Reflections on the Origin and Spread of Nationalism*, London, Verso.

Anonymous (1938) "Consumption habits of the American people", *Monthly Labor Review* 46, 608–21.

Ash, M. G. (1995) *Gestalt Psychology in German Culture, 1890-1967: Holism and the Quest for Objectivity,* New York, Cambridge University Press.

Austin, J. L. (1962) *How to Do Things With Words,* Oxford, Clarendon Press.

Babbitt, K. R. (1997) "Legitimizing nutrition education: the impact of the great depression", in Stage, S. and Vincenti, V. B. (eds) *Rethinking Home Economics: Women and the History of a Profession.* Ithaca, New York, Cornell University Press.

Banzhaf, H. S. (2006) "The other economics department: demand and value theory in early agricultural economics", in Mirowski, P. and Hands, D. W. (eds) *Agreement on Demand: Consumer Theory in the Twentieth Century.* Durham, North Carolina, Duke University Press.

Barker, D. and Kuiper, E. (eds) (2003) *Toward a Feminist Philosophy of Economics,* London, Routledge.

Barnes, B. (2001) "Practice as collective action", in Schatzki, T. R., Karin Knorr Cetina and Eike Von Savigny (ed.) *The Practice Turn in Contemporary Theory.* London, Routledge.

Barnett, C., Cloke, P., Clarke, N. and Malpass, A. (2005) "Consuming ethics: articulating the subjects and spaces of ethical consumption", *Antipode,* 37, 23–45.

Baudrillard, J. (1988) "Simulacra and simulations", in Poster, M. (ed.) *Jean Baudrillard: Selected Writings,* Stanford, California, Stanford University Press.

Becker, G. S. (1965) "A theory of the allocation of time", *Economic Journal,* 75, 493–517.

Beesten, M. M. (1998) *Where Household Needs and Political Innovations Meet: Ithaca Hours, A Local Money System.* Master's Thesis, Department of Development Sociology. Cornell University Ithaca, New York.

Belasco, W. (1989) *Appetite for Change: How the Counterculture Took on the Food Industry 1966–1988,* New York, Pantheon.

Belkin, D. (2005) Gas spike gives the Prius crowd something to crow about. *Boston Globe.*

Bentley, A. (1998) *Eating for Victory: Food Rationing and the Politics of Domesticity,* Urbana, University of Illinois Press.

Bergeron, S. and Pietrykowski, B. (1999) "Can there be genre difference in economic literature?" in Robert, F. and Garnett J. (eds) *What Do Economists Know? New Economics of Knowledge.* New York, Routledge.

Berlage, N. K. (1998) "The establishment of an applied social science: home economists, science and reform at Cornell University, 1870–1930", in Silverberg, H. (ed.) *Gender and American Social Science: The Formative Years.* Princeton, Princeton University Press.

Berman, B. (2006) Better gas mileage in a Toyota Prius. www.hybridcars.com.

Bernstein, M. (1999) "Economic knowledge, professional authority, and the state", in Robert, F. and Garnett, J. (eds) *What Do Economists Know? New Economics of Knowledge.* London, Routledge.

Bernstein, M. A. (2001) *A Perilous Progress: Economists and Public Purpose in Twentieth-Century America,* Princeton, Princeton University Press.

Bijker, W. E. (1997) *Of Bicycles, Bakelites, and Bulbs,* Cambridge, MIT Press.

Blanc, J. (1998) "Free money for social progress. Theory and practice of Gesell's accelerated money", *American Journal of Economics and Sociology,* 57, 469–83.

Boggs, J. (1970) *Racism and the Class Struggle: Further Pages from a Black Worker's Notebook,* New York, Monthly Review Press.

Borge, S. (2001) "Insidious distance", in Petrini, C. (ed.) *Slow Food: Collected Thoughts on Taste, Tradition, and the Honest Pleasures of Food.* White River Junction, Vermont, Chelsea Green Publishing.

Bourdieu, P. (1977) *Outline of a Theory of Practice,* Cambridge, Cambridge University Press.

—— (1984) *Distinction: A Social Critique of the Judgment of Taste,* Cambridge, Massachusetts, Harvard University Press.

—— (1989) "Social space and symbolic power", *Sociological Theory,* 7, 14–25.

Bowles, S. (1985) "The production process in a competitive economy: Walrasian, Neo-Hobbesian, and Marxian models", *The American Economic Review,* 75, 16–36.

—— (1998) "Endogenous preferences: the cultural consequences of markets and other economic institutions", *Journal of Economic Literature,* 36, 75–111.

Bowles, S. and Gintis, H. (1993) "The revenge of homo economicus: contested exchange and the revival of political economy", *Journal of Economic Perspectives,* 7, 83–102.

—— (2002) "Homo reciprocans", *Nature,* 415, 125–28.

—— (2008) "Social preferences, *homo economicus* and *zoon politikon*", in Goodin, R. E. and Tilly, C. (eds) *Oxford Handbook of Contextual Political Analysis.* New York, Oxford University Press.

Bowles, S., Gordon, D. M. and Weisskopf, T. E. (1983) *Beyond the Waste Land: A Democratic Alternative to Economic Decline* Garden City, New York, Anchor Press/Doubleday.

Boyer, R. (1990) *The Regulation School: A Critical Introduction,* New York, Columbia University Press.

Boyer, R. and Saillard, Y. (eds) (2002) *Regulation Theory: The State of the Art* London, Routledge.

Bradsher, K. (2002) *High and Mighty: The Dangerous Rise of the SUV,* New York, Public Affairs.

Brady, D. S. and Friedman, R. (1947) "Savings and Income Distribution", *Studies in Income and Wealth.* New York, National Bureau of Economic Research.

Bruni, L. and Sugden, R. (2007) "The road not taken: how psychology was removed from economics, and how it might be brought back", *The Economic Journal,* 117, 146–73.

Brusco, S. (1982) "The Emilian model: productive decentralisation and social integration", *Cambridge Journal of Economics,* 6, 167–84.

Bryant, R. L. and Goodman, M. K. (2004) "Consuming narratives: the political ecology of 'alternative' consumption", *Transactions of the Institute of British Geographers,* 29, 344–66.

Burke, S. (2007) Personal interview, August 2, Ithaca, New York.

CalCars (2008) CalCars: The California cars initiative. http://www.calcars.org/vehicles.html

Callon, M. (2007) "What does it mean to say the economic is performative?" in Mackenzie, D., Muniesa, F. and Siu, L. (eds) *Do Economists Make Markets?* Princeton, Princeton University Press.

Callon, M., Méadel, C. and Rabeharisoa, V. (2002) "The economy of qualities", *Economy and Society,* 31, 194–217.

Camerer, C. (1999) "Behavioral Economics: Reunifying Psychology and Economics", *Proceedings of the National Academy of Sciences,* 96, 10575–77.

Canfield, D. (1924) *The Home-Maker,* New York, Grosset & Dunlap.

Canon, H. (1942) *Development of the Dept. of Economics of the Household and Household Management as Recorded in Documents Volume I: 1900 to 1934* in New York State College of Home Economics Cornell University Library (ed.) Ithaca, New York, Accession No. 23/18/1789 (Box 2).

—— (1929a) Letter to Faith Williams dated 9-30-29. in Administration, N. R. A. A. (ed.) College Park, Maryland, Record Group 176, Box 625.

—— (1929b) Memo to Martha Van Rensselaer dated 9-24-29. in New York State College of Home Economics Cornell University Library, Ithaca, New York, Accession No. 23/3/2187.

Caro, R. (1974) *The Power Broker: Robert Moses and the Fall of New York*, New York, Knopf.

Carpenter, J. P. (2005) "Endogenous social preferences", *Review of Radical Political Economics*, 37, 63–84.

Cat, J. (2007) "Switching gestalts on gestalt psychology: on the relation between science and philosophy", *Perspectives on Science*, 15, 131–77.

Cato, M. S. (2006) "Argentina in the red: what can the UK's regional economies learn from the Argentinian banking crisis?" *International Journal of Community Currency Research*, 10, 43–55.

Chandler, A. D. (1964) *Giant Enterprise: Ford, General Motors, and the Automobile Industry*, New York, Harcourt Brace.

Chang, A. (2008) New kits turn any car into a plug-in hybrid. *Forbes*.

Chang, R. S. (2008) Are hybrids too quiet? *New York Times*. National ed.

Charness, G. and Rabin, M. (2002) "Understanding social preferences with simple tests", *The Quarterly Journal of Economics*, 117, 817–69.

Clayton, M. (2008) Squeezing the most out of a gallon. *Christian Science Monitor.*

Cohen, L. (2003) *A Consumers' Republic: The Politics of Mass Consumption in Postwar America*, New York, Alfred Knopf.

Colander, D. (2001) *The Lost Art of Economics: Essays on Economics and the Economics Profession*, Cheltenham, UK, Edward Elgar.

—— (2007) "Edgeworth's hedonimeter and the quest to measure utility", *Journal of Economic Perspectives*, 21, 215–25.

Collom, E. (2005) "Community currency in the United States: the social environments in which it emerges and survives", *Environment and Planning A*, 37, 1565–87.

Cook, I. and Crang, P. (1996) "The world on a plate: culinary culture, displacement and geographical knowledges", *Journal of Material Culture*, 1, 131–53.

Cookingham, M. (1987) "Social economics and modern reform: Berkeley, 1906–61", *History of Political Economy*, 19, 47–65.

Coşgel, M. M. (1997) "Consumption institutions", *Review of Social Economy*, 55, 153–71.

Cowan, R. S. (1983) *More Work for Mother*, New York, Basic Books.

—— (1987) "The consumption junction: a proposal for research strategies in the sociology of technology", in Bijker, W. E., Hughes, T. P. and Pinch, T. (eds) *The Social Construction of Technological Systems*. Cambridge, MIT Press.

Cowles Commission (1947) *Cowles Commission for Research in Economics Five-Year Report, 1942–1946*, Chicago, The University of Chicago.

Crang, P. (1994) "It's showtime: on the workplace geographies of display in a restaurant in southeast England", *Environment and Planning D: Society and Space* 12, 675–704

Csikszentmihalyi, M. (1990) *Flow: The Psychology of Optimal Experience*, New York, Harper & Row.

Davis, J. B. (2003) *The Theory of the Individual in Economics*, London, Routledge.

—— (2006) "The turn in economics: neoclassical dominance to mainstream Pluralism?" *Journal of Institutional Economics* 2, 1–20.

de Grazia, V. (2005) *Irresistible Empire: America's Advance Through the Twentieth Century*, Cambridge, Massachusetts, Harvard University Press.

Del Negro, M. and Stephen, J. K. (2002) "Global banks, local crises: bad news from Argentina", *Economic Review – Federal Reserve Bank of Atlanta,* 87, 89–106.

Demeulenaere, S. (2000) "Reinventing the market: alternative currencies and community development in Argentina", *International Journal of Community Currency Research,* 4.

Devault, M. L. (1991) *Feeding the Family: The Social Organization of Caring and Gendered Work,* Chicago, University of Chicago Press.

Dickens, D. (1949) "Food Patterns of White and Negro Families, 1936–1948", *Social Forces,* 27, 425–30.

Didier, E. (2007) "Do statistics 'perform' the economy?" in Mackenzie, D., Muniesa, F. and Siu, L. (eds) *Do Economists Make Markets?* Princeton, Princeton University Press.

Dolfsma, W. (1999) "The consumption of music and the expression of VALUES: a social economic explanation for the advent of pop music", *American Journal of Economics and Sociology,* 58, 1019–46.

—— (2002) "Preferences – How institutions affect consumption", *Review of Social Economy,* 36, 449–57.

Dolfsma, W. (ed.) (2007) *Consuming Symbolic Goods: Identity and Commitment, Values and Economics,* London, Routledge.

Donath, S. (2000) "The Other Economy: A Suggestion for a Distinctly Feminist Economics", *Feminist Economics,* 6, 115–23.

Dorfman, J. (1959) *The Economic Mind in American Civilization, 1918–1933,* New York, Viking Press.

Dorr, R. C. (1924) *A Woman of Fifty,* New York, Funk & Wagnalls Company.

Douglas, M. and Isherwood, B. (1979) *The World of Goods,* New York, Basic Books.

Duany, A. M. and Plater-Zyberk, E. (1992) "The second coming of the American small town", *Wilson Quarterly,* 16, 19–50.

Duesenberry, J. S. (1949) *Income, Saving and the Theory of Consumer Behavior,* Cambridge, Massachusetts, Harvard University Press.

Duly, A. (2003) "Consumer spending for necessities", in US Department of Labor (ed.) *Consumer Expenditure Survey Anthology, 2003.* Washington, DC, Government Printing Office.

Dupuis, E. M. (2000) "Not in my body: rBGH and the rise of organic milk", *Agriculture and Human Values* 17, 285–95.

Earl, P. E. (1986) *Lifestyle Economics: Consumer Behaviour in a Turbulent World,* Brighton, Sussex, Wheatsheaf Books.

—— (1990) "Economics and psychology: a survey", *Economic Journal,* 100, 718–55.

—— (2005) "Economics and psychology in the twenty-first century", *Cambridge Journal of Economics,* 29, 909–26.

Earl, P. E. and Potts, J. (2004) "The market for preferences", *Cambridge Journal of Economics,* 28, 619–33.

East, M. (1980) *Home Economics: Past, Present, and Future,* Boston, Allyn and Bacon.

Edgeworth, F. Y. (1881) *Mathematical Psychics: An Essay on the Application of Mathematics to the Moral Sciences,* London, C. Kegan Paul and Company.

Edwards, R. (1979) *Contested Terrain: The Transformation of the Workplace in the Twentieth Century,* New York, Basic Books.

Eglash, R., Croissant, J. L., Chiro, G. D. and Fouche, R. (eds) (2004) *Appropriating Technology: Vernacular Science and Social Power,* Minneapolis, University of Minnesota Press.

England, P. (1993) "The separative self: androcentric bias in neoclassical assumptions", in Ferber, M. A. and Nelson, J. A. (eds) *Beyond Economic Man: Feminist Theory and Economics.* Chicago, University of Chicago Press.

England, P. and Folbre, N. (1999) "The cost of caring", *Annals of the American Academy of Political and Social Science,* 561, 39–51.

Ettlinger, N. (2004) "Toward a critical theory of untidy geographies: the spatiality of emotions in consumption and production", *Feminist Economics,* 10, 21–54.

Etzioni, A. (1986) "The case for a multiple utility conception", *Economics and Philosophy* 2, 159–83.

—— (2004) "The post affluent society", *Review of Social Economy,* 62, 407–20.

Ewen, S. (1996) *PR! A Social History of Spin,* New York, Basic Books.

Falk, P. and Campbell, C. (eds) (1997) *The Shopping Experience,* London, Sage Publications.

Fehr, E. and Fischbacher, U. (2002) "Why social preferences matter – the impact of non-selfish motives on competition, cooperation and incentives", *The Economic Journal,* 112, C1-C33.

Fehr, E., Kirchsteiger, G. and Riedl, A. (1993) "Does fairness prevent market clearing? An experimental investigation", *Quarterly Journal of Economics,* 108, 437–59.

—— (1998) "Gift exchange and reciprocity in competitive experimental markets", *European Economic Review,* 42, 1–34.

Fehr, E. and Schmidt, K. M. (1999) "A theory of fairness, competition, and cooperation", *The Quarterly Journal of Economics,* 114, 817–68.

Ferber, E. (1995) *So Big,* Urbana, Illinois, University of Illinois Press.

Ferber, M. and Nelson, J. A. (eds) (1993) *Beyond Economic Man,* Chicago, University of Chicago Press.

Ferber, R. (1973) "Consumer economics, a survey", *Journal of Economic Literature,* 11, 1303–42.

Ferree, M. M. (1991) "The gender division of labor in two-earner marriages: dimensions of variability and change", *Journal of Family Issues,* 12, 158–80.

Fine, B. (1995) "From political economy to consumption", in Miller, D. (ed.) *Acknowledging Consumption: A Review of New Studies.* London, Routledge.

—— (2002) "'Economic imperialism': a view from the periphery", *Review of Radical Political Economics,* 34, 187–201.

Fine, B., Heasman, M. and Wright, J. (1996) *Consumption in an Age of Affluence,* London, Routledge.

Fine, B. and Leopold, E. (1993) *The World of Consumption,* London, Routledge.

Fischler, C. (1988) "Food, self and identity", *Science Information* 27, 275–92.

Floro, M. S. (1999) "Double day/second shift", in Peterson, J. and Lewis, M. (eds) *The Elgar Companion to Feminist Economics.* Cheltenham, UK, Edward Elgar

Folbre, N. (1994) *Pays for the Kids? Gender and the Structures of Constraint,* New York, Routledge.

—— (1998) "The 'sphere of women' in early twentieth-century economics", in Silverberg, H. (ed.) *Gender and American Social Science* Princeton, Princeton University Press.

—— (2001) *The Invisible Heart: Economics and Family Values,* New York, New Press.

Folbre, N. (2005) "'Holding Hands at Midnight': The Paradox of Caring Labor", *Feminist Economics,* 1, 73-92.

Forget, E. L. (1995) "American women economists 1900–940", in Mary Ann Dimand, R. W. D., and Evelyn L. Forget (ed.) *Women of Value: Feminist Essays on the History of Women in Economics.* Brookfield, Vermont, Edward Elgar.

—— (1996) "Margaret Gilpin Reid: a Manitoba home economist goes to Chicago", *Feminist Economics,* 2, 1–16.

—— (2001) "Margaret Gilpin Reid (1896–1991)", in Dimand, R., Dimand, M. A. and Forget, E. L. (eds) *A Biographical Dictionary of Women Economists.* Northampton, Massachusetts, Edward Elgar.

Foucault, M. (1980) *Power/Knowledge: Selected Interviews and Other Writings, 1972–1977,* New York, Pantheon.

Frank, R. (2005).The Mysterious Disappearance of James Duesenberry. *New York Times* (1857–current file), June 9, http://www.proquest.com/ (accessed October 3, 2008).

Frank, R. H. (1999) *Luxury Fever: Money and Happiness in an Era of Excess,* Princeton, New Jersey, Princeton University Press.

Frank, R. H., Gilovich, T. and Regan, D. T. (1993) "Does studying economics inhibit cooperation?" *Journal of Economic Perspectives,* 7, 159–71.

Frey, B. S., Pommerehne, W. W., Schneider, F. and Gilbert, G. (1984) "Consensus and dissension among economists: An empirical inquiry", *The American Economic Review,* 74, 986–94.

Fridell, M., Hudson, I. and Hudson, M. (2008) "With friends like these: the corporate response to fair trade coffee", *Review of Radical Political Economics,* 40, 8–34.

Friedman, M. (1957) *A Theory of the Consumption Function,* Princeton, Princeton University Press.

Fullbrook, E. (2003) *The Crisis in Economics,* London, Routledge.

Fuller, L. and Smith, V. (1991) "Consumers' reports: management by customers in a changing economy", *Employment, Work & Society,* 5, 1–16.

Fuller, S. (2000a) *The Governance of Science,* Buckingham, Open University Press.

—— (2000b) *Thomas Kuhn: A Philosophical History for Our Times,* Chicago, University of Chicago Press.

Gabaccia, D. R. (1998) *We Are What We Eat: Ethnic Food and the Making of Americans,* Cambridge, Harvard University Press.

Gabriel, Y. and Lang, T. (1995) *The Unmanageable Consumer: Contemporary Consumption and Its Fragmentations,* Thousand Oaks, California, Sage Publishers.

Galbraith, J. K. (1958) *The Affluent Society,* Boston, Houghton Mifflin Publishers.

Gallegati, M. and Kirman, A. P. (eds) (1999) *Beyond the Representative Agent,* Cheltenham, UK, Edward Elgar.

Gartman, D. (1986) *Auto Slavery: The Labor Process in the American Automobile Industry, 1897–1950,* New Brunswick, New Jersey, Rutgers University Press.

George, D. (2004) *Preference Pollution: How Markets Create the Desires We Dislike,* Ann Arbor, Michigan, University of Michigan Press.

Gibson-Graham, J. K. (1996) *The End of Capitalism (as we knew it): A Feminist Critique of Political Economy,* Cambridge, Massachusetts, Blackwell Publishers.

Gibson-Graham, J. K. (2006) *A Postcapitalist Politics,* Minneapolis, University of Minnesota Press.

Gieryn, T. (1983) "Boundary-work and the demarcation of science from non-science", *American Sociological Review* 48, 781–95.

Gieryn, T. F. (1999) *Cultural Boundaries of Science: Credibility on the Line,* Chicago, University of Chicago Press.

Gilboy, E. W. (1938) "The propensity to consume", *The Quarterly Journal of Economics,* 53, 120–40.

—— (1939) "The propensity to consume: reply", *The Quarterly Journal of Economics,* 53, 633–8.

Gintis, H. (1976) "The nature of labor exchange and the theory of capitalist production", *Review of Radical Political Economics,* 8, 36–54.

—— (1989a) "Financial markets and the political structure of the enterprise", *Journal of Economic Behavior & Organization,* 11, 311–22.

—— (1989b) "The power to switch: on the political economy of consumer sovereignty", in Bowles, S., Edwards, R. and Shepherd, W. G. (eds) *Unconventional Wisdom: Essays in Honor of John Kenneth Galbraith.* New York, Houghton-Mifflin.

Glickman, L. B. (1997) *A Living Wage: American Workers and the Making of Consumer Society,* Ithaca, New York, Cornell University Press.

Glover, P. (1996) *Hometown Money: How to Enrich Your Community with Local Currency,* Ithaca, New York, Greenplanners.

Goffman, E. (1959) *The Presentation of Self in Everyday Life,* Garden City, New York, Doubelday.

Goldstein, C. M. (2003) "Home economics: mediators", in Lerman, N. E., Oldenziel, R. and Mohun, A. P. (eds) *Gender and Technology: A Reader.* Baltimore, Johns Hopkins University Press.

—— (2006) "Educating consumers, representing consumers: reforming the marketplace through scientific expertise at the Bureau of Home Economics, United States Department of Agriculture, 1923–40", in Chatriot, A., Chessel, M. E. and Hilton, M. (eds) *The Expert Consumer: Associations and Professionals in Consumer Society.* Aldershot UK, Ashgate.

Goodman, A. C. (1998) "Andrew Court and the invention of hedonic price analysis", *Journal of Urban Economics,* 44, 291–8.

Goodman, D. and Dupuis, E. M. (2002) "Knowing food and growing food: beyond the production-consumption debate in the sociology of agriculture", *Sociologia Ruralis,* 42, 5–22.

Goodman, M. K. (2004) "Reading fair trade: political ecological imaginary and the moral economy of fair trade foods", *Political Geography,* 23, 891–915.

Gordon, D. M., Edwards, R. and Reich, M. (1982) *Segmented Work, Divided Workers: The Historical Transformation of Labor in the United States,* Cambridge, Cambridge University Press.

Gorz, A. (1999) *Reclaiming Work: Beyond the Wage-Based Society,* Cambridge, Polity Press.

Gramsci, A. (1971) *Selections from the Prison Notebooks,* New York, International Publishers.

Grapard, U. (2001) "The trouble with women in economics: a postmodern perspective on Charlotte Perkins Gilman", in Cullenberg, S., Amariglio, J. and Ruccio, D. F. (eds) *Postmodernism, Economics and Knowledge.* London, Routledge.

Greco, T. H. (2001) *Money: Understanding and Creating Alternatives to Legal Tender,* White River Junction, Vermont, Chelsea Green Publishers.

Gregson, N., Crewe, L. and Brooks, K. (2002) "Shopping, space, and practice", *Environment and Planning D: Society and Space,* 20, 597–617.

Gualerzi, D. (2001) *Consumption and Growth: Recovery and Structural Change in the US Economy,* Cheltenham, UK, Edward Elgar.

Gunn, C. (2004) *Third-Sector Development: Making Up for the Market,* Ithaca, New York, Cornell University Press.

Guthman, J. (2002) "Commodified meanings, meaningful commodities: re-thinking production-consumption links through the organic system of provision", *Sociologia Ruralis* 42, 295–311.

—— (2003) "Fast food/organic food: reflexive tastes and the making of 'yuppie chow'", *Social and Cultural Geography,* 4, 45–58.

Guy, C. (2002) "Rituals of pleasure in the land of treasures: wine consumption and the making of French identity in the late nineteenth century", in Belasco, W. and Scranton, P. (eds) *Food Nations: Selling Taste in Consumer Societies.* New York, Routledge.

Habermas, J. (1984) *The Theory of Communicative Action, Volume 1: Reason and the Rationalization of Society,* Boston, Beacon Press.

Hall, P. A. and Soskice, D. W. (2001) *Varieties of Capitalism: The Institutional Foundations of Comparative Advantage,* Oxford, Oxford University Press.

Harding, S. (1986) *The Science Question In Feminism,* Ithaca, Cornell University Press.

—— (1995) "Can feminist thought be more objective?" *Feminist Economics,* 1, 7–32.

—— (2004) "Rethinking standpoint epistemology: what is 'strong objectivity'?" in Harding, S. (ed.) *The Feminist Standpoint Theory Reader.* London, Routledge.

Harvey, D. (1989) *The Condition of Postmodernity,* Oxford, Basil Blackwell.

Hayden, D. (1978) "Two utopian feminists and their campaigns for kitchenless houses", *Signs,* 4, 274–90.

Heilbroner, R. A. and Milberg, W. (1995) *The Crisis of Vision in Modern Economic Thought.,* Cambridge, Cambridge University Press.

Helleiner, E. (2000) "Think globally, transact locally: green political economy and the local currency movement", *Global Society,* 14, 35–51.

Hendrickson, M. K. and Heffernan, W. D. (2002) "Opening spaces through relocalization: locating potential resistance in the weaknesses of the global food system", *Sociologia Ruralis,* 42, 347–69.

Hershberg, E. (2002) "Why Argentina crashed – and is still crashing", *NACLA Report on the Americas,* 36, 30–35.

Hess, D. (1997) *Science Studies: An Advanced Introduction,* New York, New York University Press.

Hewitson, G. J. (1999) *Feminist Economics: Interrogating the Masculinity of Rational Economic Man,* Cheltenham, UK, Edward Elgar.

Hirsch, F. (1976) *Social Limits to Growth,* Cambridge, Massachusetts, Harvard University Press.

Hirschfield, M. L. (1997) "Methodological stance and consumption theory: a lesson in feminist methodology", in Davis, J. B. (ed.) *New Economics and Its History.* Durham, NC, Duke University Press.

Hirschman, A. O. (1970) *Exit, Voice, and Loyalty,* Cambridge, Harvard University Press.

—— (1984) "Against parsimony: three easy ways of complicating some categories of economic discourse", *The American Economic Review,* 74, 89–96.

Hochschild, A. and Machung, A. (2003) *The Second Shift,* New York, Penguin.

Hochschild, A. R. (1983) *The Managed Heart,* Berkeley, University of California Press.

Hodgson, G. M. (2001) *How Economics Forgot History: The Problem of Historical Specificity in Social Science,* London, Routledge.

Hodgson, G. M. (2003) "The hidden persuaders: institutions and individuals in economic theory", *Cambridge Journal of Economics,* 27, 159–75.

—— (2007a) "Evolutionary and institutional economics as the new mainstream?" *Evolutionary and Institutional Economics Review,* 4, 7–25.

—— (2007b) "Meanings of methodological individualism", *Journal of Economic Methodology,* 14, 211–26.

Holloway, L., Kneafsey, M., Venn, L., Cox, R., Dowler, E. and Tuomainen, H. (2007) "Possible food economies: a methodological framework for exploring food production-consumption relationships", *Sociologia Ruralis,* 47, 1–19.

Holm, P. (2007) "Which way is up on Callon?" in Mackenzie, D., Muniesa, F. and Siu, L. (eds) *Do Economists Make Markets? On the Performativity of Economics.* Princeton, Princeton University Press.

Holman, W. J., Jr. (2005) Business world: Prius follies, take two. *Wall Street Journal.*

Hooker, C. (1997) "Ford's sociology department and the Americanization campaign and the manufacture of popular culture among line assembly workers c.1910–17", *Journal of American Culture,* 20, 47–53.

Horowitz, D. (1998) "The emigré as celebrant of American consumer culture", in Strasser, S., McGovern, C. and Judt, M. (eds) *Getting and Spending: European and American Consumer Societies in the Twentieth Century.* Cambridge, Cambridge University Press.

Hounshell, D. (1984) *From the American System to Mass Production, 1800–1932,* Baltimore, Johns Hopkins University Press.

Hoyt, E. E. (1928) *The Consumption of Wealth,* New York, Macmillan.

—— (1944) "The place of gestalt theory in the dynamics of demand", *American Journal of Economics and Sociology,* 4, 81–85.

Hudson, I. and Hudson, M. (2003) "Removing the veil: commodity fetishism, fair trade, and the environment", *Organization & Environment,* 16, 413–30.

Hughes, T. P. (1989) *American Genesis: A Century of Invention and Technological Enthusiasm,* New York, Viking.

Igo, S. E. (2007) *The Averaged American: Surveys, Citizens and the Making of a Mass Public* Cambridge, Massachusetts, Harvard University Press.

Ingham, G. (2004) *The Nature of Money,* Cambridge, UK, Polity Press.

Inglehart, R. F. (2008) "Changing values among western publics 1970–2006", *West European Politics,* 31, 130–46.

Itazaki, H. (1999) *The Prius that Shook the World,* Tokyo, Nikkan Kogyo Shimbun Ltd.

Jackson, K. T. and Ballon, H. (eds) (2007) *Moses and the Modern City: The Transformation of New York,* New York, W. W. Norton.

Jackson, P. (2004) "Local consumption cultures in a globalizing world", *Transactions of the Institute of British Geographers,* 29, 165–78.

Jacob, J., Brinkerhoff, M., Jovic, E. and Wheatley, G. (2004a) "HOUR town – Paul Glover and the genesis and evolution of Ithaca HOURS", *International Journal of Community Currency Research,* 8, 29–41.

—— (2004b) "The social and cultural capital of community currency, an Ithaca HOURS case study survey", *International Journal of Community Currency Research.*

Jenkins, N. H. (1994) Slow food fights back. *Washington Post.* Washington DC.

Jessop, B. (1997) "Twenty years of the (Parisian) regulation approach: the paradox of success and failure at home and abroad", *New Political Economy,* 2, 503–26.

Johnston, J. (2008) "The citizen-consumer hybrid: ideological tensions and the case of Whole Foods market", *Theory and Society,* 37, 229–70.

Joseph, P. E. (2001) "Black liberation without apology: reconceptualizing the Black Power movement", *The Black Scholar,* 31, 2–20.

Kahneman, D. (1994) "New challenges to the rationality assumption", *Journal of International and Theoretical Economics,* 150, 18–36.

—— (2003) "Maps of bounded rationality: psychology for behavioral economics", *The American Economic Review,* 93, 1449–75.

—— (2003) "A Perspective on judgment and choice mapping bounded rationality", *American Psychologist,* 58, 697–720.

Kahneman, D. and Snell, J. (1997) "Predicting a changing taste: do people know what they will like?" in Goldstein, W. M. and Hogarth, R. M. (eds) *Research on Reason and Judgment in Decision Making.* Cambridge, Cambridge University Press.

Kain, J. F. and Quigley, J. M. (1970) "Measuring the value of housing quality", *Journal of the American Statistical Association,* 65, 532–48.

Katona, G. (1942) *War Without Inflation: The Psychological Approach to Problems of War Economy,* New York, Columbia University Press.

—— (1944) "The role of the frame of reference in war and post-war economy", *The American Journal of Sociology,* 49, 340–47.

—— (1945) *Price Control and Business,* Bloomington, Indiana, Principia Press.

—— (1947) "Contribution of psychological data to economic analysis", *Journal of the American Statistical Association,* 42, 449–59.

—— (1951) *Psychological Analysis of Consumer Behavior,* New York, McGraw-Hill.

—— (1960) *The Powerful Consumer,* New York, McGraw-Hill.

—— (1961) "Consumers – Wasters or Investors?" *Challenge,* 4, 14–16.

—— (1963) "The relationship between psychology and economics", in Koch, S. (ed.) *Psychology: A Study of Science, Volume 6. Investigations of Man as Socius: Their Place Psychology and the Social Sciences.* New York, McGraw-Hill.

—— (1972) "The human factor in economic affairs", in Campbell, A. and Converse, P. E. (eds) *The Human Meaning of Social Change.* New York, Russell Sage Foundation.

—— (1980) Letter to Harold T. Shapiro. Ann Arbor, Michigan, George Katona Papers, Bentley Historical Library, University of Michigan.

Katznelson, I. and Pietrykowski, B. (1991) "Rebuilding the American state: evidence from the 1940s", *Studies in American Political Development,* 5, 301–39.

Kaufman, B. (2006) "Integrating emotions into economic theory", in Altman, M. (ed.) *Handbook of Contemporary Behavioral Economics: Foundations and Developments.* Armonk, New York, M.E. Sharpe.

Kayatekin, S. A. (2001) "Sharecropping and feudal class processes in the postbellum Mississippi delta", in Gibson-Graham, J. K., Resnick, S. and Wolff, R. (eds) *Re/Presenting Class: Essays in Postmodern Marxism.* Durham, North Carolina, Duke University Press.

Killerby, P. and Wallis, J. (2002) "Social capital and social economics", *Forum for Social Economics,* 32, 21–32.

Kirman, A. (2000) "Demand theory and general equilibrium: from explanation to introspection, a journey down the wrong road", in Mirowski, P. and Hands, D. W. (eds) *Agreement on Demand: Consumer Theory in the Twentieth Century.* Durham, North Carolina, Duke University Press.

Kirman, A. P. (1992) "Whom or what does the representative individual represent?" *The Journal of Economic Perspectives,* 6, 117–36.

Kirman, A. (2006) "Demand Theory and General Equilibrium: From Explanation to Introspection, a Journey Down the Wrong Road", in Mirowski, P. and Hands, D. W. (eds) *Agreement on Demand: Consumer Theory in the Twentieth Century.* Durham, North Carolina, Duke University Press

Kiss, D. E. and Beller, A. H. (2000) "Hazel Kyrk: putting the economics into home economics", *Kappa Omicron Nu Forum,* 11, 25–42.

Klamer, A. (2007a) "Does this have to be our future?" in Colander, D. (ed.) *The Making of an Economist Redux.* Princeton, NJ, Princeton University Press.

—— (2007b) *Speaking of Economics,* London, Routledge.

Klamer, A. and McCloskey, D. N. (1988) "Economics in the human conversation", in Klamer, A., McCloskey, D. N. and Solow, R. M. (eds) *The Consequences of Economic Rhetoric.* Cambridge, Cambridge University Press.

Klein, L. R. and Mooney, H. W. (1953) "Negro-White savings differentials and the consumption function problem", *Econometrica,* 21, 425–56.

Kline, R. (2003) "Resisting consumer technology in rural America: the telephone and electrification", in Oudshoorn, N. and Pinch, T. (eds) *How Users Matter: The Co-Construction of Users and Technology.* Cambridge, MIT Press.

Kline, R. and Pinch, T. (1996) "Users as agents of technological change: the social construction of the automobile in the rural United States", *Technology and Culture,* 37, 763–95.

Kline, R. R. (1997) "Agents of modernity: home economists and rural electrification in the United States, 1925–50", in Stage, S. and Vincenti, V. B. (eds) *Rethinking Home Economics: Women and the History of a Profession.* Ithaca, New York, Cornell University Press.

Kneeland, H., Schoenberg, E. H. and Friedman, M. (1936) "Plans for a study of the consumption of goods and services by American families", *Journal of the American Statistical Association,* 31, 135–40.

Knorr-Cetina, K. (1985) *The Manufacture of Knowledge: an Essay on the Constructivist and Contextual Nature of Science* Amsterdam, Elsevier.

Kochan, T. A., Katz, H. C. and McKersie, R. B. (1986) *The Transformation of American Industrial Relations,* New York, Basic Books.

Korsmeyer, C. (1999) *Making Sense of Taste: Food and Philosophy,* Ithaca, New York, Cornell University Press.

Krueger, A. O. (1991) "Report of the commission on graduate education in economics", *Journal of Economic Literature,* 29, 1035–53

Krumholz, N., Janice M. Cogger and John H. Linner (1975) "The Cleveland policy planning report", *American Institute of Planning Journal* 41, 298–304.

Krumholz, N. and Forester, J. (1990) *Making Equity Planning Work,* Philadelphia, Temple University Press.

Kuhn, T. (1970) *The Structure of Scientific Revolutions,* Chicago, University of Chicago Press.

Kummer, C. (2002) *The Pleasures of Slow Food* San Francisco, Chronicle Books.

Kupiec, B. and Revell, B. (1998) "Specialty and artisanal cheeses today: the product and the consumer", *British Food Journal,* 100, 236–42.

Kyrk, H. (1923) *A Theory of Consumption,* New York, Houghton Mifflin Company.

Laclau, E. and Mouffe, C. (1985) *Hegemony and Socialist Strategy,* London, Verso.

Lamont, M. and Molnar, V. (2002) "The study of boundaries in the social sciences", *Annual Review of Sociology,* 28, 167–95.

Lamoreaux, N. R. (2003) "Rethinking the transition to capitalism in the early American Northeast", *The Journal of American History,* 90, 437–61.

Lancaster, K. J. (1971) *Consumer Demand: A New Approach,* New York, Columbia University Press.

Lane, R. E. (1991) *The Market Experience,* Cambridge, Cambridge University Press.

—— (2000) *The Loss of Happiness in Market Societies,* New Haven, Connecticut, Yale University Press.

Lasn, K. (2000) "Culture jamming", in Schor, J. B. and Holt, D. B. (eds) *The Consumer Society Reader.* New York, New Press.

Latour, B. (1988) *Science in Action: How to Follow Scientists and Engineers through Society* Cambridge, MA, Harvard University Press.

Lauden, R. (2001) "A plea for culinary modernism: why we should love new, fast, processed food", *Gastronomica,* 1, 36–44.

Laufer, W. S. (2003) "Social accountability and corporate greenwashing", *Journal of Business Ethics,* 43, 253–61.

Lazear, E. P. (2000) "Economic imperialism", *Quarterly Journal of Economics,* 115, 99–146.

Lazonick, W. (1979) "Industrial relations and technical change: The Case of the Self-Acting Mule", *Cambridge Journal of Economics,* 3, 231–62.

—— (1990) *Competitive Advantage on the Shop Floor,* Cambridge, Harvard University Press.

Leamer, E. (2007) "Housing *is* the business cycle", *Housing, Housing Finance, and Monetary Policy.* Jackson Hole, Wyoming, Federal Reserve Bank of Kansas City.

Lee, L., Frederick, S. and Airely, D. (2006) "Try it, you'll like it: the influence of expectation, consumption, and revelation on preferences for beer", *Psychological Science,* 17, 1054–8.

Lee, M. J. (1993) *Consumer Culture Reborn,* London, Routledge.

Lee, R. (1996) "Moral money? LETS and the social construction of local economic geographies in southeast England", *Environment and Planning A,* 28, 1377–94.

Leidner, R. (1999) "Emotional Labor in Service Work", *Annals of the American Academy of Political and Social Science,* 561, 81-95.

Lerman, N. E., Oldenziel, R. and Mohun, A. P. (2003) "Introduction: interrogating boundaries", in Lerman, N. E., Oldenziel, R. and Mohun, A. P. (eds) *Gender & Technology: A Reader.* Baltimore, Johns Hopkins University Press.

Lester, R. A. (1946) "Shortcomings of marginal analysis for wage-employment problems", *The American Economic Review,* 36, 63–82.

Levine, D. P. (1998) *Subjectivity in Political Economy: Essays on Wanting and Choosing,* London, Routledge.

Lewin, S. B. (1996) "Economics and psychology: lessons for our own day from the early twentieth century", *Journal of Economic Literature,* 34, 1293–1323.

Leyshorn, A., Lee, R. and Williams, C. C. (eds) (2003) *Alternative Economic Spaces,* London, Sage.

Libby, B. (1984) "Women in economics before 1940", *Essays in Economics and Business History: Selected Papers from the Economic and Business History Society,* 3, 273–90.

Lipietz, A. (1988) "Accumulation, crises and ways out", *International Journal of Political Economy,* 18, 10–43.

Little, I. M. D. (1949) "A reformulation of the theory of consumer's behaviour", *Oxford Economic Papers,* 1, 90–9.

Lloyd, V. and Weissman, R. (2001) "Against the workers: how IMF and world bank policies undermine labor power and rights", *Multinational Monitor,* 22, 7–11.

Lobdell, R. A. (2000) "Hazel Kyrk", in Dimand, R., Dimand, M. A. and Forget, E. L. (eds) *A Biographical Dictionary of Women Economists.* Northampton, Massachusetts, Edward Elgar.

Lockie, S. (2002) "'The invisible mouth': mobilizing 'the consumer' in food production-consumption networks", *Sociologia Ruralis,* 42, 278–94.

Lockie, S. and Kitto, S. (2000) "Beyond the farm gate: production-consumption networks and agri-food research", *Sociologia Ruralis,* 40, 3–19.

Lowe, M. and Crewe, L. (1996) "Shop work: image, customer care, and the restructuring of retail employment", in Wrigley, N. and Lowe, M. (eds) *Retailing, Consumption, and Capital: Towards a New Retail Geography.* Essex, Longman.

Lupton, D. (1996) *Food, the Body and the Self,* London, Sage.

Lutz, M. A. and Lux, K. (1979) *The Challenge of Humanistic Economics,* Menlo Park, California, Benjamin/Cummings Publishing.

Lynch, K. (1960) *The Image of the City,* Cambridge, Massachusetts, MIT Press.

Lynch, K. (1975) *The Image of the City,* Cambridge, Massachusetts, MIT Press.

Lyson, T. A. (2004) *Civic Agriculture: Reconnecting Farm, Food, and Community,* Medford, Massachusetts, Tufts University Press.

Müller, H. (1999) "From Dollarisation to Euroisation: The Future of the Euro as an International Substitution Currency", *Intereconomics,* 34, 286-296.

Machlup, F. (1946) "Marginal analysis and empirical research", *The American Economic Review,* 36, 519–54.

Macy, M. W. and Flache, A. (1995) "Beyond rationality in models of choice", *Annual Review of Sociology,* 21, 73–91.

Madden, K. K. (2002) "Female contributions to economic thought, 1900–940", *History of Political Economy,* 34, 1–30.

Maier, N. R. F. (1930) "Reasoning in humans. I. On direction", *Journal of Comparative Psychology* 10, 115–43.

Marglin, S. (1974) "What do bosses do? The origins and functions of hierarchy in capitalist production", *Review of Radical Political Economics,* 6, 61–112.

Marglin, S. A. (2008) *The Dismal Science: How Thinking Like an Economist Undermines Community,* Cambridge, Harvard University Press.

Marx, K. (1964) *Economic and Philosophic Manuscripts of 1844,* New York, International Publishers.

—— (1973) *Grundrisse,* New York, Vintage Press.

—— (1977) *Capital, Volume I,* New York, Vintage Press.

Mason, R. (1998) *The Economics of Conspicuous Consumption: Theory and Thought Since 1700,* Cheltenham, UK, Edward Elgar.

Matthaei, J. (2001) "Healing ourselves, healing our economy: paid work, unpaid work and the next stage of feminist economic transformation", *Review of Radical Political Economics,* 33, 461–94.

Maurer, B. (2003) "Uncanny exchanges: the possibilities and failures of 'making change' with alternative monetary forms", *Environment and Planning D: Society and Space,* 21, 317–40.

McCall, L. (2005) "The complexity of intersectionality", *Signs,* 30, 1771–1800.

McCloskey, D. (1987) *The Rhetoric of Economics,* Madison, Wisconsin, University of Wisconsin Press.

McCloskey, D. M. (1994) *Knowledge and Persuasion in Economics,* Cambridge, Cambridge University Press.

McCloskey, D. and Klamer, A. (1995) "One quarter of GDP is persuasion", *The American Economic Review,* 85, 191–95.

McCloskey, D. N. (2006) *The Bourgeois Virtues: Ethics for an Age of Commerce,* Chicago, University of Chicago Press.

McCracken, G. (1990) *Culture & Consumption,* Bloomington, Indiana University Press.

—— (2005) *Culture and Consumption II,* Bloomington, Indiana University Press.

McDonough, T. (2008) "Social structures of accumulation theory: the state of the art", *Review of Radical Political Economics,* 40, 153–73.

Mendershausen, H. (1940) "Differences in family savings between cities of different size and location, whites and negroes", *Review of Economics and Statistics*, 22, 122–37.

Merrill, M. (1976) "Cash is good to eat: self-sufficiency and exchange in the rural economy of the United States", *Radical History Review*, 3, 42–71.

Meyer, S. (1981) *The Five Dollar Day: Labor Management and Social Control in the Ford Motor Company, 1908–1921*, Albany, New York, State University of New York Press.

Miele, M. and Murdoch, J. (2002) "The practical aesthetics of traditional cuisines: slow food in Tuscany", *Sociologia Ruralis* 42, 312–28.

Milberg, W. S. and Pietrykowski, B. (1994) "Objectivism, relativism and the importance of rhetoric for Marxist economics", *Review of Radical Political Economics*, 26, 84–108.

Miller, D. (ed.) (1995) *Acknowledging Consumption: A Review of New Studies*, London, Routledge.

Miller, D. (2002) "Turning Callon the right way up", *Economy and Society*, 31, 218–33.

Miller, J. (2003) "Why economists are wrong about sweatshops and the antisweatshop movement", *Challenge*, 46, 93–122.

Minkler, L. (1999) "The problem with utility", *Review of Social Economy* 57, 4–24.

Mirowski, P. (1998) *More Heat Than Light: Economics as Social Physics, Physics as Nature's Economics* Cambridge, Cambridge University Press.

—— (2000) "Twelve theses concerning the history of postwar price theory", in Mirowski, P. and Hands, D. W. (eds) *Agreement on Demand: Consumer Theory in the Twentieth Century*. Durham, North Carolina, Duke University Press.

—— (2002) *Machine Dreams: Economics Becomes a Cyborg Science*, Cambridge, Cambridge University Press.

—— (2005) "How Positivism Made a Pact with the Postwar Social Sciences in the United States", in Steinmetz, G. (ed.) *The Politics of Method in the Human Sciences*. Durham, North Carolina, Duke University Press.

—— (2007) The Mirage of an Economics of Knowledge, Version 3.0. (unpublished paper)

Mirowski, P. and Hands, D. W. (1998) "A paradox of budgets: the postwar stabilization of American neoclassical demand theory", in Morgan, M. S. and Rutherford, M. (eds) *From Interwar Pluralism to Postwar Neoclassicism. Supplemental Issue of History of Political Economy, Volume 30*. Durham, North Carolina, Duke University Press.

Mirowski, P. and Nik-Khah, E. (2007) "Markets made flesh: performativity, and a problem in science studies, augmented with consideration of the FCC auctions", in Mackenzie, D., Muniesa, F. and Siu, L. (eds) *Do Economists Make Markets? On the Performativity of Economics*. Princeton, Princeton University Press.

Mitchell, T. (2004) "Economists and the economy in the twentieth century", in Steinmetz, G. (ed.) *The Politics of Method in the Human Sciences: Positivism and Its Epistemological Others*. Durham, North Carolina, Duke University Press.

Mitchell, W. C. (1912) "The backward art of spending money", *The American Economic Review*, 2, 269–81.

Modigliani, F. (1986) "Life cycle, individual thrift, and the wealth of nations", *The American Economic Review*, 76, 297–313.

Mohammed, E. A. C. (2004) "Pounds of flesh, the merchants of Parma & ham-lets: a review of the Parma ham litigation across Canada and the U.K.", *Intellectual Property Journal*, 18, 443–52.

Moisander, J. and Pesonen, S. (2002) "Narratives of sustainable ways of living: constructing the self and the other as a green consumer", *Management Decisions*, 40, 329–42.

Mom, G. (2004) *The Electric Vehicle: Technology and Expectations in the Automobile Age,* Baltimore, Johns Hopkins University Press.

Monroe, D. (1927) "The family in Chicago: a study of selected census data", *Journal of Home Economics,* 19, 617–22.

—— (1930) "Open forum: homemakers and the 1930 census", *Journal of Home Economics,* 22, 479–83.

—— (1932) *Chicago Families: A Study of Unpublished Census Data,* Chicago, University of Chicago Press.

—— (1937) "Levels of living of the nation's families", *Journal of Home Economics,* 29, 665–70.

—— (1944) "Preparing for Social Action", *Journal of Home Economics* 36, 65–68.

—— (1974) "Pre-Engel studies and the work of Engel: the origins of consumption research", *Home Economics Research Journal* 3, 43–65.

Montanari, M. (2001) "Unnatural cooking", in Petrini, C. (ed.) *Slow Food: Collected Thoughts on Taste, Tradition, and the Honest Pleasures of Food.* White River Junction, Vermont, Chelsea Green Publishing.

Moody, K. (1997) *An Injury to All: The Decline of American Unionism,* London, Verso.

Mootry, M. K. (1995) "Introduction", in Ferber, E. (ed.) *So Big.* Urbana, University of Illinois Press.

Morgan, J. N. (1972) "A quarter century of behavioral research in economics, persistent programs and diversions", in Strumpel, B., Morgan, J. N. and Zahn, E. (eds) *Human Behavior in Economic Affairs: Essays in Honor of George Katona.* San Francisco, Jossey-Bass Inc.

Morgan, M. S. and Rutherford, M. (1998) "American economics: the character of the transformation", in Morgan, M. S. and Rutherford, M. (eds) *From Interwar Pluralism to Postwar Neoclassicism. Annual Supplement to Volume 30, History of Political Economy.* Durham, North Carolina, Duke University Press.

Moss, M. (2007) *Shopping as an Entertainment Experience,* Lanham, Maryland, Lexington Books.

Mount, C. (1999) *Different Roads: Automobiles for the Next Century,* New York, Museum of Modern Art.

Murray, R. (1992) "Fordism and post-Fordism", in Jencks, C. (ed.) *The Post-Modern Reader.* London, Academy Editions.

Muth, R. F. (1966) "Household production and consumer demand functions", *Econometrica,* 34, 699–708.

National Labor Committee (2008) The Toyota you don't know: the race for the bottom in the auto industry. New York, National Labor Committee.

Nelson, E. (1980) "Hazel Kyrk", in Sicherman, B. and Green, C. H. (eds) *Notable American Women: The Modern Period.* Cambridge, Harvard University Press.

Nelson, J. A. (1993) "The study of choice or the study of provisioning? Gender and the definition of economics", in Ferber, M. A. and Nelson, J. A. (eds) *Beyond Economic Man: Feminist Theory and Economics.* Chicago, University of Chicago Press.

—— (1996) *Feminism, Objectivity and Economics,* New York, Routledge.

Nerad, M. (1999) *The Academic Kitchen,* Albany, New York, State University of New York Press.

Neuman, M. (1998) "Does planning need the plan?" *Journal of the American Planning Association,* 64, 208–20.

Nixon, W. (2003) "Better than speed", *Mother Earth News,* 52–4.

North, P. (2007) *Money and Liberation: The Micropolitics of Alternative Currency Movements,* Minneapolis, University of Minnesota Press.

Offe, C. and Heinze, R. G. (1992) *Beyond Employment: Time, Work and the Informal Economy,* Philadelphia, Temple University Press.

Offer, A. (1997) "Between the Gift and the Market: The Economy of Regard", *Economic History Review,* 50, 450–76.

Offer, A. (2006) *The Challenge of Affluence,* Oxford, Oxford University Press.

Ogletree, S. M. and Drake, R. (2007) "College students' video game participation and perceptions: gender differences and implications", *Sex Roles,* 56, 537.

Olkin, I. (1991) "A Conversation with W. Allen Wallis", *Statistical Science,* 6, 121–40.

Ollman, B. (1971) *Alienation: Marx's Conception of Man in Capitalist Society,* Cambridge, Cambridge University Press.

Olney, M. L. (1998) "When your word is not enough: race, collateral, and household credit", *Journal of Economic History,* 58, 408–31.

Orenstein, P. (2004) Food fighter. *New York Times.* Late ed. New York City.

O'Shaughnessy, J. and O'Shaughnessy, N. J. (2003) *The Marketing Power of Emotion,* New York, Oxford University Press.

Oudshoorn, N. and Pinch, T. (2003) "Introduction: how users and non-users matter", in Oudshoorn, N. and Pinch, T. (eds) *How Users Matter: The Co-Construction of Users and Technology.* Cambridge, MIT Press.

Pacione, M. (1997) "Local exchange trading systems as a response to the globalisation of capitalism", *Urban Studies,* 34, 1179–99.

Parker, M. and Slaughter, J. (1988) *Choosing Sides: Unions and the Team Concept,* Boston, South End Press.

Parr, J. (2003) "Economics and homes: agency", in Lerman, N. E., Oldenziel, R. and Mohun, A. P. (eds) *Gender and Technology: A Reader.* Baltimore, Johns Hopkins University Press.

Paxson, H. (2008) "Post-Pasteurian cultures: the microbiopolitics of raw-milk cheese in the United States", *Cultural Anthropology,* 23, 15–47.

Pearson, R. (2003) "Argentina's barter network: new currency for new times?" *Bulletin of Latin American Research,* 22, 214–30.

Pereyra, F. (2007) "Exploring gender divisions in a community currency scheme: the case of the barter network in Argentina", *International Journal of Community Currency Research,* 11, 98–111.

Persky, J., Ranney, D. and Wiewel, W. (1993) "Import substitution and local economic development", *Economic Development Quarterly,* 7, 18–29.

Petrini, C. (2001a) "Building the ark", in Petrini, C. (ed.) *Slow Food: Collected Thoughts on Taste, Tradition, and the Honest Pleasures of Food.* White River Junction, Vermont, Chelsea Green Publishing.

—— (2001b) *Slow Food: The Case for Taste,* New York, Columbia University Press.

—— (2005) *Slow Food Revolution: A New Culture of Eating and Living,* New York, Rizzoli.

Pietrykowski, B. (1994) "Consuming culture: postmodernism, post-fordism and economics", *Rethinking Marxism,* 7, 62–80.

—— (1995a) "Beyond contested exchange: the importance of consumption and communication in market exchange", *Review of Social Economy,* 53, 215–41.

—— (1995b) "Fordism at Ford: spatial decentralization and labor segmentation at the Ford motor company, 1920–50", *Economic Geography,* 71, 383–401.

—— (1995c) "Gendered employment in the U.S. auto industry: a case study of the Ford Motor Co. Phoenix plant, 1922–40", *Review of Radical Political Economics*, 27, 39–48.

—— (1996) "Alfred Schutz and the economists", *History of Political Economy*, 28, 219–44.

—— (1999) "Beyond the Fordist/post-Fordist dichotomy: working through *the second industrial divide*", *Review of Social Economy*, 57, 177–98.

—— (2004) "You are what you eat: the social economy of the slow food movement", *Review of Social Economy*, 62, 307–21.

—— (2007a) "Different roads: automobiles for the next century": revisiting the 1999 museum of modern art exhibit. University of Michigan-Dearborn.

—— (2007b) "Exploring new directions for research in the radical political economy of consumption", *Review of Radical Political Economics*, 39, 257–83.

—— (2008) "The curious popularity of the Toyota Prius in the United States", in Schmitt, G. and Canzler, W. (eds) *Zukünfte des Automobils: Aussichten und Grenzen der autotechnischen Globalisierung* Berlin, Sigma.

Pigou, A. C. (1917) "The value of money", *The Quarterly Journal of Economics*, 32, 38–65.

Pinch, T. J. and Bijker, W. E. (1989) "The social construction of facts and artifacts: or how the sociology of science and the sociology of technology might benefit each other", in Pinch, T. J. and Bijker, W. E. (eds) *The Social Construction of Technological Systems: New Directions in the Sociology and History of Technology.* Cambridge, MIT Press.

Piore, M. J. and Sabel, C. F. (1984) *Second Industrial Divide: Possibilities for Prosperity,* New York, Basic Books.

Piven, F. F. and Cloward, R. (1971) *Regulating the Poor: The Functions of Public Welfare,* New York, Vintage

Pollan, M. (2003) "Cruising the ark of taste", *Mother Jones*, 28, 75–77.

Portes, A. and Mooney, M. (2002) "Social capital and community development", in Guillén, M. F., Collins, R., England, P. and Meyer, M. (eds) *The New Economic Sociology: Developments in an Emerging Field.* New York, Russell Sage Foundation.

Prasch, R. E. (2007) "Professor Lester and the neoclassicals: the 'marginalist controversy' and the postwar academic debate over minimum wage legislation: 1945–50", *Journal of Economic Issues*, 41, 809–25.

Putnam, R. D. (1993) *Making Democracy Work,* Princeton, Princeton University Press.

Rabin, M. (1994) "Cognitive dissonance and social change", *Journal of Economic Behavior and Organization*, 23, 177–94.

—— (1998) "Psychology and economics", *Journal of Economic Literature*, 36, 11–46.

—— (2002) "A perspective on psychology and economics", *European Economic Review*, 46, 657–85.

Raff, D. M. G. (1988) "Wage determination theory and the five-dollar day at Ford", *The Journal of Economic History*, 48, 387–99.

Ragin, C. C. (2000) *Fuzzy Set Social Science,* Chicago, University of Chicago Press.

Reckwitz, A. (2002) "Toward a theory of social practices: a development in culturalist theorizing", *European Journal of Social Theory*, 5, 243–63.

Redmond, W. H. (2007) "Home equity, fungibility and consumption: the increasing rationalization of society", *Review of Radical Political Economics*, 39, 201–13.

Reid, M. G. (1942) *Consumers and the Market,* New York, F.S. Crofts.

Resnick, S. and Wolff, R. (1987) *Knowledge and Class: A Marxian Critique of Political Economy,* Chicago, University of Chicago Press.

—— (1988) "Marxian theory and the rhetoric of economics", in Klamer, A., McCloskey, D. N. and Solow, R. M. (eds) *The Consequences of Economic Rhetoric.* Cambridge, Cambridge University Press.

Restaurant Opportunities Center (2005) *Behind the Kitchen Door: Pervasive Inequality in New York City's Thriving Restaurant Industry.* New York City, Restaurant Opportunities Center of New York (ROC-NY).

Richmond, M. L. (1997) "'A lab of one's own': the Balfour biological laboratory for women at Cambridge University, 1884–1914", *Isis,* 88, 422–55.

Rodríguez-Garavito, C. (2005) "Global governance and labor rights: codes of conduct and anti-sweatshop struggles in global apparel factories in Mexico and Guatemala", *Politics & Society,* 33, 203–33.

Rose, F. (1930) *Annual Report of the College of Home Economics.* Ithaca, New York, New York State College of Home Economics, Accession No. 23/18/1789, Box 2.

Rose, F. and Stocks, E. H. (1969) *A Growing College: Home Economics at Cornell University,* Ithaca, New York, Cornell University Press.

Rösl, G. (2006) "Regional currencies in Germany – local competition for the Euro", *Series 1: Economic Studies.* Deutsche Bundesbank.

Rossiter, M. W. (1980) "Women's work in science, 1880–1910", *Isis,* 71, 381–98.

—— (1982) *Women Scientists in America: Struggles and Strategies to 1940,* Baltimore, Johns Hopkins University Press.

—— (1997) "The men move in: home economics in higher education, 1950–70", in Stage, S. and Vincenti, V. B. (eds) *Rethinking Home Economics: Women and the History of a Profession.* Ithaca, New York, Cornell University Press.

Ruccio, D. M. and Amariglio, J. (2003) *Postmodern Moments in Modern Economics,* Princeton, Princeton University Press.

Rumbo, J. D. (2002) "Consumer resistance in a world of advertising clutter: the case of *Adbusters*", *Psychology and Marketing,* 19, 127–48.

Rutherford, M. (2000) "Institutionalism between the wars", *Journal of Economic Issues,* 34, 291–303.

Rutkoff, P. M. and Scott, W. B. (1986) *New School: A History of the New School for Social Research,* New York, Free Press.

Sabel, C. F. and Zeitlin, J. (1985) "Historical alternatives to mass production: politics, markets and technology in nineteenth-century industrialization", *Past and Present,* 108, 133–76.

Sabel, C. F. and Zeitlin, J. (1997) *World of Possibilities: Flexibility and Mass Production in Western Industrialization,* Cambridge, Cambridge University Press.

Sacks, J. (2002) *The Money Trail: Measuring Your Impact on the Local Economy Using the LM3,* London, New Economics Foundation.

Samuels, W. J. (2000) "Introduction to the problem of the history of the interwar period", in Samuels, W. J. and Biddle, J. E. (eds) *Research in the History of Economic Thought and Methodology.* New York, JAI Press.

Samuelson, P. A. (1938) "A note on the pure theory of consumer's behaviour", *Economica,* 5, 61–71.

—— (1948) "Consumption theory in terms of revealed preference", *Economica,* 15, 243–53.

Sayer, A. (2000) "Moral economy and political economy", *Studies in Political Economy,* 61, 79–104.

—— (2003) "(De)commodification, consumer culture, and moral economy", *Environment and Planning D: Society and Space,* 21, 341–57.

—— (2004) "Moral economy", *Department of Sociology On-Line Papers.* Lancaster, UK, Lancaster University.

Scharf, V. (1991) *Taking the Wheel: Women and the Coming of the Motor Age,* Albuquerque, New Mexico, University of New Mexico Press.

Schatzki, T. R. (2001) "Introduction: practice theory", in Schatzki, T. R., Cetina, K. K. and Savigny, E. V. (eds) *The Practice Turn in Contemporary Theory.* London, Routledge.

Schlosser, E. (2005) *Fast Food Nation* New York, Harper Perennial

Schneider, G. (2004) Toyota's Prius proving to be the hotter ride in hybrids. *Washington Post.*

Schor, J. B. (1998) *The Overspent American: Upscaling, Downshifting and the New Consumer,* New York, Basic Books.

—— (2004) *Born to Buy: The Commercialized Child and the New Consumer Culture,* New York, Scribner.

Schraven, J. (2000) "The economics of local exchange trading systems: a theoretical perspective", *International Journal of Community Credit Research,* 4.

Schuller, T., Baron, S. and Field, J. (2000) "Social capital: a review and critique", in Baron, S., Field, J. and Schuller, T. (eds) *Capital: Critical Perspectives.* Cambridge, Cambridge University Press.

Schutz, A. (1967) *The Phenomenology of the Social World,* Evanston, Illinois, Northwestern University Press.

—— (1964) "The well-informed citizen", in Broderson, A. (ed.) *Collected Papers, Volume II: Studies in Social Theory,* The Hague, Martin Nijhoff.

Schwartz, B. (2004) "The tyranny of choice", *Scientific American,* 15, 44–49.

Scitovsky, T. (1976) *The Joyless Economy: An Inquiry into Human Satisfaction and Consumer Dissatisfaction,* New York, Oxford University Press.

Scranton, P. (1997) *Endless Novelty: Specialty Production and American Industrialization, 1865–1925,* Princeton, Princeton University Press.

Seiz, J. (1991) "The bargaining approach and feminist methodology", *Review of Radical Political Economics,* 23, 22–9.

Sekine, T. T. (2004) "Socialism beyond market and productivism", in Albritton, R., Bell, S., Bell, J. R. and Westra, R. (eds) *New Socialisms: Futures Beyond Globalization.* London, Routledge.

Sen, A. (1993) "Capability and well-being", in Sen, A. and Nussbaum, M. (eds) *The Quality of Life.* New York, Oxford University Press.

Sen, A. K. (1977) "Rational fools: a critique of the behavioral foundations of economic theory", *Philosophy and Public Affairs,* 6, 317–44.

Sent, E.-M. (2004) "Behavioral economics: how psychology made its (limited) way back into economics", *History of Political Economy,* 36, 735–60.

Sewell, W. H., Jr. (1992) "A theory of structure: duality, agency, and transformation", *The American Journal of Sociology,* 98, 1–29.

Seyfang, G. (2001) "Working for the Fenland dollar: an evaluation of local exchange trading schemes as an informal employment strategy to tackle social exclusion", *Work Employment Society,* 15, 581–93.

Shaw, H. J. (2006) "Food deserts: towards the development of a classification", *Geografiska Annaler, Series B: Human Geography* 88, 231–347.

Sheller, M. (2004) "Automotive emotions: feeling the car", *Theory Culture Society,* 21, 221–42.

Shields, R. (ed.) (1992) *Lifestyle Shopping: The Subject of Consumption,* London, Routledge.

Silverberg, H. (1998) "Introduction: toward a gendered social science history", in Silverberg, H. (ed.) *Gender and American Social Sciences*. Princeton, Princeton University Press.

Sklar, K. K. (1998) "The consumer's white label campaign of the national consumers' league, 1898–1918", in Strasser, S., McGovern, C. and Judt, M. (eds) *Getting and Spending: European and American Consumer Societies in the Twentieth Century*. Cambridge, Cambridge University Press.

Slater, D. (2002) "From calculation to alienation: disentangling economic abstractions", *Economy and Society*, 31, 234–49.

Slow Food (2008) Slow Food USA. http://www.slowfoodusa.org/index.html

Smith, T. (1994) *Making the Modern: Industry, Art, and Design in America* Chicago, University of Chicago Press.

Sokal, M. M. (1989) "Gestalt psychology in America in the 1920s and 1930s", in Poggi, S. (ed.) *Gestalt Psychology: Its Origins, Foundations and Influence*. Florence, Italy, Leo S. Olschki Publishers.

Soper, K. and Thomas, L. (2006) "'Alternative hedonism' and the critique of 'consumerism'" (Working Paper No. 31). *Cultures of Consumption Working Paper Series*. London, Birkbeck College.

Southerton, D. (2001) "Consuming kitchens: taste, context, and identity formation", *Journal of Consumer Culture*, 1, 179–203.

Stage, S. (1997) "Introduction – home economics: what's in a name", in Stage, S. and Vincenti, V. B. (eds) *Rethinking Home Economics: Women and the History of a Profession*. Ithaca, New York, Cornell University Press.

Stage, S. and Vincenti, V. B. (eds) (1997) *Rethinking Home Economics: Women and the History of a Profession*, Ithaca, New York, Cornell University Press.

Stanley, L. (1936) Letter to W. Frank Persons dated 1-11-36. in National Archives and Records Administration (ed.) College Park, Maryland, Record Group 176, Department of Labor Correspondence with Other Government Departments and Bureaus 1933–37.

Starr, M. (2007) "Saving, spending and self-Control: cognition versus consumer culture", *Review of Radical Political Economics*, 39, 214–29.

Stapleford, T. A. (2007) "Market visions: expenditure surveys, market research, and economic planning in the new deal", *The Journal of American History*, 94, 418–44.

Steinberg, R. J. and Figart, D. M. (1999) "Emotional labor since *The Managed Heart*", *Annals of the American Academy of Political and Social Science 561*, 8–26.

Steinmetz, G. (ed.) (2005) *The Politics of Method in the Human Sciences: Positivism and its Epistemological Others*, Durham, North Carolina, Duke University Press.

Sterner, R. M. E. (1943) *The Negro's Share: A Study of Income, Consumption, Housing and Public Assistance*, New York, Harper.

Stevenson, R. W. and Kaufman, L. (2001) After the attacks: the economy. *New York Times*. Final Edition ed. New York City.

Stewart, H. and Blisard, N. (2008) *Are Lower Income Households Willing and Able to Budget for Fruits and Vegetables?* Washington DC, United States Department of Agriculture.

Stigler, G. J. (1950) "The development of utility theory. II", *The Journal of Political Economy*, 58, 373–96.

Stigler, G. J. and Becker, G. (1977) "De gustibus non est disputandum", *American Economic Review*, 67, 76–90.

Stille, A. (2001) "Slow food: an Italian answer to globalization", *The Nation*, 273, 11–16.

Strasser, S. (1982) *Never Done: A History of American Housework,* New York, Pantheon Books.

Strasser, S., McGovern, C. and Judt, M. (eds) (1998) *Getting and Spending: European and American Consumer Societies in the Twentieth Century,* Cambridge, Cambridge University Press.

Strassmann, D. (1993) "Not a free market: the rhetoric of disciplinary authority in economics", in Ferber, M. A. and Nelson, J. A. (eds) *Beyond Economic Man.* Chicago, University of Chicago Press.

Su, B. W. (2004) "The U.S. economy to 2012: signs of growth", *Monthly Labor Review,* 127, 23–36.

—— (2007) "The U.S. economy to 2016: slower growth as boomers begin to retire", *Monthly Labor Review,* 130, 13–32.

Sullivan, T. A., Warren, E. and Westbrook, J. L. (2006) "Less stigma or more financial distress: an empirical analysis of the extraordinary increase in bankruptcy filings", *Stanford Law Review,* 59, 213.

Talen, E. (1999) "Sense of community and neighbourhood form: an assessment of the social doctrine of new urbanism", *Urban Studies,* 36, 1361–79.

Taylor III, A. (2006) The birth of the Prius. *Fortune.*

Tedlow, R. S. (1990) *New and Improved: The Story of Mass Marketing in America,* New York, Basic Books.

Thaler, R. H. (1992) *The Winner's Curse: Paradoxes and Anomalies of Economic Life,* Princeton, Princeton University Press.

—— (2000) "From homo economicus to homo sapiens", *Journal of Economic Perspectives,* 14, 133–41.

Thaler, R. H. and Johnson, E. J. (1991) "Gambling with the house money and trying to break even: the effects of prior outcomes on risky choices", in Thaler, R. H. (ed.) *Quasi-Rational Economics.* New York, Russell Sage Foundation.

Thaler, R. H. and Shefrin, H. (1981) "Economic theory of self-control", *Journal of Political Economy,* 89, 392–406.

Theien, I. (2006) "Shopping for the 'people's home': consumer planning in Norway and Sweden after the Second World War", in Chatriot, A., Chessel, M.-E. and Hilton, M. (eds) *The Expert Consumer: Associations and Professionals in Consumer Society.* Aldershot UK, Ashgate.

Thomas, J. J. (1989) "Early economic history of the consumption function", *Oxford Economic Papers,* 41, 131–49.

—— (2000) "Elizabeth Waterman Gilboy", in Dimand, R., Dimand, M. A. and Forget, E. L. (eds) *A Biographical Dictionary of Women Economists.* Cheltenham, UK, Edward Elgar.

Thompson, C. J. (2000) "A new puritanism?" in Schor, J. (ed.) *Do Americans Shop Too Much?* Boston, Beacon Press.

Thompson, E. P. (1993) *Customs in Common: Studies in Traditional and Popular Culture,* New York, New Press.

Thompson, E. T. (1975) *Plantation Societies, Race Relations and the South: The Regimentation of Populations,* Durham, North Carolina, Duke University Press.

Throne, A. C. (1995) "Women mentoring women in economics in the 1930s", in Dimand, M. A., Dimand, R. W. and Forget, E. L. (eds) *Women of Value: Feminist Essays on the History of Women in Economics.* Brookfield, Vermont, Edward Elgar.

Tiemstra, J. P. (1992) "Theories of regulation and the history of consumerism", *International Journal of Social Economics,* 19, 3–27.

Tobin, J. (1972) "Wealth, liquidity, and the propensity to consume", in Strumpel, B., Morgan, J. N. and Zahn, E. (eds) *Human Behavior in Economic Affairs: Essays in Honor of George Katona*. San Francisco, Jossey-Bass.

US Census Bureau (2008) State and County QuickFacts. US Government.

Underhill, P. (1999) *Why we Buy: The Science of Shopping,* New York, Simon and Schuster.

University of Gastronomic Sciences (2008) Program Presentation.

Urry, J. (2008) "Governance, flows, and the end of the car system?" *Global Environmental Change*, 18, 343–9.

—— (2005) "The 'system' of automobility", in Featherstone, M., Thrift, N. and Urry, J. (eds) *Automobilities*. Thousand Oaks, California, Sage Publications.

van Velzen, S. (2003) "Hazel Kyrk and the ethics of consumption", in Barker, D. K. and Kuiper, E. (eds) *Toward a Feminist Philosophy of Economics*. London, Routledge.

Van Rensselaer, M. (1929) Letter dated 10-16-1929. in Monroe, D. (ed.) *New York State College of Home Economics Department of Household Economics and Management Records* Ithaca, New York, New York State College of Home Economics, Department of Household Economics and Management Records 23-2-749 Box 6-4. Division of Rare and Manuscripts Collection, Cornell University Library.

Vardy, J. (2001) Shopping is patriotic, leaders say. *National Post.* Toronto.

Veblen, T. (1953) *The Theory of the Leisure Class,* New York, Penguin.

Wagner, H. R. (1983.) *Alfred Schutz: An Intellectual Biography,* Chicago, University of Chicago Press.

Walker, K. E. (1969) "Homemaking still takes time", *Journal of Home Economics,* 61, 621–24.

Walker, R. (2004) The hidden (in plain sight) persuaders. *New York Times Sunday Magazine.*

Wallis, W. A. (1935) "The influence of color on apparent size", *Journal of General Psychology,* 13, 193–99.

Wallis, W. A. and Friedman, M. (1942) "The empirical derivation of indifference functions", in Lange, O., McIntyre, F. and Yntema, T. O. (eds) *Studies in Mathematical Economics and Econometrics*. Chicago, University of Chicago Press.

Ward, B. and Lewis, J. (2002) *Plugging the Leaks: Making the Most of Every Pound that Enters Your Local Economy,* London, New Economics Foundation.

Warde, A. (2005) "Consumption and theories of practice", *Journal of Consumer Culture,* 5, 131–53.

Ward's Automotive Group (2004, 2005, 2006) *Ward's Automotive Yearbook*. Southfield, Michigan.

Wärneryd, K.-E. (1982) "The life and work of George Katona", *Journal of Economic Psychology,* 2, 1–31.

Warren, J. (1964) *Oral History of Jean Warren*. Ithaca, New York, New York State College of Home Economics, Department of Household Economics and Management Records 47-2-O.H.70 Division of Rare and Manuscripts Collection, Cornell University Library.

Watkins, M. W. (1920) "The labor situation in Detroit", *The Journal of Political Economy,* 28, 840–52.

Weisskopf, T. E., Bowles, S., Gordon, D. M., Baily, M. N. and Rees, A. (1983) "Hearts and minds: a social model of U.S. productivity growth", *Brookings Papers on Economic Activity,* 1983, 381–450.

Wertheimer, M. (1955) "Gestalt theory", in Ellis, W. D. (ed.) *A Source Book of Gestalt Psychology.* London, Routledge & Kegan Paul.

Wilk, R. (2002) "Food and Nationalism: The Origins of 'Belizean Food'", in Belasco, W. and Scranton, P. (eds) *Food Nations: Selling Taste in Consumer Societies.* New York, Routledge.

Wilkinson, J. (2007) "Fair trade: dynamic and dilemmas of a market oriented global social movement", *Journal of Consumer Policy,* 30, 219–39.

Williams, C. C. (1996) "Local purchasing schemes and rural development: an evaluation of local exchange and trading systems (LETS)", *Journal of Rural Studies,* 12, 231–44.

—— (2005) "Unraveling the meanings of underground work", *Review of Social Economy,* 63, 1–18.

Winner, L. (1986) "Do artifacts have politics?" in Winner, L. (ed.) *The Whale and the Reactor.* Chicago, University of Chicago Press.

Winokur, L. A. (2008) "Encore (a special report); cooking up a revolution: at age 64, celebrated chef Alice Waters has a new mission: educating the nation's youth about food", *Wall Street Journal.*

Womack, J. P., Jones, D. T. and Roos, D. (1991) *The Machine That Changed the World: The Story of Lean Production,* New York, Harper Perennial.

Yi, Y.-A. (1996) "Margaret G. Reid: life and achievements", *Feminist Economics,* 2, 17–36.

Yonay, Y. P. (1994) "When black boxes clash: competing ideas of what science is in economics, 1924–39", *Social Studies of Science,* 24, 39–80.

—— (1998) *The Struggle Over the Soul of Economics: Institutionalist and Neoclassical Economists in America Between the Wars,* Princeton, New Jersey, Princeton University Press.

Zafirovski, M. (2000) "The rational choice generalization of neoclassical economics reconsidered: any theoretical legitimation for economic imperialism?" *Sociological Theory,* 18, 448–71.

Zelizer, V. A. (1994) *The Social Meaning of Money,* New York, Basic Books.

Zenk, S. N., Schulz, A. J. and Israel, B. A. (2005) "Neighborhood racial composition, neighborhood poverty, and the spatial accessibility of supermarkets in metropolitan Detroit", *American Journal of Public Health,* 95, 660–67.

Index

advertising 5, 44, 72, 76, 78; advertisers 3, 11, 12, 65, 93, 111; buzz marketing 11, 76, 111; Prius hybrid automobile 101, 110–11

agency 39, 82; agency/structure relation in consumption practices 33; Regulation School 79, 85–6; *see also* agent

agent 11, 20, 63, 76, 90, 95, 135, 136, 143, 144, 156; actor-network theory 13, 87–8, 90–8; composite agent 61; economic agents 2, 3, 20, 41, 53, 55, 61–2, 64, 69, 77, 85, 125, 129, 157; 'representative agent' 1, 14, 24, 26, 61; *see also* agency; consumer

alternative currency 13, 98, 129–42; advantages 133, 140–1, 150; alternative consumption behavior 140–2; and local economies 132–3, 158; and non-capitalist spaces of exchange 135–40, 150 (American system of non-capitalist household production 138–9, 158); circulating goods and services 129–32, 133, 136–7, 158; demurrage 130–1; ethical/political consumption dissonance 150–1; Euro 140; Fisher, Irving 131, 158; goal 150; Ithaca HOURS 130, 135–6, 137, 138, 140, 141–2, 150 (Glover, Paul 138); labor 131, 135, 138, 139, 141; Linton, Michael 130, 131; local currencies 130–1, 138; local currency in Argentina 133–5; local exchange trading systems (LETS) 130, 131, 134, 135, 138, 140, 150 (Britain 130, 131, 134, 140–1); Marx, Karl 136–7, 158; money 129, 136–7, 138, 140, 158 (economic functions 136–7, 139, 142, 158; social functions 129; 'social money' 129–30); moral economy 150–1;

social relationships 130, 133, 134, 135, 140, 141, 150, 151; time dollars 130, 135–6, 137, 138, 140, 141–2, 150; types of 130; US dollar 133, 140; value of the currency 131, 133, 135, 151; *see also* capitalism

Argentina: 2001–2 economic crisis 133–4; local currency in Argentina 133–5; 'prosumer' 134–5; Red Global de Trueque (RGT) 134–5

Austria: economists 16, 25

automobile 145; advertising 65, 101, 110–11; gender division of consumption 86, 112, 114; Prius hybrid automobile 10, 99–114; Sloanism 86; sport utility vehicle (SUV) 102–3; United States 9, 10, 99, 100, 101, 102–3, 110, 149; *see also* green automobility

behavioral economics 7, 13, 14, 20–3, 26, 54–5, 56, 65, 85–6, 150; behavioral turn in economics 23, 54–5; ethical consumption 13, 143–52; foundational principles 77; from psychological economics to behavioral economics 74–8; Gestalt school 74–7; Kahneman, Daniel 63, 65, 155; limitations 98; political consumption 13, 143–52; political dimension 78; preferences 56, 75, 78; research 126, 150; Simon, Herbert 54; unanswered questions 77; *see also* Katona, George

Bourdieu, Pierre: consumption 33; cultural capital 120, 121; food consumption 120, 121, 123; *habitus* 7, 33, 51, 52–3, 115; sociological theory of taste 53

Britain 121; local exchange trading systems (LETS) 130, 131, 134, 140–1;